Taking Charge of Your Financial Future

LAWRENCE LYNN
Editor

CB
CONTEMPORARY BOOKS

Library of Congress Cataloging-in-Publication Data

Taking charge of your financial future / Lawrence Lynn, editor.
p. cm.
Includes bibliographical references and index.
ISBN 0-8092-2908-0
1. Finance, Personal. 2. Investments. I. Lynn, Lawrence.
HG179.T338 1998
332.024—dc21 97-51634
CIP

Cover and interior design by Scott Rattray

Published by Contemporary Books
A division of NTC/Contemporary Publishing Group, Inc.
4255 West Touhy Avenue, Lincolnwood (Chicago), Illinois 60646-1975 U.S.A.

Printed in the United States of America
International Standard Book Number: 0-8092-2908-0
15 14 13 12 11 10 9 8 7 6 5 4 3 2 1

Contents

Acknowledgments v

Introduction vii

1 Planning and Objectives
Lawrence Lynn 1

2 Monitoring Your Stocks
James H. Galbraith 17

3 Bonds and Other Fixed-Income Obligations
Otto Glaser 35

4 Investment Companies
Lawrence Lynn and James H. Galbraith 49

5 Monitoring and Controlling Options
Lawrence Lynn 63

6 Technical Analysis for Monitoring Investments
John R. Markle 83

7 Life Insurance and Annuities
Lynn E. Marx and George S. Eckhardt, Jr. 103

8 Retirement Plans, Reports, and Withdrawals
Kenneth Altvater 131

9 The Registered Investment Adviser
Lawrence Lynn 145

10 Tangible Assets and Real Estate
Robert Frater and Charles Smith 159

11 Conclusions and Summary
Lawrence Lynn 175

Appendix: Important Information Locators 183

Bibliography 191

Index 193

Acknowledgments

WHETHER FICTION or nonfiction, most books are only nominally created by author(s) or editor(s) named on the title page. In actuality they are the efforts of many other human beings with whom the authors have shared either experiential or anecdotal events over possibly prolonged time periods. I know this is the case with books on finance and investments.

The true credit for this book belongs to the many people with whom I've shared thoughts on investment monitoring, control, or other aspects of the total investment experience. Certainly, as a teacher in public-school venues and in private-corporation venues such as Schlumberger, Inc. and British Petroleum, Ltd., I've been queried extensively on how to stay on top of one's investment program. These question-and-answer sessions were an extension of parallel discussions during my investment brokerage years at Merrill Lynch and Drexel Burnham Lambert. Thus, I can safely say that, while I have acknowledged the most important sources of queries regarding monitoring or control, those cited below are only a limited list of people who contributed to the thinking in this book.

First I must recognize the major contributions made to this work by Linda Bilmes-Hakim, Renate Donovan, Aliana Poe, and Temple Moore, all of whom contributed not only thoughtful questions but also general encouragement and background. Also, a special thanks goes to Marie Madrid of the Harris County Library Association for her gracious help.

At British Petroleum, Ltd., thanks for the helpful thinking from David Clarke and Timothy Cook. From Schlumberger, Inc. and its many subsidiaries and divisions, I must cite Neil Hammond, Laurent Coquilleau, David Mathison, Laurent Muller, Maurice Mienville, David Malone, Bill Shepherd, and Stuart Schaaf.

From my good students at Fluor, Ltd., I must cite the helpful comments and questions from Louis Gambucci, Suru Parekh, and Greg Cowan, and from Environmental Resources Management the ever thought-provoking discussions with Annette Brewster. I must also express my appreciation for their general help and encouragement to my literary agent, David Hiatt, and my editor, Rich Hagle. They pushed whenever my efforts flagged.

Finally and most important, I appreciate the quiet patience and moral support from my wife, Dori Lynn, and from Randi Davisson of Richard J. Fruth and Associates, Inc., as well as the editing skill of Barbara Reschke.

As to the source of any errata to be found in this book, I lay sole and total claim to such offenses as unfortunately may be found.

Lawrence Lynn

Introduction

SUPPOSE FOR A moment that you were in the position of my friend Joe Doaks, whose Uncle Harry had recently passed away in Chicago. It so happens that Joe is the principal heir of Uncle Harry's estate. Furthermore, he is the one responsible for collating all of Harry's estate ingredients and evaluating and reporting them for probate before the proper court in Chicago. Now we must assume, unfortunately, that Harry did not have and use this book to stay on top of his estate during his life. Neither did Joe.

When Joe gets into the mess, he discovers that Harry's estate is in stock, bonds, real estate, and proprietary interests here and there in Illinois, Indiana, and Iowa. Poor Joe. He must determine the basis for many of Harry's holdings while knowing hardly anything about them. He may have to assume high bases in the absence of data to the contrary and may walk away from Harry's large deductible losses in certain areas. In a word, he's up the proverbial creek with nary a paddle. Harry never did put much emphasis on monitoring or control of one's estate ingredients. Wasn't it enough to try to make a buck?

Even a worse thought . . . suppose you had a bad heart attack or stroke and became a pseudo-vegetable. Can your spouse—if you have one handy—pull together your financial interests in such a manner that you can find enough energy left to help with monitoring and exercising control where necessary over those securities, ongoing options, warrants, real estate partnerships, etc., while you are laid up for a prolonged period, perhaps the rest of your life?

What if the person doing all this mental searching is yourself? Do you remember who your insurance agent is for the homeowner's policy? Yes, it's that guy who was so friendly at the last church social. You remember him, don't you? What the heck was his name? And how much did you pay for those shares in Intel and Compaq Computer; are you at the point of long-term capital gain, or is it still short-term? Your bonds in XYZ Corporation have been called in by the corporation? But didn't they come with ten years of call protection, and it has been only five years since issuance? Isn't there an error in the early call? What was the guaranteed period certain with that high interest rate on that tax-deferred annuity? How long should you defer taking regular checks from it before it might be considered annuitized and taxable?

Aren't there many questions that turn up frequently for which you find the information is . . . where? Oh, you left it at the office. No, not that, it's in the credenza drawer with the car licenses because insurance is related, or is it? The data on the convertibility of the bonds should be available through the broker you used back then to get them . . . what was that dude's name?

There are a jillion excuses for not having all the pertinent information in one location . . . in a financial logbook of sorts. The convenient modus operandi is to have all the key data written down and collated logically as shown in this book. This approach prevents a search job like Joe's or the imaginary example of your spouse. Nor do you have to organize a search team to find the data for yourself to properly supervise, monitor, and control your own financial activities, whether stocks, options, real estate, benefit plan payments, or anything.

The purpose of this book is to help you systematize your records, utilize your system, and discipline yourself to stay on top of your financial activities. It should enable you to make periodic entries and survey what has occurred previously to the benefit of your profit picture. In retirement it should help you avoid actions that might shift you into extremely costly tax-penalty areas. It should help you recall whom to talk to in hours of need, not to mention critical phone numbers and other important data. It should also help to prepare you for visits to your tax accountant and for making gifts to your children, grandchildren, charities, and so on. In all, it should greatly help you monitor and control the estate that you worked so hard to build.

1 Planning and Objectives

Lawrence Lynn

AT FIRST GLANCE, the two nouns in the chapter title might seem identical or at least overlapping, but they are not.

What is a **plan**? It is an organized system of thoughts and steps by which a set of objectives may be achieved. Moreover, a plan normally must be not only organized, but also intelligently written. A plan that you hold in your thoughts is usually not a plan but a hope, a daydream, or an inchoate set of goals. A true plan lends itself to critique and monitoring over time.

The origination of true planning is lost in antiquity. Possibly Alexander the Great had a plan before he went off on his campaigns. It is likely that Julius Caesar had organized plans. Certainly major corporations such as Du Pont and General Electric have plans. In fact, they have planning teams composed of well-educated and trained groups of people from diverse disciplines.

Planning of an organized nature probably originated with the military, then extended into governance of countries or empires, church bodies, and others. Planning is a necessary ingredient in the work of any successful football or baseball coach today. The coach must ask, "What will we do if we get the ball on the twenty-yard line with a first down and ten yards to go?" The answer must set an **objective:** to score a touchdown immediately or achieve another first down as an intermediate goal.

We may conclude then, that the first step of planning is to be able to set some objectives. This is true whether you are planning a summer driving vacation or an estate or earnings plan. Your objective may be to achieve an estate of some dollar amount at age fifty-five to permit early retirement, or to achieve a nest egg of some amount by the time the kids are ready for college. Your objective could be to achieve replicable earnings for your widowed mother whom you are helping with advice, if not money. You may want her to live comfortably in a nice retirement community or, possibly, if she is suffering from a disability, a community with medical facilities.

Perhaps your objective is to direct your estate to the point where it is capable of generating a fixed amount per month at your normal sixty-five-year retirement age. This should be supplemented with your Social Security payment because your corporate employer's pension plan is woefully inadequate. All in all, the number of possible objectives for your financial plan is infinite.

In addition to your objectives, you must honestly determine the answer to the question, Where are we, or where am I, financially now? In other words, you must have a good understanding of how your estate is disposed now, and possibly also how it got there.

A good starting point is offered in the Investment-Objective Worksheet. Figure 1.1 is a completed example, filled out for a mythical couple, John and Mary Investor. The Investors have a total of $58,378 in stocks, subdivided among British Petroleum, Ltd. (BP), Investment Company of America (ICA), Thermo Electron (TMO), Hormel and Company, Inc. (HRL), Ohio Edison (OEC), and Sunshine Mining Co. (SSC). The Ohio stock is an income-oriented investment vehicle. The mining company falls under speculation, and the others are planned to produce long-term growth.

As you can see, Mr. and Mrs. Investor are very growth oriented, because about three-quarters of their portfolio is allocated that way. Some correction may be in order, because they want 30 percent of their assets to be income oriented. At present, they have only 15 percent so directed.

You, too, can start by filling out an Investment-Objective Distribution Analysis. Figure 1.2 is a blank worksheet for you to copy and fill in.

Figure 1.1 Investment Objective Worksheet: Completed Example

Name: John & Mary Investor   Date: 03/10/97

Growth			Income			Speculation		
Item*	Present Value $	Annual Yield $	Item*	Present Value $	Annual Yield $	Item*	Present Value $	Annual Yield $
BP	$6,825	$157	OEC	$8,750	$604	SSC	$5,500	$0
ICA	$20,240	$484						
TMO	$12,863	$0						
HRL	$4,200	$101						
Total	(A) $44,128	(B) $742		(C) $8,750	(D) $604		(E) $5,500	(F) $0
Annual Yield %		1.70%	Annual Yield %		6.90%	Annual Yield %		0%

Total Value	[(A) + (C) + (E)]	(G) $	58,378
Total Yield $	[(B) + (D) + (F)]	(H) $	1,346
Total Annual Yield %	[(H) / (G) × 100]		2.30 %

Distribution by Objective		Actual %	Desired %
Growth	[(A) / (G) × 100]	76	60
Income	[(C) / (G) × 100]	15	30
Speculation	[(E) / (G) × 100]	9	10

*Abbreviations: BP=British Petroleum; ICA=Investment Company of America; TMO=Thermo Electron; HRL=Hormel; OEC=Ohio Edison; SSC=Sunshine Mining.

Figure 1.2 Investment Objective Worksheet

Name: ______________________________ Date: ____________

Growth			Income			Speculation		
Item	Present Value $	Annual Yield $	Item	Present Value $	Annual Yield $	Item	Present Value $	Annual Yield $
Total	(A)	(B)		(C)	(D)		(E)	(F)
Annual Yield %		%	Annual Yield %		%	Annual Yield %		%

Total Value	[(A) + (C) + (E)]	(G)	$ ____________
Total Yield $	[(B) + (D) + (F)]	(H)	$ ____________
Total Annual Yield	[(H) / (G) × 100]		____________ %

Distribution by Objective		Actual %	Desired %
Growth	[(A) / (G) × 100]		
Income	[(C) / (G) × 100]		
Speculation	[(E) / (G) × 100]		

Investment Objectives

Like the Investors, you begin planning by organizing your present position into the three major categories of investment: growth of principal, present or deferred income, and speculation. Every dollar you have invested is poised to accomplish one or more of these things. If, for example, you have CDs, surely they are intended for current income and capital preservation. A single-premium tax-deferred annuity is expected to generate a specific amount of deferred income—so many dollars per year or month. In contrast, you hold that piece of undeveloped land either for highly probable (you hope) long-term growth or for speculation, depending on its location and other specifics. Maybe you should divide it between the two categories.

Furthermore, you need to understand what general route or routes to achieving your objectives are most logical and acceptable for you. You also need to include the aspirations of your spouse. Is she or he oriented toward secure current income such as can be provided by U.S. Treasury bonds? Or do either of you prefer relatively secure long-term growth? Decide together on the relative percentage of each of these categories for the routes most comfortable for the two of you.

For instance, you might decide that the percentages of growth, income, and speculative investments should be in the proportions 33:33:34. Or you might choose something like 70:20:10. In setting your desired ratios, you must take into consideration aspects such as your age, health, size of your estate, and value judgments. When you get to that stage, place these three percentages in the column under "Desired" in the lower right-hand corner of Figure 1.2.

Value Judgments

Now take a closer look at yourself. For this, you need to refer to the value judgments or characteristics listed in Figure 1.3, the Value Selection Chart. The scale there has been devised to help you find the proper balance between the values shown.

The purpose of this chart is to help you fine-tune your values. It describes different investment vehicles as extreme examples for each end of the scale. For example, if you prefer hands-on management of an asset, perhaps you would enjoy the personal management of rental houses or fix-'em-ups, which you might buy, improve, and resell as fast as possible. If you dislike personal participation in asset management, you may be more inclined to mutual funds, which are professionally managed.

John and Mary Investor, who completed Figure 1.1, also completed the Value Selection Chart. Their choices were consistent with their investments. They selected a 6 for line 1, a 3 for line 2, a 2 for line 3, a 6 for line 4, and a 7 for line 5.

In the blank Value Selection Chart (Figure 1.4), select the point on each value line that best reflects your desires and capabilities. As you consider where you belong on these lines, you are helping yourself decide what investment vehicles would be

Figure 1.3 Value Selection Chart: Completed Example

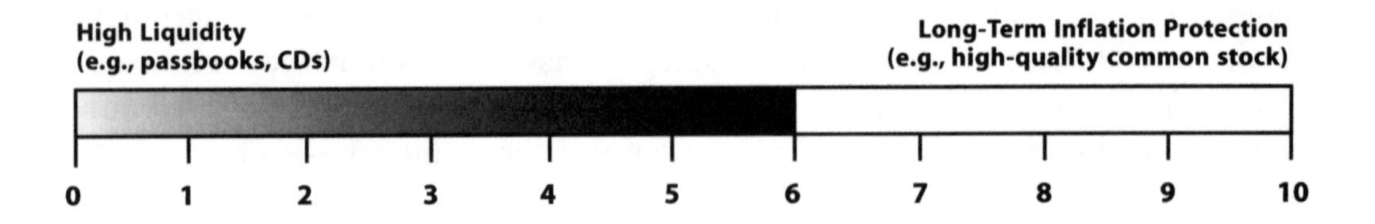

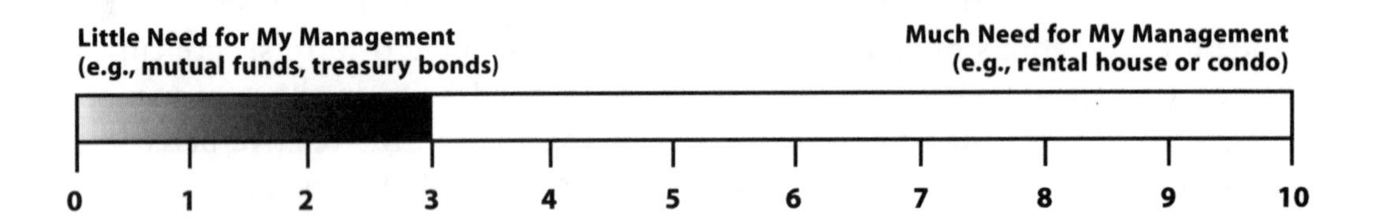

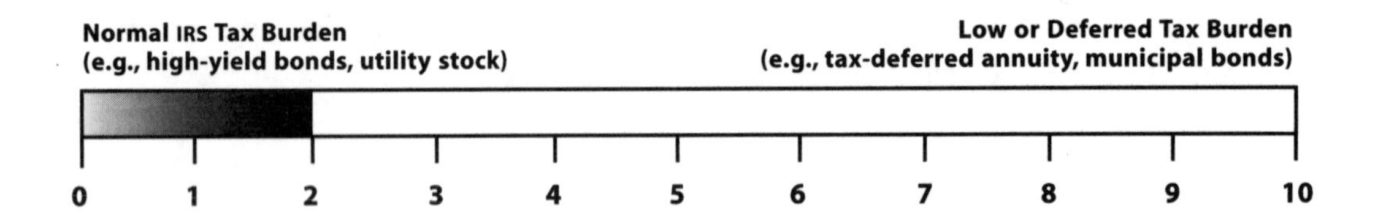

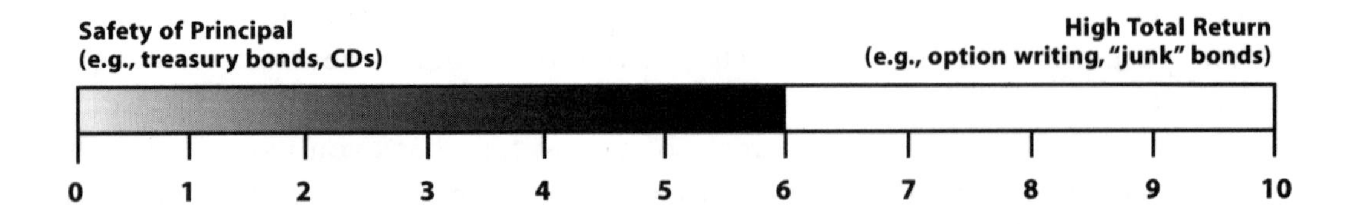

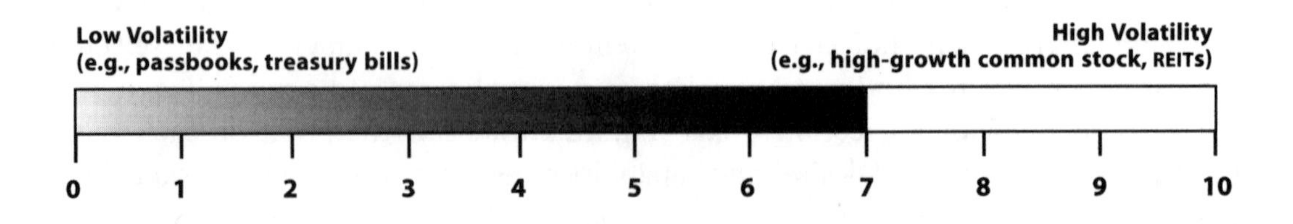

Figure 1.4 Value Selection Chart

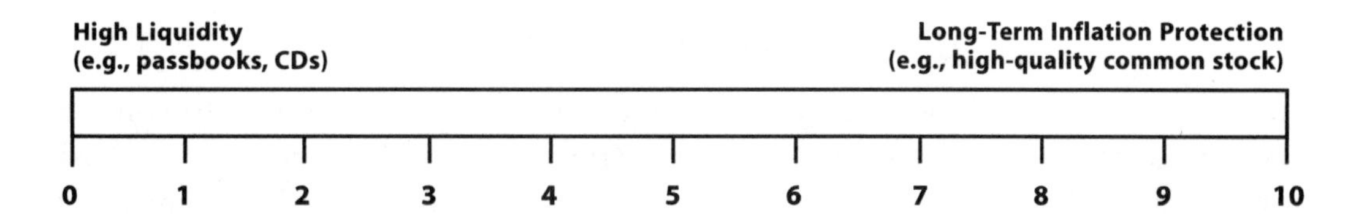

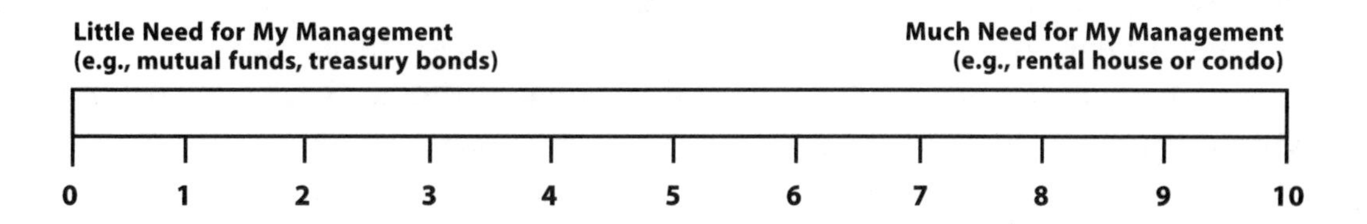

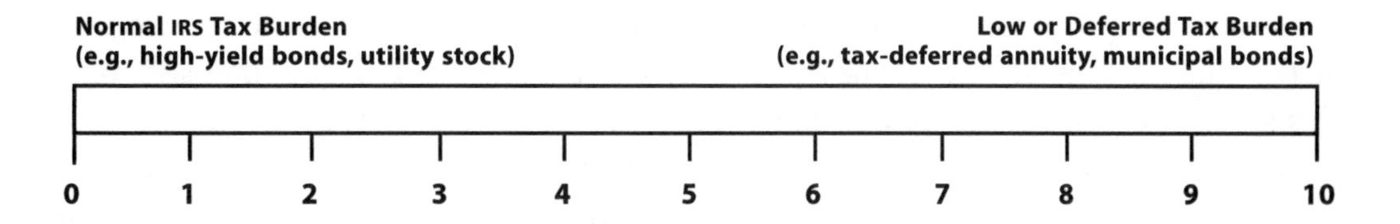

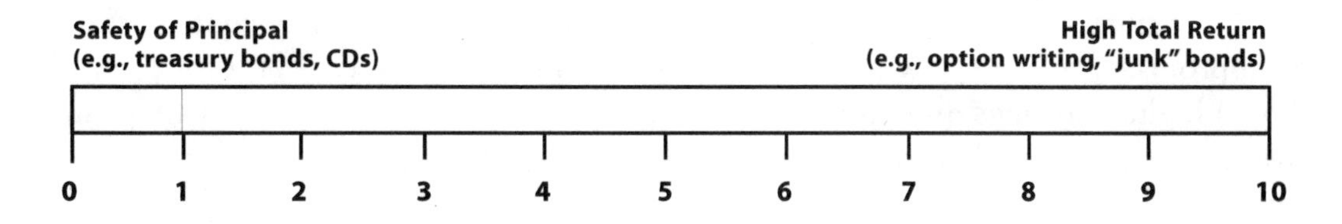

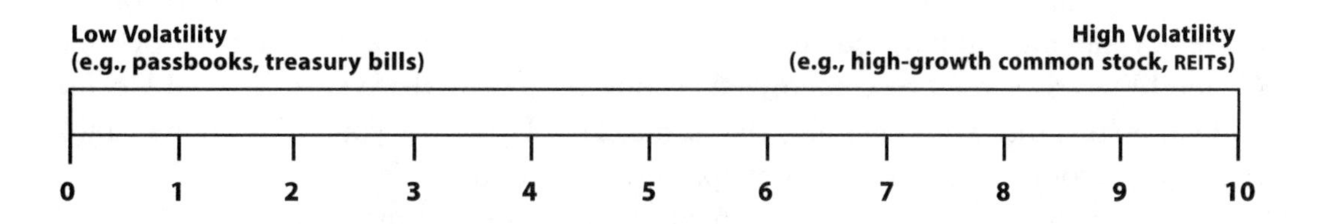

appropriate. If you are not averse to high volatility, you might select commodities. If you are highly averse to volatility, you should consider CDs and Treasury instruments, or something in between.

Risk Versus Return

Another way to help decide where to place yourself on the value line is to consider risk versus return. Consider first of all the returns you might expect on the basis of your own risk tolerance. To get a quick measurement of your risk tolerance, ask yourself if you can sleep nights when the market is going down and it looks as if you are losing your nest egg. As you get more experience with investing, you will find that the market is always fluctuating, and normally over the long run your estate will grow, along with your risk tolerance.

One of your goals in investing is to preserve your principal. This also means your purchasing power, which is affected by inflation. As a lower limit on your return, you might consider the inflation rate, which reasonably varies from about 3 percent to 5 percent.

For an idea of the return you might expect for a given level of risk, see Figure 1.5. This graph presents a relative relationship between total return and risk. If you desire the lowest risk of losing your principal, you will tend to lock into candidates such as passbook accounts, CDs, and government paper of various types. If you desire the higher returns generated by investments located along the upper regions of the line, you must risk using the chancier and more knowledge-intensive vehicles such as commodities or raw-land ventures.

As you can see from the selections they made in Figures 1.1 and 1.3, John and Mary Investor are moderately conservative. Their expectations regarding return on their investments lie in the range of 10 percent to 12 percent, as demonstrated by their use of selected common stock, selected mutual funds, utilities, and one potentially high-growth speculative stock.

Over time, with experience and success, your risk tolerance may change. What is appropriate for you now may not be when you have a greater total estate and (I hope) higher earnings and more workable knowledge and experience. At that time you may want to review your risk-reward stance by making use of Figure 1.5.

Your Estate Today

When you have decided on the relative weights for each of the three categories shown in Figure 1.2, list each of your assets in its proper column and record its current value and annualized return. For example, we can agree that a stock like General Electric should be categorized as long-term growth. Sysco Inc. and Hormel and Company, Inc. would fall into that same class. However, your CDs are inevitably there for income, as are your municipal bonds and annuities.

You may consider companies such as Marvel Entertainment and Callaway Golf as growth oriented, but they should be classified as speculative. So, too, are any

Figure 1.5 Risk vs. Reward for Typical Investments

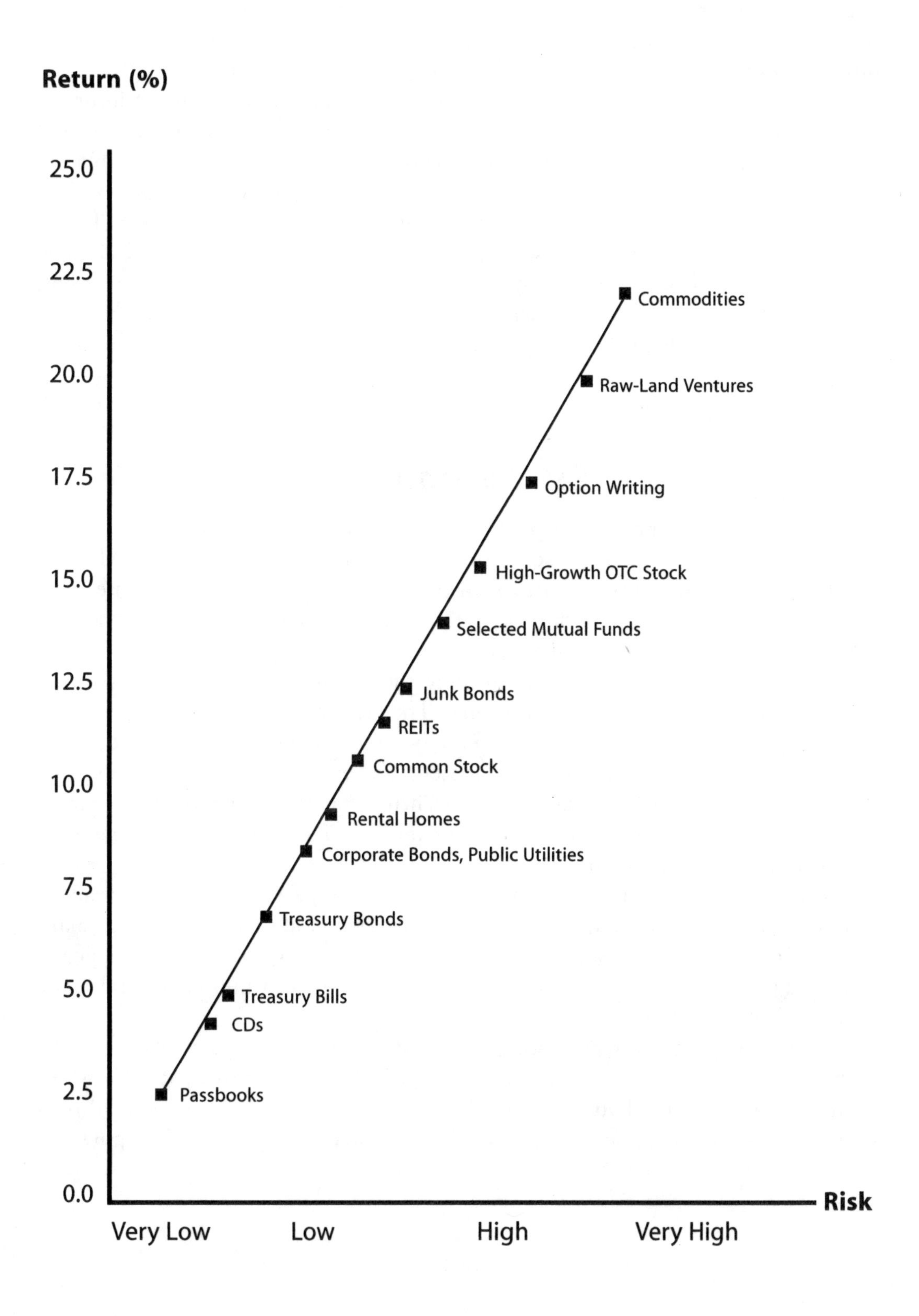

commodity items such as gold and silver, as well as most unlisted stocks. Certainly, all "penny" stocks are considered speculative.

Some items may have to be split. One might be a rental house that generates a decent level of current income. If you are convinced the investment is oriented safely toward growth of principal, then classify it partly as growth. If it is somewhat unsafe, however, then classify it partly or totally as speculative.

After classifying your estate by item, add the respective columns of information to get totals. Now determine what parts were aimed for growth, income, and speculation. Compare these actual figures with the desired figures you established before itemizing. Do the desired objectives diverge from what you are doing today?

Another valuable piece of information this table provides is the overall yield from your estate. Is this in line with your perceived needs when compared with typical yields for stock, bonds, rental property, and annuities? If so, great; if not, some modifications may be in order.

Make copies of Figure 1.2 so you can repeat this process every six months or annually.

Estate Monitor

The next step in the process of planning is to create a picture of where you are now and where you would like to be several years hence. Use the Estate Monitor graph shown in Figure 1.6 to chart the history of your total estate and estate earnings. You plot the year along the horizontal axis and the estate income as well as total estate value on the vertical axis.

This graph is semi-logarithmic, meaning the horizontal axis is linear (equally spaced) and the vertical axis is logarithmic. The vertical axis contains three cycles. The first begins at $1,000 and ends at $10,000. The second begins at $10,000 and ends at $100,000. The third begins at $100,000 and ends at $1,000,000. Thus, each cycle is ten times greater than the previous. When you plot compound rates of return with such a log scale, they appear as a straight line. This makes it much easier to make projections into the future.

To illustrate, Figure 1.7 plots data for Mr. Oilman, a seismologist with an oil drilling and service company. He is thirty-seven years old and is earning a salary of $73,500 per year. His estate earnings were $8,000 in 1989, and this gradually increased to $12,900 by the end of 1994. Table 1.1 lists his earnings and total estate at the end of each year.

To see how the point representing $8,000 at the end of 1989 was placed on the graph, move along the horizontal axis to the vertical line that crosses at 1989. Move up this vertical line until you come to the value $8. The point is represented by a solid square at this location. This process was repeated for each point in Figure 1.7.

Figure 1.6 Estate Monitor

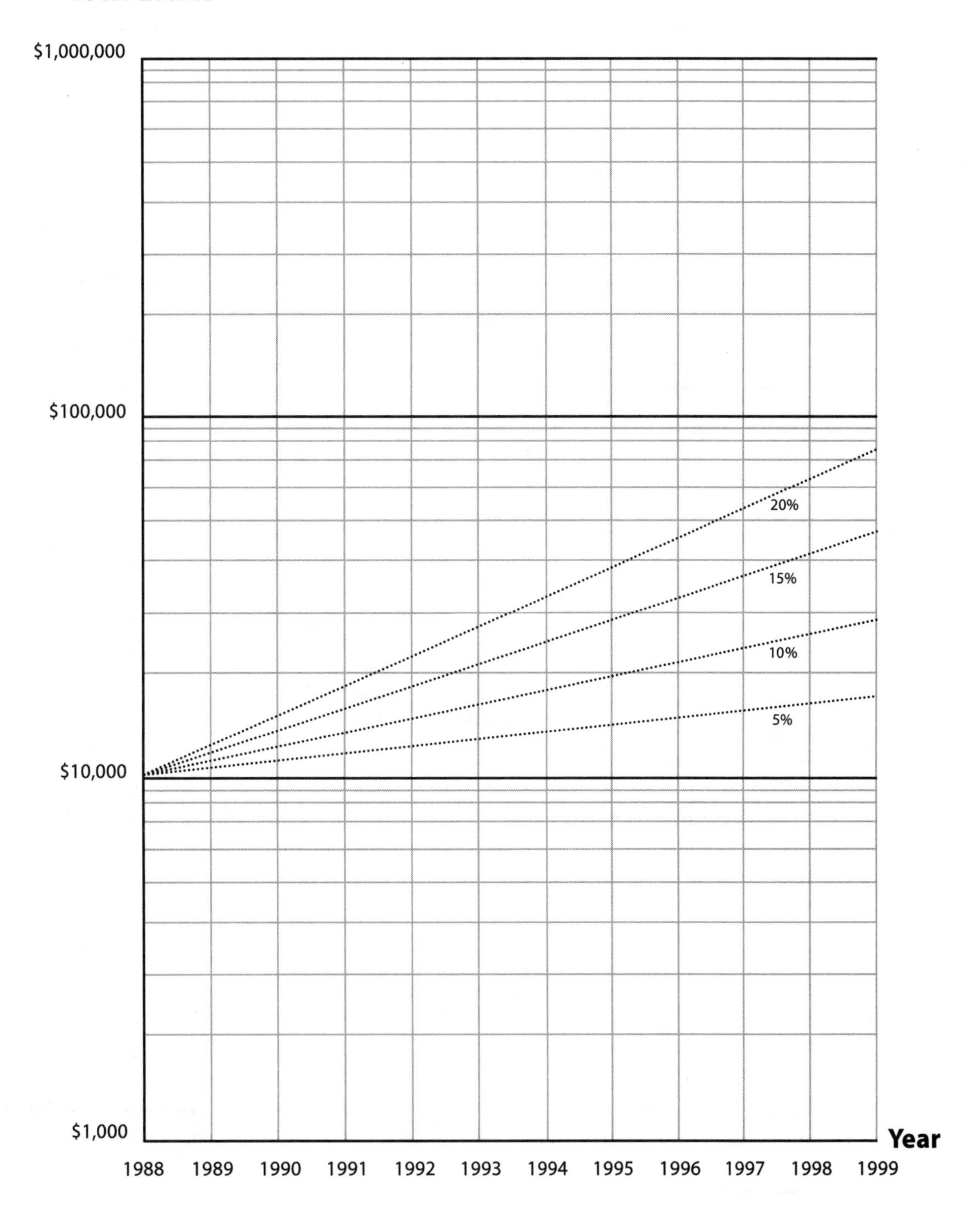

Figure 1.7 Estate Monitor: Completed Example

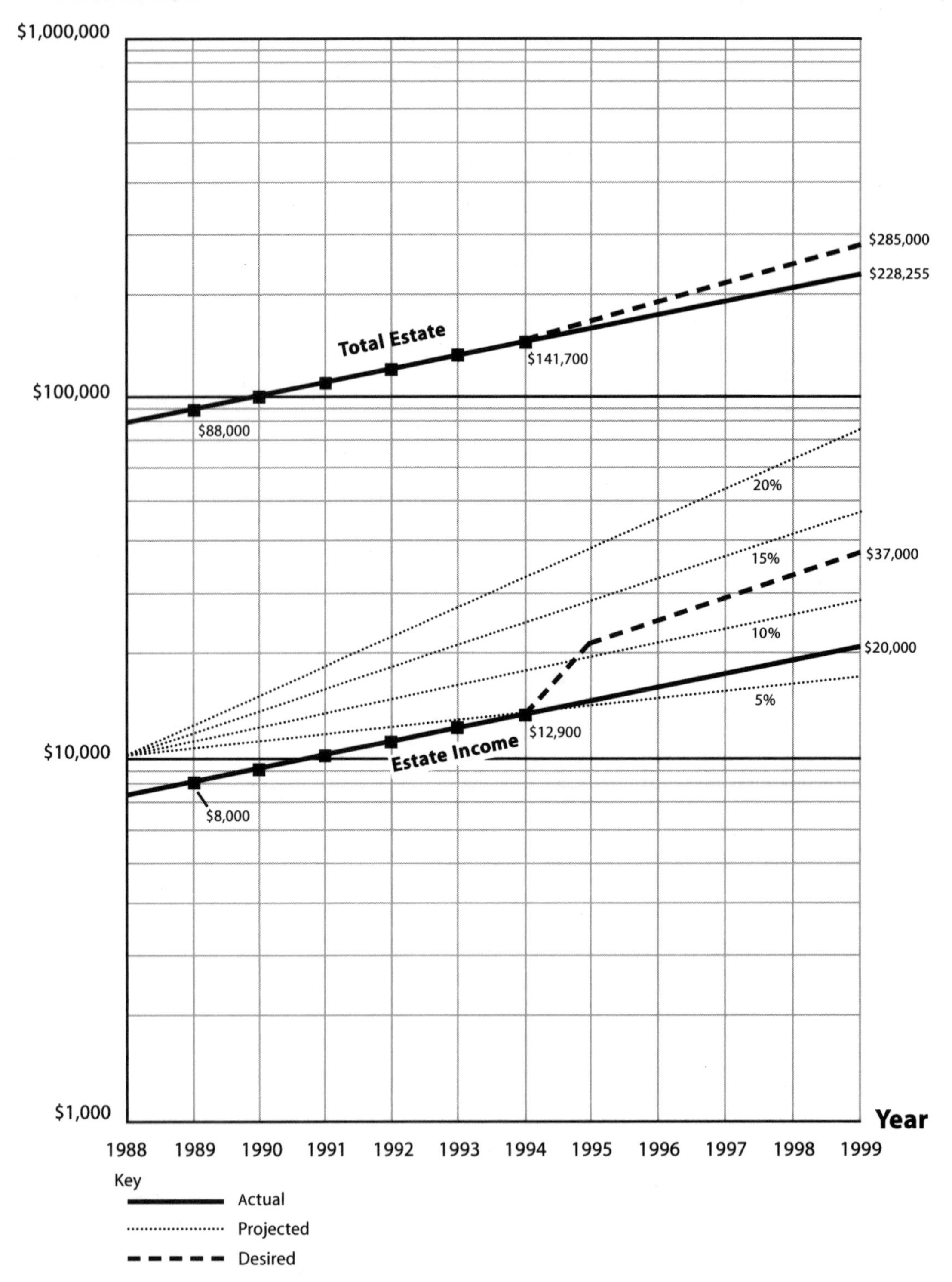

Table 1.1

Estate Income and Total Estate: Data for Figure 1.7

End of Year	Estate Income		Total Estate	
	Actual	Desired	Actual	Desired
1988	$7,273		$80,000	
1989	$8,000		$88,000	
1990	$8,800		$96,801	
1991	$9,680		$106,481	
1992	$10,648		$117,129	
1993	$11,713		$128,843	
1994	$12,885	$12,885	$141,727	$141,727
1995	$14,173	$21,259	$155,900	$162,986
1996	$15,590	$24,448	$171,491	$187,434
1997	$17,149	$28,115	$188,640	$215,549
1998	$18,864	$32,332	$207,504	$247,882
1999	$20,751	$37,182	$228,255	$285,064

Mr. Oilman's total estate, worth $88,000 in 1989, consists mostly of common stock, some bonds and CDs, a real estate partnership, a small rental house, and a small vested pension fund. His firm has no profit-sharing plan, and he has no IRA. As you can see, he has invested steadily at a 10 percent rate. He has been only an investor, not a spender, so at the end of 1994, the estimated worth of his estate was about $142,000.

This chart depicts the first part of planning. Mr. Oilman could have developed the data for his estate from the Investment Objective Worksheet (Figure 1.2). Try to work out your own figures and lines for the Estate Monitor. After establishing your total estate and estate earnings, place those numbers on a copy of Figure 1.6, just as I have done for Mr. Oilman. If the scales are not correct for you, you may simply change them to match the numbers that fit your case.

From Figure 1.7, Mr. Oilman extrapolated his data and found that, if he continued investing at the same rate as in the past, his estate would grow to $228,255 by the end of 1999, five years later. However, he has loftier ambitions. He wants to reach beyond the $20,000 income his estate would generate by the end of 1999. Therefore, he has a gap between what he wants to achieve and what he will have if he continues earning and saving at the same rate as the past five years. He would like to have an estate of over $500,000 by the time he reaches his late forties because he wants to reorder his life and change careers.

To accomplish his objectives, he must decide on investment alternatives whose total returns average about 15 percent per year. This is what planning seeks to do. By 1999 he should have a total estate of about $285,000. By the year 2004 he should reach his goal. Do the calculations yourself. Take the last number in the desired column for total estate in Table 1.1 and multiply by 1.15. This is the value for the end of year 2003. Then multiply that value by 1.15 again to get the next year's value. Repeat this process until you get the value $498,579 for the end of 2004.

Actionable Items

This final section provides an outline of nine actions you need to take and some considerations you need to think about when creating and implementing your plan.

1. Determine where you are now financially. Be honest with yourself. If you cheat, you're only cheating yourself. Also understand your strengths and weaknesses, your senses of value and balance. Determine your inclination toward risk or risk avoidance.

2. Estimate what you will achieve if you simply continue living and investing as you have for the last five, ten, or more years, depending on your age. (Use Figure 1.6)

3. Estimate where you really want to be. Try to be both realistic and optimistic. Don't be a stick-in-the-mud, but don't assume you may become the King of England or the owner of DeBeers Diamonds. You probably won't achieve either of those two goals in your lifetime. When you chart your desires, you are entering lines equivalent to the bold dashed lines in Figure 1.7. Now you can see your planning gaps.

4. Once you have found your planning gaps, try to select several investments that will give you the return necessary to put you on the trend you set for yourself. Record them in a list, and write down the reason you might want to use them. To help you make your selections, you could consult a basic investment book, such as Lawrence Lynn's *How to Invest Today.*

   So, what did you pick? Real estate, rental houses? But you have no experience with real estate. High-yield bonds? But the only bonds you have used are Series EE savings bonds. Obviously, you have a lot of learning ahead of you. Your first step is to find the expertise available to you. Study at the library or attend an adult-education class in your nearby community college. Are you ready to find an experienced money manager or financial planner to assist you?

Do you need to set up a trust structure or to select some form of tax shelter? If so, you may need help from an attorney, a tax expert, or even an insurance expert, depending on what you select.

Possibly, your objective was just too optimistic, and you can't take the risks or spend the time and efforts needed to master these new techniques.

When you have completed your selections, evaluate each investment type independently. What are the benefits to you if you use it? Don't try to be exact; just rough estimates will be sufficient.

5. If you think you can successfully use the tools you have selected and have found the correct expertise to guide you at an affordable cost, when will the results be achieved? Prepare a schedule or timetable.

6. Decide whose job it is going to be to carry out this plan. In my own family, my wife oversees our real estate activities with only minimal input from me. I take care of bonds, stocks, pension funds, collecting Social Security, and our option-trading program. She stays away from these activities except for helping me monitor our overall progress.

7. How much of your resources will this plan take, and can you really risk it? Dare you take these resources away from what they are doing now, whether in passbook accounts, CDs, or other low-risk vehicles? Can you tolerate this new use of funds if your resources are quite limited? Should you set up some smaller-scale financial "pilot plan" as a test device to confirm the approach and limit the consequences of errors as you learn?

8. Reassess the plan. Can you really carry it out? If so, prepare to work on the first intermediate steps and prepare a schedule for the whole plan. Your schedule should be for a specific period of time, such as one year, five years, or ten years.

9. Start using your plan. Periodically, such as every quarter, half year, or year, check your progress by category and overall. Eventually you will need to revise the plan. It was either too pessimistic or too optimistic and requires correction.

The rest of this book will help you implement your plan, select specific vehicles along the way, and validate your progress segment by segment as well as for the overall plan. Remember, a plan is only as good as its objectives. Good luck!

2 Monitoring Your Stocks

James H. Galbraith

A TYPICAL INVESTMENT portfolio is made up of many different investments, including stocks, bonds, and mutual funds. In this chapter, we will look at how to select common stock for your portfolio and monitor the progress of this component of your estate.

Selecting Stocks

There are many reasons why people choose a particular stock for their portfolio; it should be more than just a suggestion from an acquaintance. The reasons for buying a particular stock in the first place should include, among other things, sound management of the underlying company, a favorable outlook for the industry, and an attractive relative value. The next section will examine some of the key indicators of the health of a company and its management, present charts for monitoring the progress of these companies over time, and show you how to keep track of the progress of your stock portfolio as a whole.

To be sure, many investors consider the earnings of a company the best indicator of its health. However, this incomplete approach to stock selection and monitoring can eventually lead to trouble. A company's annual report contains seven basic parts, all of which you should review carefully each year. Two fundamentally important sections are the income statement and balance sheet. These two sections contain valuable information for deriving the key indicators for the health of the company.

Figure 2.1 summarizes the formulas for deriving these indicators. A more thorough discussion of their meaning can be found in Lawrence Lynn's book, *How to Invest Today*. In this chapter we will discuss how to calculate them and what we would expect their values to be if they were a measure of a well-run, healthy organization.

Prepurchase Analysis

Before you invest in a specific stock, you should have sound fundamental reasons for doing so. Many of these reasons should come from the financial report made by the company. You can record these data on a copy of Figure 2.2. Later, as you monitor the progress of your investment, you must refer back to this form to verify that the reasons for purchasing the stock have not changed significantly. As an example, Figure 2.3 presents data for SYSCO Inc., a Houston-based company engaged in marketing and distributing a wide range of food and related products to the food-service or "away-from-home-eating" industry from outlets in the United States and Canada. Later, I will briefly discuss the meaning of this information.

Most U.S. companies publish quarterly as well as annual reports. If this is the case, you may want to keep records of their progress at that frequency. To compare each period with the previous periods, use a properly designed monitor such as the one in Figure 2.4. The performance monitor in Figure 2.5 has been filled out with data for SYSCO.

Key Indicators

Investors measure the health of a company with fifteen key indicators. These are defined in terms of basic data from the company's financial statements, so let's begin with a review of financial basics.

Figure 2.1 Formulas for Deriving Key Indicators

$$\text{Current Ratio} = \frac{\text{Current Assets}}{\text{Current Liabilities}}$$

$$\text{Turnover Ratio} = \frac{\text{Sales}}{\text{Average Inventory}}$$

$$\text{Book Value} = \frac{\text{Stockholders' Equity—Intangibles—Preferred Stock}}{\text{Common Shares Outstanding}}$$

$$\text{Bond Ratio} = \frac{\text{Long-Term Debt}}{\text{Total Capitalization}}$$

$$\text{Preferred Stock Ratio} = \frac{\text{Par Value of Preferred Stock}}{\text{Total Capitalization}}$$

$$\text{Common Stock Ratio} = \frac{\text{Common Stock} + \text{Paid-in Capital} + \text{Retained Earnings}}{\text{Total Capitalization}}$$

$$\text{Leverage} = \frac{\text{Long-Term Debt} + \text{Preferred Stock}}{\text{Stockholders' Equity}}$$

$$\text{Earnings per Share} = \frac{\text{Net Earnings}}{\text{Common Shares Outstanding}}$$

$$\text{Interest Coverage} = \frac{\text{Operating Profit} + \text{Other Income}}{\text{Interest Expense}} \times 100$$

$$\text{Price/Earnings Ratio} = \frac{\text{Market Price per Share}}{\text{Earnings per Share}}$$

$$\text{Return on Equity} = \frac{\text{Net Earnings}}{\text{Last Year's Stockholders' Equity}} \times 100$$

$$\text{Return on Investment} = \frac{\text{Operating Earnings}}{\text{Last Year's Total Debt} + \text{Total Equity}} \times 100$$

$$\text{Operating Profit Margin} = \frac{\text{Operating Earnings}}{\text{Sales}} \times 100$$

$$\text{Net Profit Margin} = \frac{\text{Net Earnings}}{\text{Sales}} \times 100$$

$$\text{Dividend Yield} = \frac{\text{Dividend per Share}}{\text{Market Price per Share}} \times 100$$

Figure 2.2 Prepurchase Financial Analysis

Symbol: ______________________ Exchange traded: __________

Company: ______________________ Date: ________________

Reason for evaluation: ______________ Price: $____________/share

Key Indicator	Value	Comments
Current ratio*		
Turnover ratio		
Book value		
Bond capitalization ratio		
Preferred stock capitalization ratio		
Common stock capitalization ratio		
Leverage		
Earnings per share (EPS)*		
Interest coverage		
Price/earnings ratio (P/E)*		
Return on equity (ROE)		
Return on investment (ROI)		
Operating profit margin*		
Net profit margin		
Dividend yield		

* Critical indicators.

Figure 2.3 Prepurchase Financial Analysis: Completed Example

Symbol: SYY Exchange traded: NYSE

Company: SYSCO Inc. Date: 03/12/92

Reason for evaluation: High consistent growth rate Price: $24.25 /share

Key Indicator	Value	Comments
Current ratio*	1.87	Close to 2; quite healthy
Turnover ratio	18	High, rapid turnover of inventories
Book value	$6.95	Price is about 6 times book value
Bond capitalization ratio	45.80%	Slightly low, but financially sound
Preferred stock capitalization ratio	0%	No preferred stock outstanding
Common stock capitalization ratio	54.20%	Conservative
Leverage	0.6	Low debt, conservatively operated
Earnings per share (EPS)*	$1.67	Positive increase each year for 10 years
Interest coverage	6.1	Very healthy
Price/earnings ratio (P/E)*	26	Premium P/E due to performance
Return on equity (ROE)	16.70%	Excellent
Return on investment (ROI)	22.00%	Excellent
Operating profit margin*	3.60%	Sound for its industry
Net profit margin	3.10%	Sound for its industry
Dividend yield	0.50%	Positive increase each year for 10 years

* Critical indicators.

Figure 2.4 Stock Performance Monitor

Symbol: ______ No. of shares: ____________ Exchange traded: ____________

Company: ______________________________ Date of purchase: ____________

Purchase price/share: __________ Type: ___Growth ___Income ___Speculation

Year								
Growth Rate								
Sales (%)								
Earnings (%)								
Dividend (%)								
Price (%)								
Price and Earnings								
High price per share ($)								
Low price per share ($)								
Earnings per share ($)								
Book value ($)								
Profit margin before tax (%)								
Net profit margin (%)								
Return on equity (%)								
Return on investment (%)								
Financial Ratios								
Current ratio								
Turnover ratio								
High price/earnings ratio								
Low price/earnings ratio								
Bond ratio								
Preferred stock ratio								
Common stock ratio								
Leverage								
Interest coverage								
Dividend yield (%)								

Figure 2.5 Stock Performance Monitor: Completed Example

Symbol: SYY No. of shares: 1,000 Exchange traded: NYSE

Company: SYSCO Inc. Date of purchase: 06/13/85

Purchase price/share: $4.50 Type: X Growth ___Income ___Speculation

Year	1985	1986	1987	1988	1989	1990	1991	1992
Growth Rate								
Sales (%)	13.70	20.70	15.20	19.90	56.30	10.80	7.40	9.10
Earnings (%)	7.40	13.80	6.10	28.60	33.30	21.70	13.70	12.10
Dividend (%)	13.90	12.10	23.00	16.60	14.10	15.90	24.20	42.80
Price (%)	16.00	46.60	22.40	−3.00	64.90	20.00	23.40	17.30
Price and Earnings								
High price per share ($)	5.80	8.50	10.40	9.70	16.00	19.20	23.70	27.80
Low price per share ($)	4.00	5.60	5.60	6.50	9.20	12.80	15.00	20.60
Earnings per share ($)	0.29	0.33	0.35	0.45	0.60	0.73	0.83	0.93
Book value ($)	1.97	2.25	2.55	3.01	3.54	4.20	4.96	5.69
Profit margin before tax (%)	3.58	3.39	3.35	2.95	2.58	2.85	3.08	3.17
Net profit margin (%)	1.92	1.84	1.69	1.98	1.58	1.75	1.89	1.94
Return on equity (%)	16.00	16.00	14.00	17.00	18.90	19.00	18.00	17.00
Return on investment (%)	12.00	12.00	12.00	15.00	9.00	10.00	11.00	11.00
Financial Ratios								
Current ratio	2.12	2.03	2.03	1.87	1.80	1.83	1.87	1.89
Turnover ratio								
High price/earnings ratio	20.00	25.80	29.70	21.60	26.70	26.30	28.20	29.90
Low price/earnings ratio	13.80	17.00	16.00	14.40	15.30	17.50	17.90	22.20
Bond ratio	0.24	0.21	0.18	0.15	0.49	0.43	0.37	0.32
Preferred stock ratio								
Common stock ratio	0.76	0.79	0.82	0.85	0.51	0.57	0.63	0.68
Leverage	0.32	0.26	0.22	0.17	0.96	0.76	0.59	0.46
Interest coverage	8.66	9.65	11.02	10.26	2.92	3.73	5.00	6.36
Dividend yield (%)	1.19	0.96	1.17	1.16	0.93	0.76	0.80	0.83

For a newly formed company to survive, it must have assets to operate. It needs funding to acquire these assets. This funding may come from private sources or public participation. The company may acquire funds by taking on debt (liability) or giving up equity (selling stock), or ownership in the company. The combination of total debt and total equity used to run the company is called total assets, as depicted at the top in Figure 2.6. Debt can be short-term (payable in less than one year) or long-term. Equity can be common or preferred stock.

A company like SYSCO Inc. is in business to make money by selling its products. Before it can sell products, however, the company must create its infrastructure. It will use the acquired funds in three general ways, shown at the bottom in Figure 2.6. The first is to purchase fixed assets: land, buildings, and equipment for storage and movement of the products. Second, it purchases raw products (inventory), which would be considered part of current assets. Finally, the company runs its daily operations with current assets. These items, as well as intangibles (which will not exist when the company gets started), constitute the total assets of the company.

A company stays in business and grows by selling its product at a price high enough to cover the cost of buying the raw product and getting it to the customer. If the difference between the sale price and the total cost to deliver it is high enough, the company makes a profit. As the company grows, its stock goes up in value, creating additional capital, and the company retains some of its profit (retained earnings). This increase in total stockholders' equity is shown in Figure 2.7.

The firm uses its revenues from sales and any miscellaneous sources ("other income") as shown in Figure 2.8. Sales revenues must cover operating expenses of the business, cost of physical goods (cost of sales), interest expenses, and taxes. The remainder contributes to profits.

Current Ratio

The first key indicator we will present is called the current ratio. The **current ratio** is the ratio of the current assets to the current liabilities. It is a measure of a company's working-capital position.

Acceptable values for current ratio vary with industry. Utilities can withstand current ratios less than 1.5, owing to their stable customer base. They can pass most costs on to their utility users, customers who must have their services. Many analysts believe that a current ratio of 2 is a comfortable margin for a company to run its business effectively. SYSCO has consistently maintained a current ratio near 2, which is in the comfort zone.

Turnover Ratio

The second key indicator is **turnover ratio**. To calculate this, divide sales by average inventory. This lets you know the number of times that goods were purchased and resold that year. Again, the value is meaningful when considered within a given industry. SYSCO's ratio for 1992–1995 was about 18, which is very good.

Figure 2.6 Total Assets at Initiation

Sources of Assets

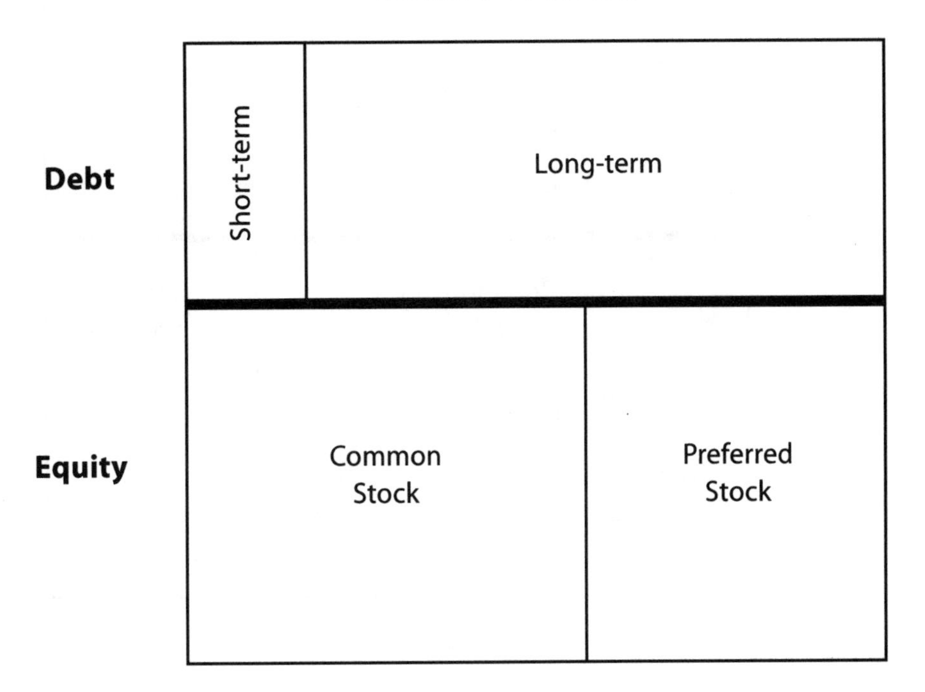

Types of Assets

Intangibles

Current Assets

Fixed Assets

Figure 2.7 Total Assets After Growth

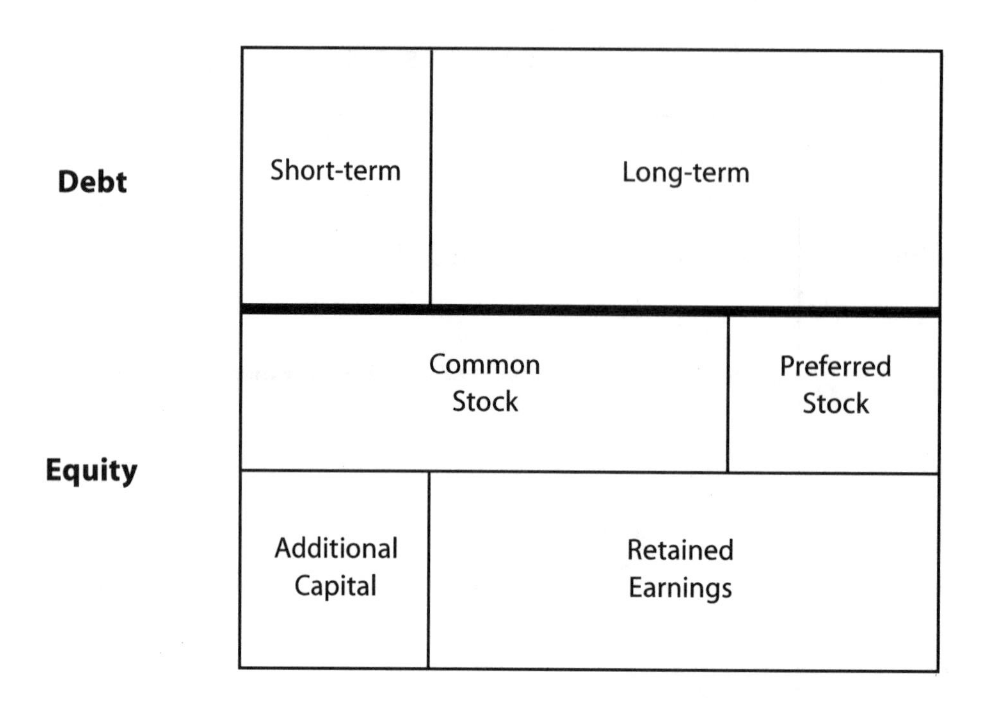

Figure 2.8 Distribution of Income

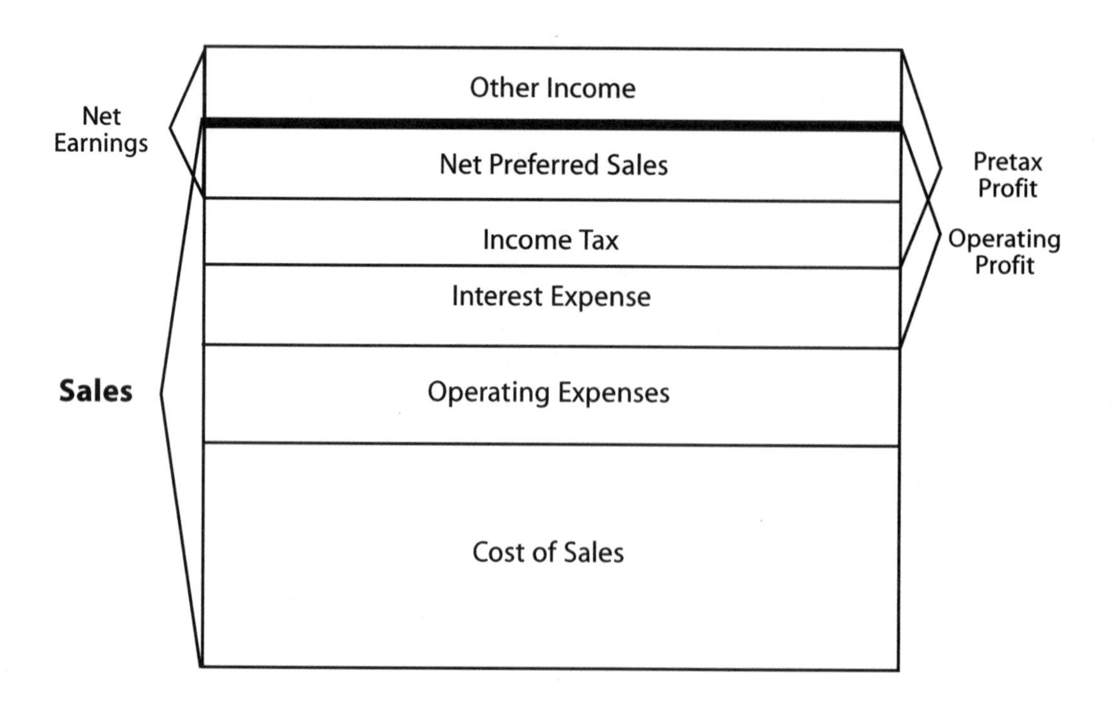

Book Value

The company's **book value** is normally thought of as the theoretical value of a share of common stock. To measure it, divide common-stock holders' equity by the number of common shares outstanding. Common-stock holders equity consists of stock sold by the corporation as well as that part of earnings retained for growth. SYSCO's book value has been going up consistently since this monitor started in 1988 (see Figure 2.5).

Capitalization Indicators

A company's total capitalization is the sum of all the long-term funds it has available. It represents the total amount of money that the company has raised through the sale of all bonds and preferred and common stock, plus additional paid-in capital and accumulated retained earnings (less intangibles if you are a purist).

Three key indicators relate to capitalization: the bond ratio, the preferred stock ratio, and the common stock ratio. The **bond ratio** is the ratio of the value of long-term debt (bonds) divided by the total capitalization. Similarly, the **preferred stock ratio** is the ratio of the par value of the preferred stock to capitalization. However, the **common stock ratio** is the proportion of the combined value of common stock, capital surplus (paid-in capital), and retained earnings to total capitalization. This is because capital surplus (additional paid-in capital) and retained earnings support the common stock.

A high ratio for either the bonds or preferred stock should be a red flag. A high debt ratio implies that less funds will remain for common shareholders during years when earnings are low. How high is too high? This depends on both the industry and management. SYSCO has maintained a bond ratio below 0.5 (50 percent) with a minimum of 0.15 (15 percent).

Leverage

The next indicator, **leverage**, can be viewed as the use of other people's money to increase your profits. That is to say, you borrow money at a given rate and earn more money at a higher rate. Leverage is the ratio of the combined total of long-term debt and preferred stock outstanding to the total stockholders' equity.

How much leverage is too much or too risky is a managerial decision. If you overleverage your equity, you may not be able to meet interest payments on borrowed money during hard times. In general, a company with a leverage of about 1:1 is probably not using margin to its fullest. If the leverage gets to 4:1, the situation could be precarious if the company manufactures goods. Utility companies, however, can withstand this kind of leverage. You are well advised to stay clear of a company that uses too much leverage. SYSCO's leverage was somewhat low in the earlier years. It increased only to a maximum of nearly 1 in 1989.

Earnings per Share

One of the most commonly known and used indicators is **earnings per share** (EPS). It is especially useful when its value is monitored over time to show a trend. Earnings are derived from sales, that is, the revenue received by the company from selling a product or service. The most common way to derive EPS is to divide the net earnings by the number of outstanding shares of common stock at the end of the fiscal year.

Earnings per share alone should not be used to determine whether the price of a stock is reasonable. If the company has earnings that grow about 20 percent per year and appears likely to continue to grow at that high rate for the next few years, you would probably be likely to invest in that company. This would be better than investing in a company with volatile earnings, that is, high earnings one year and low the next.

More investors have greater confidence in a consistent company than in a volatile one, and they have greater expectations of an increase in the market price for its common shares. Consequently, watch the *trend* of earnings, not just absolute earnings. SYSCO has shown excellent management through consistent high increases in earnings from year to year.

Interest Coverage

A company should be able to meet all its interest payments comfortably for the year and still have enough earnings to show a profit, pay dividends, and grow. The interest expense is the interest paid to bondholders for money borrowed. These expenses come from the operating profit, which is derived by subtracting the cost of sales and operating expenses from revenue (see Figure 2.8).

Interest coverage lets us know the number of times the interest could be covered by the profits generated.To derive interest coverage, use the income statement. Divide the sum of operating profit and other income by the interest expense.

As a rule of thumb, interest coverage should be 3 or greater. Clearly, SYSCO has maintained a high comfortable interest coverage over the years, and continues to do so.

Price/Earnings (P/E) Ratio

The **price/earnings ratio** (P/E) is the multiple derived by dividing the current stock price by the primary earnings per share (EPS). The P/E depends on a number of factors. These include recent earnings, the historic trend for earnings, the position of the company in its industry, and the recognition of the company and its industry by investors.

The P/E should never be used in isolation to evaluate a stock, but should be used in conjunction with the other indicators as well as the historical trends. The earnings trend is significant for the investor's expectation for the future. With high expectations come high P/E ratios; investors expect earnings to continue to increase. SYSCO, because of its persistent increases in earnings and sales, commands a high P/E. A decline in the P/E may represent a good buying opportunity. If you monitor your stock in this way, you can spot these bargain opportunities.

Return on Equity

Another measure of the worth of a stock is **return on equity** (ROE), which is calculated by dividing the net earnings by the previous year's stockholders' equity. This indicator is industry dependent but may also be compared to the average ROE generated by other U.S. companies. SYSCO has maintained a nearly constant high ROE over the years.

Return on Investment

Another measure of how good a return a company has obtained is its **return on investment** (ROI). This differs from ROE in several ways. First, it is based on net income *before* interest charges. Second, ROI uses net worth (total stockholders' equity) combined with long-term debt rather than the common owners' equity. That is, net worth also includes the equity of the preferred-stock holders. High ROI is usually an excellent indicator of efficient management. Conversely, low ROI may indicate poor management or inefficient use of resources and personnel by management.

Profit Margins

Profitability may also be measured in terms of profit margin. The **operating profit margin** is the operating profit divided by the total sales. Investors are interested in knowing how this margin has changed from year to year. The trend of the operating margin, especially over the last five years, is a good indicator of the health of a company. A drop in this item, even when sales increase, could mean that the company is not properly managing costs or cannot increase product prices enough to meet increased costs. SYSCO gives a ten-year summary of its pretax return on sales instead of operating margin or net profit ratio. This performance measure has essentially remained steady at near 3 percent over that time span, indicating consistency of performance.

The **net profit margin** is similar to the operating profit margin, except that, it uses the profit number obtained after income tax has been paid (see Figure 2.8).

Dividend Yield

The last indicator is the **dividend yield**. It is the percentage of the price per share that the dividend represents. The dividend is the portion of the profits that are paid to common-stock holders. It is tangible evidence that a company is profitable. To calculate dividend yield, divide the dividend per share by the recent price per share.

Gains from Stock Ownership

There are several ways you can realize gains from your purchase of a stock. The most common two are increases in the price of the stock and receipt of dividends. A company can reinvest its profits in the company for growth, or pay them out to the shareholders, or both. Growth companies like SYSCO Inc. usually return a small amount to investors in the form of dividends and plow the rest back into the company as retained earnings. Companies such as utilities are more income oriented. They tend to pay higher dividends to their stockholders because the potential for growth is more limited. SYSCO has paid a dividend that has, since 1982, increased steadily each year from six cents per share to twenty-four cents per share. Even so, it remains low.

Growth Rate

The **growth rate** is the change in a monitored parameter (such as sales, earnings, dividend, or price) over time. This change is usually specified as a percentage of the initial value. Thus, if an indicator such as earnings remains the same as in the previous year, then the growth rate is zero. If the amount this year is less than for the previous year, then the growth is negative. A good growth company would have high positive values on the order of 10 percent or more.

There are several ways to look at the growth values. You could simply record the changes, as is done near the top of Figure 2.4. Or you could use a graph to present a picture of the change, as has been done for SYSCO in Figure 2.9. The points graphed in Figure 2.9 are based on data in Figure 2.5, the Performance Monitor for SYSCO. You can find the price of your stocks on your monthly brokerage report or in the newspaper.

Stock Portfolio Monitor

Having purchased a number of stocks, you need to keep track of their price gain as well as the overall price gain of your portfolio. To do this, you can use copies of the Stock Portfolio Monitor shown in Figure 2.10. When you purchase a stock, record the symbol for the company in the first column and the number of shares in the second column. Use the remaining columns to enter its total value at the end of each month.

Figure 2.9 Selected Growth Rates for SYSCO

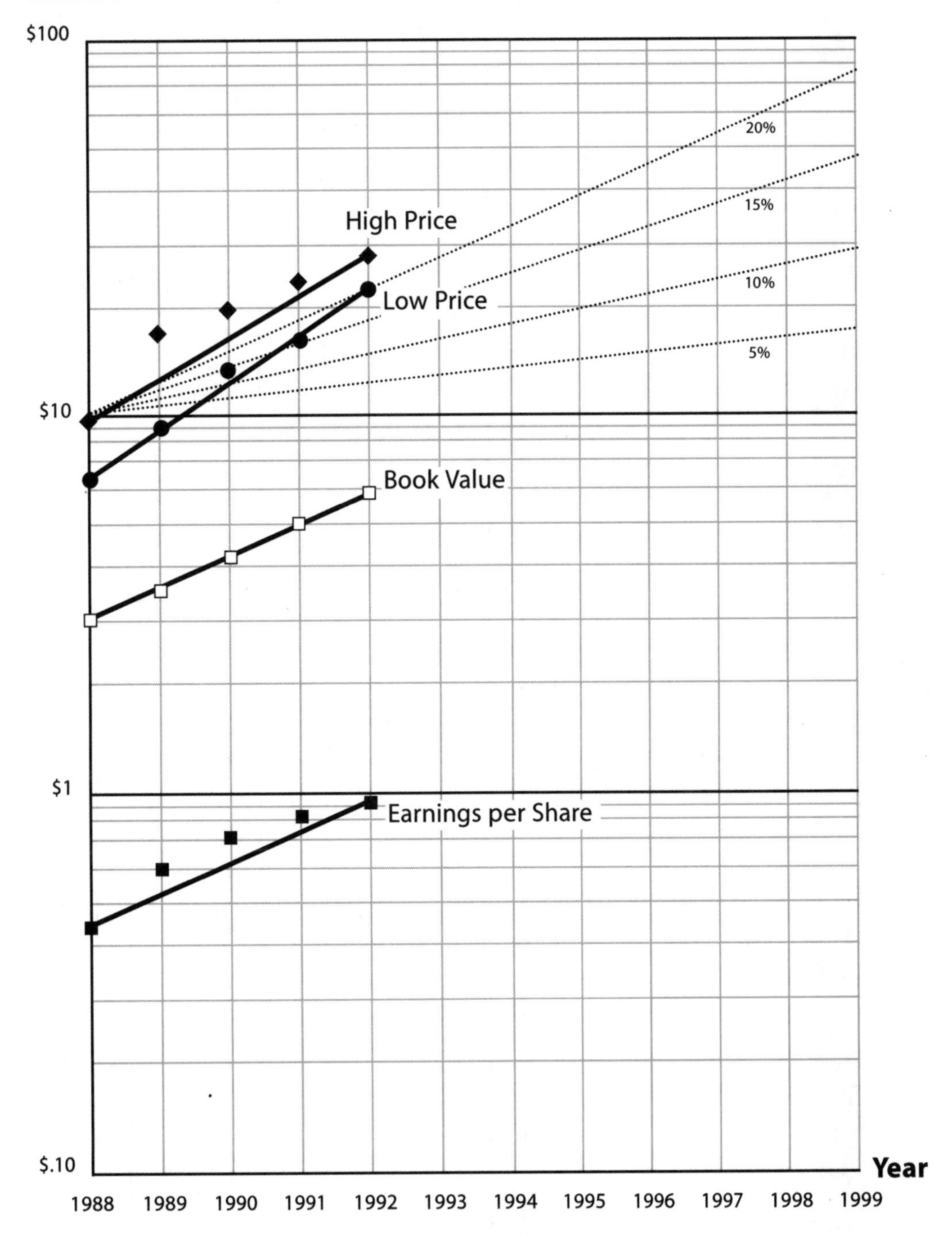

Figure 2.10 Stock Portfolio Monitor

Year: ________

Symbol	Shares	Jan	Feb	Mar	Apr	May	Jun	Jul	Aug	Sep	Oct	Nov	Dec

Frequently, in addition to common stock as shown in Figure 2.10, you also hold shares of one or more mutual funds. If you are holding shares in a mutual fund composed of stock, you might list these funds along with your common and preferred stock in Figure 2.10 or separately as illustrated in Chapter 4. On the other hand, if your mutual funds are principally made up of bonds—either corporate, federal, or municipal—you should include those funds in the Bond Monitor as shown in Chapter 3. For most meaningful monitoring, do not mix bond funds with stock funds.

If we try to judge the results of the sample stock portfolio given in Figure 2.11, we can see steady good performance by all items except Homestake Mining Company (HM). Should the investor have removed HM from the portfolio in light of its lackluster performance? In this case, the portfolio owner pondered such a deletion and replacement, but decided to hold because its key indicators remained sound. Also, he felt the market as a whole was getting into treacherous new high ground and that gold issues such as HM would endure if the market plummeted. His decision was correct because the market did crater on October 19, 1987, "Black Monday," but gold issues held up. In fact, in 1987 HM increased beyond its 1986 high, and the market value of his 1,000 shares surpassed $46,575. Consequently, the monitoring plus the key determinants helped the owner make a sound decision.

What do you do if you sell off some of the shares in your stock portfolio and invest in others? The best idea is to footnote the event of the sale or a purchase. If you use footnotes, place an asterisk or two on the modified items. An example might be as follows:

*Sold	500 shares Winn-Dixie, Inc.
Added	700 shares American Barrick
	300 shares Schlumberger, Inc.

The performance log for your stock (common and preferred) is only one of the elements of monitoring your overall portfolio performance. We will pick up the question of overall performance in Chapter 11, after we have completed the discussion of bonds, real estate, and other investment vehicles you may be using.

Figure 2.11 Stock Portfolio Monitor: Completed Example

Year: 1986

Symbol	Shares	Jan	Feb	Mar	Apr	May	Jun	Jul	Aug	Sep	Oct	Nov	Dec
BAX	1,000	$10,000	$17,875	$18,500	$19,375	$20,250	$18,250	$19,125	$17,624	$15,500	$18,875	$18,500	$19,250
CL	10,000	$327,500	$350,000	$380,000	$398,880	$397,500	$415,000	$410,000	$398,750	$363,750	$386,250	$442,500	$408,750
GTE	1,000	$48,750	$50,500	$53,000	$50,500	$50,125	$56,500	$54,750	$58,250	$53,875	$61,000	$61,250	$58,375
HM	1,100	$46,575	$41,850	$44,325	$40,725	$40,950	$45,100	$46,550	$55,000	$62,150	$28,600	$28,875	$27,912
UCL	400	$9,250	$8,950	$8,200	$8,700	$8,650	$7,050	$8,050	$8,700	$8,650	$9,700	$10,400	$10,650
UT	1,500	$37,313	$42,375	$43,500	$41,250	$41,438	$43,688	$43,125	$46,312	$40,125	$41,437	$42,375	$38,250
WIN	2,900	$87,400	$90,000	$95,100	$95,700	$101,100	$111,000	$115,800	$122,100	$105,600	$133,125	$124,062	$133,038
Total	17,900	$566,788	$601,550	$642,625	$655,130	$660,013	$696,588	$697,400	$706,736	$649,650	$678,987	$727,962	$696,225

BAX = Baxter International CL = Colgate-Palmolive GTE = General Telephone & Electric, Inc. HM = Homestake Mining Company
UCL = Unocal Corp. UT = United Telecommunications WIN = Winn-Dixie

3 Bonds and Other Fixed-Income Obligations

Otto Glaser

A SERIOUS INVESTOR with a well-founded plan will have some investments in "serious money" vehicles. These may well include sound top-quality stocks or mutual funds. However, your portfolio should also include some proportion in fixed-income investments, perhaps 10 percent to 40 percent of your estate, depending on your age, health, size of estate, and your recurring income.

There are several reasons for making fixed-income investments. They help to provide stability and have a lower volatility than most stocks and some real estate. They usually provide more current income, taxable or tax-exempt, than stock and have a greater loan value should you want to borrow using them as collateral.

Fixed-income obligations are of many types. These include corporate bonds, short-term commercial paper, municipal bonds, government bonds, notes, and bills, as well as certificates of deposit (CDs) from banks or savings and loan institutions (S&Ls), nonbank savings institutions, and credit unions. Passbook savings or CDs can be considered as short-maturity bonds or bond surrogates.

Before selecting which bond issue or issues to purchase, you should systematically evaluate the value and performance of each.

Selection Criteria

To select bonds, begin by keeping records using copies of the Bond Monitor form in Figure 3.1. For each bond, fill in the basic facts at the top of the form. Most of these items are self-evident. The coupon percentage is the amount of interest stipulated by the issuer at the time the bond is first issued. This usually remains constant over the life of the bond and should be compared to the yield-to-call, if there is a call feature, and to the yield-to-maturity.

If you then record the results of your selection process for each bond you buy, Figure 3.1 will be a convenient way to monitor your own bonds. It's worth completing to help you focus on what you are getting into and why, so you should fill out one of these sheets for each bond you own. At a later date, you should refer to this sheet to judge your prescience.

Factors you need to consider when buying bonds include interest rate, purchasing power (inflation), marketability, liquidity, legislative, call, and reinvestment.

Bond Rating

The first criterion for bond selection is the bond rating. The bond issuer has a certain credit rating, which is based on the issuer's ability to make interest and principal payments. The two main agencies that rate bonds are Moody's and Standard and Poor's. Standard and Poor's investment-grade ratings are AAA, AA, A, and BBB. Anything below these grades is considered speculative grade, and is rated BB, B, CCC, CC, C, or D. These bonds are commonly referred to by the pejorative of "junk" bonds.

Bonds rated D are traded "flat," meaning they are in default and are not paying any current interest. Unless you have good reason to believe that a D-rated bond is about to be rerated higher, avoid it. The lower the credit rating, however, the higher the yield. The difference in yield between ratings changes, so you have to review the yields available to decide the quality level to buy.

Figure 3.1 Bond Monitor

Company: ______________________ Symbol: __________

Coupon: __________ % No. of bonds: ________ Exchange traded: ________

Purchase price/bond: $ ________ Total cost: $ ________ Date of purchase: ________

Yield-to-maturity: ________ % Current yield: ________ % Date of maturity: ________

Yield-to-call: __________ % Terms of call: ______________________

Year								
Quarter	1st	2nd	3rd	4th	1st	2nd	3rd	4th
Interest Received								
Date								
Payment ($)								
Year-to-date ($)								
Criteria								
Bond rating								
Date of pricing								
Bond price ($)								
Government bond price ($)								
Current yield (%)								

Notes	
Accrued interest paid	
Equivalent government bond	
Price of government bond at purchase	
Rating service used	

Short-term note ratings on corporate and municipal issues are made by Moody's. Commercial paper is rated P1, P2, P3, and NP, where the *P* stands for "prime" paper, and P1 is the highest rating. The municipal bonds have the ratings MIG1 to MIG4, where MIG stands for "Moody's Investment Grade."

Maturity Date

Also consider the bond's maturity date. Maturities are available from a few months to 100 years.

Your decision regarding maturity is based on two considerations. The first is your prediction of interest-rate fluctuations. Longer maturities generally pay more but have more price volatility for a given change in interest. If you think, correctly, that the interest rate will change little or go lower, buying a longer maturity will bring in more interest dollars. But if you think interest rates will increase, shorter maturities, although they will pay less, will result in less price risk or loss in current value. Also, as the short-term issues mature, you will be able to reinvest the principal at the higher rate.

The second consideration is the time when you will want to use the funds invested. You can easily select bond maturities that match the date you need the money. For example, if the money is designated for your son's college education beginning in the year 2005, get that maturity.

Interest Rate

Still another selection criterion is the interest rate the bond pays. Bonds can be selected in such a way that they pay above or below the coupon interest rate. Of course, this will cause the bond to be priced above (at a premium) or below (at a discount) its maturity value, which is normally par or $1,000.

You must, therefore, consider current yield, yield-to-maturity, and coupon interest. The current yield takes into consideration the current market price of the bond. It is calculated as follows:

Current Yield = Yearly Interest in Dollars / Price

Yield-to-maturity is the combined effect of the coupon interest rate and the premium or discount in the overall yield calculation. If the bond is discounted, the formula is this:

Yield-to-Maturity = (Yearly Income + Discount) / Average Price

If the bond is bought at a premium, the formula is as follows:

Yield-to-Maturity = (Yearly Income – Premium) / Average Price where average price is half the sum of the purchase price plus redemption price. The higher the interest rate, the less the bond price will change when interest rates fluctuate. Bonds purchased above or below par value can create taxable capital gains or losses at maturity. Bond prices are expressed in percent of par value ($1,000), so a bond quoted at 98 is 98 percent of par value, or $980.

Call Feature

The fourth selection criterion is the call feature. The call feature describes the terms under which the issuer can pay off the bond before maturity. To calculate the yield-to-call, use the same formula as yield-to-maturity, but use the redemption price at the call date instead of at maturity.

In general, bonds are not called unless the issuer can borrow new money at a lower interest rate than the rate being paid on the outstanding bond. Because a bond call usually works against the bond owner, you should carefully review the terms before you purchase. You want the issuer to either pay a substantial penalty for early call or include a provision against an early call for a period of, say, ten years.

Examples

With these principles in mind, compare the sample Bond Monitor forms for Du Pont (Figure 3.2), General Electric (Figure 3.3), Nuveen (Figure 3.4), and Bond Fund of America, part of the American Funds group or family of funds, (Figure 3.5).

Monitoring

When a bond is purchased, the buyer pays accrued interest to the seller. If a bond pays interest every six months and you purchase the bond between payments, then you must pay the seller whatever interest has accrued up to the date of purchase. This interest payment should be subtracted from your first interest payment to determine the net interest received for the first payment period. Use the Interest Received part of Figure 3.1 to record interest paid at purchase and interest later received.

Monitor bonds for rating, price, and current-yield changes in comparison to yields on alternative investments. You can easily monitor each of your bonds by comparing the price of your bond to a U.S. government bond with a similar maturity. As long as the price difference between your bond and the government bond stays about the same, the credit quality of your bond probably has not changed.

Rating changes are published in Standard and Poor's and Moody's monthly bond guides. Most brokers have one or both available and will be pleased to give you the ratings of your bonds. If both your bond and the government bond changed about the same amount, then it is most likely that interest rate changes caused your bond to change in price.

Figure 3.2 Bond Monitor: Du Pont Example

Company: Du Pont — Symbol: DD01

Coupon: 6.00 % — No. of bonds: 20 — Exchange traded: NYSE

Purchase price/bond: $ 1,000 — Total cost: $ 20,000 — Date of purchase: 11/10/93

Yield-to-maturity: 6.00 % — Current yield: 6.00 % — Date of maturity: 12/01/01

Yield-to-call: N/A % — Terms of call: Noncallable

Year	1993				1994			
Quarter	1st	2nd	3rd	4th	1st	2nd	3rd	4th
Interest Received								
Date				12/1		6/1		12/1
Payment ($)				600		600		600
Year-to-date ($)				600				1,200
Criteria								
Bond rating				AA	AA	AA	AA	
Date of pricing				12/31	3/31	6/30	9/30	
Bond price ($)				98.625	93.875	91.00	90.00	
Government bond price ($)				111.56	105.03	101.59	100.16	
Current yield (%)								

Notes

Accrued interest paid	$553.33
Equivalent government bond	7.5% due 11/15/01
Price of government bond at purchase	$112.22
Rating service used	S&P

Figure 3.3 Bond Monitor: GE Example

Company: General Electric Symbol: GE 98

Coupon: 7.88 % No. of bonds: 40 Exchange traded: OTC

Purchase price/bond: $109.156 Total cost: $ 43,662.40 Date of purchase: 11/10/93

Yield-to-maturity: 5.00 % Current yield: 7.08 % Date of maturity: 09/15/98

Yield-to-call: N/A % Terms of call: Noncallable

Year	1993				1994			
Quarter	1st	2nd	3rd	4th	1st	2nd	3rd	4th
Interest Received								
Date					3/15		9/15	
Payment ($)					1,575		1,575	
Year-to-date ($)					1,575		3,150	
Criteria								
Bond rating				AAA	AAA	AAA	AAA	
Date of pricing				12/31	3/31	6/30	9/30	
Bond price ($)				109.25	104.72	91.00	100.88	
Government bond price ($)				110.75	106.34	103.75	102.44	
Current yield (%)								

Notes	
Accrued interest paid	$280.00
Equivalent government bond	7.88% due 04/15/98
Price of government bond at purchase	$111.22
Rating service used	S&P

Figure 3.4 Bond Monitor: Nuveen Example

Company: Nuveen National Insured Series #200 Symbol: N/A

Coupon: N/A % No. of bonds: 100 units Exchange traded: OTC

Purchase price/bond: $117.76 Total cost: $ 11,776.00 Date of purchase: 11/10/93

Yield-to-maturity: N/A % Current yield: 6.20 % Date of maturity: N/A

Yield-to-call: N/A % Terms of call: Noncallable

Year	1993				1994			
Quarter	1st	2nd	3rd	4th	1st	2nd	3rd	4th
Interest Received								
Date				12/31		6/30		
Payment ($)				362.7		362.7		
Year-to-date ($)								
Criteria								
Bond rating	AAA	(Insured)						
Date of pricing				12/31	3/31	6/30	9/30	
Bond price ($)				114.29	109.42	108.78	108.28	
Government bond price ($)	N/A							
Current yield (%)				6.3	6.6	6.7	6.7	

Notes

Accrued interest paid	$140.00
Equivalent government bond	N/A
Price of government bond at purchase	N/A
Rating service used	N/A

Figure 3.5 Bond Monitor: American Funds Example

Company: American Funds Bond Fund of America   Symbol: ABNDX

Coupon: N/A %   No. of bonds: 200   Exchange traded: OTC

Purchase price/bond: $ 117.76   Total cost: $ 11,776.00   Date of purchase: 11/10/93

Yield-to-maturity: N/A %   Current yield: 7.30 %   Date of maturity: N/A

Yield-to-call: N/A %   Terms of call: Noncallable

Year	1993				1994			
Quarter	1st	2nd	3rd	4th	1st	2nd	3rd	4th
Interest Received								
Date				12/31	3/31	6/30	9/30	
Payment ($)				52.50	52.50	52.50	52.50	
Year-to-date ($)						105.00	157.50	
Criteria								
Bond rating	N/A							
Date of pricing				12/31	3/31	6/30	9/30	
Bond price ($)				14.45	13.65	13.19	13.03	
Government bond price ($)	N/A							
Current yield (%)				7.30	7.70	8.00	8.10	

Notes	
Accrued interest paid	N/A
Equivalent government bond	N/A
Price of government bond at purchase	N/A
Rating service used	N/A

To help monitor your holdings of bonds and other fixed-income investments, consider using the summary form in Figure 3.6. You can get the price of these issues from your brokerage firm's monthly statements, and you should periodically check on the ratings with the broker if you can't find these numbers in a guide book such as Standard & Poor's *Monthly Bond Guide*.

The completed sample in Figure 3.7 illustrates an investor who held 20 Du Pont bonds, 40 GE bonds, 100 units of Nuveen National Insured Series #200, and 200 shares of Bond Fund of America. Note how this investor recorded the price at the end of each quarter to determine the current value of this part of her portfolio. If she had noted a new bond rating, she would have highlighted it with an asterisk.

Should your collection of interest be diminished, or should a bond receive a lower bond rating, obviously your bond is in trouble. By investigating the issuer's latest data, you may discover a reason to continue holding, to sell, or perhaps even to dollar-cost-average and take advantage of a bargain by buying more. Dollar-cost-averaging is simply the act of buying an investment at constant intervals over a period of time to take advantage of the fluctuations in price. In theory, on the average, you will buy more times at a low price than at a high.

By using the form in Figure 3.8, you can keep track of your interest received on an annual basis. Bonds usually pay every six months, so you typically enter interest in alternate quarters. Some trust certificates and bond mutual funds, however, pay monthly, requiring more frequent entries for these investments. Figure 3.9 is a completed example.

Bonds add stability to a portfolio and provide a steady source of income. In past years major changes have occurred in interest rates, requiring careful monitoring of bond portfolios. This chapter gives you the tools to accomplish this task.

Figure 3.6 Summary of Fixed-Income Securities

Description	Date: ______		Date: ______		Date: ______		Date: ______	
	Price	Value	Price	Value	Price	Value	Price	Value
Bonds								
Mutual Funds								
Unit Trusts								
CDs								
Passbook Savings								
Totals								

Figure 3.7 Summary of Fixed-Income Securities: Completed Example

Description	Date: 12/31/93		Date: 3/31/94		Date: 6/30/94		Date: 9/30/94	
	Price	Value	Price	Value	Price	Value	Price	Value
Bonds								
20,000 Du Pont 6% 12/1/01	98.625	$19,725	93.875	$18,775	91.000	$18,200	90.000	$18,000
40,000 GE 7.875% 9/15/98	109.250	$43,700	104.719	$41,888	101.969	$40,788	100.875	$40,350
Mutual Funds								
200 Bond Fund of America	14.450	$2,890	13.650	$2,730	13.190	$2,638	13.030	$2,606
Unit Trusts								
100 Nuveen Nat. Insurance Series 200	114.290	$11,429	109.420	$10,942	108.750	$10,875	108.280	$10,828
CDs								
Passbook Savings								
$2,000 at 3%		$2,000		$2,015		$2,030		$2,046
Totals								
		$79,744		$76,350		$74,531		$73,830

Figure 3.8 Record of Interest Received

Year: ____________

Security	Amount	Jan	Feb	Mar	Apr	May	Jun	Jul	Aug	Sep	Oct	Nov	Dec	Total

Figure 3.9 Record of Interest Received: Completed Example

Year: ________

Security	Amount	Jan	Feb	Mar	Apr	May	Jun	Jul	Aug	Sep	Oct	Nov	Dec	Total
Bonds														
Du Pont 6% 12/1/03	20						$600.00						$600.00	$1,200.00
GE 7.875% 9/15/98	40			$1,575.00						$1,575.00				$3,150.00
Unit Trusts														
Nuveen Series 200	100					$362.70						$362.70		$725.40
Mutual Funds														
Bond Fund of America	200	$17.50	$17.50	$17.50	$17.50	$17.50	$17.50	$17.50	$17.50	$17.50	$17.50	$17.50	$17.50	$210.00
Totals		$17.50	$17.50	$1,592.50	$17.50	$380.20	$617.50	$17.50	$17.50	$1,592.50	$17.50	$380.20	$617.50	$5,285.40

4 Investment Companies

Lawrence Lynn and
James H. Galbraith

SOME PEOPLE BLITHELY think that if they own investments in so-called "investment companies," they are not required to monitor them. After all, those investments are managed by professionals, aren't they? Yes, and some are very well managed indeed, whereas the management of others ranges from mediocre to feeble. It is wise, therefore, to remain informed about those investments. It is especially important to be aware of a management change; the new manager may not follow the same asset-allocation strategy and philosophy as the original, or with the same skills.

There are, broadly speaking, only three major types of investment companies in wide use today: the unit investment trust, closed-end investment companies, and open-end (mutual) investment companies. Regardless of the type of investment company in which you have invested, you should monitor your holdings in roughly the same manner. Be aware of such items as how your investment is performing relative to the progress you want, what kind of periodic payments (capital-gains distributions, dividends, interest) the company makes, and how its performance measures up.

The Fund Monitor

For each of the funds you want to monitor, use a copy of Figure 4.1 (for a closed-end fund) or Figure 4.2 (for an open-end fund). Record information on a quarterly or annual basis. If you record quarterly, you will have room for six years of data. If you record annually, you have room for twenty-four years of data. These fund monitors are divided into two sections. The first section is used to record the basic information about the fund. It includes the company name, its symbol, the number of shares you purchased, the cost per share, the market value or net asset value (NAV), the total cost, a note to indicate whether you are reinvesting dividends or taking income, the commission if it is a closed-end fund or load if it is a mutual fund, the date of purchase, the objective of the fund, and the percentage of stocks, bonds, and foreign investments.

The second section, which is repeated three times, is where you record your quarterly or annual results. The following discussion includes guidelines for entering and interpreting information in this section.

Unit Investment Trusts

The first type of investment companies, unit investment trusts, are frequently put together by major brokerage houses such as A. G. Edwards & Sons, Inc., Merrill Lynch, Prudential Securities, and Dean Witter. To illustrate their modus operandi with a tax-exempt unit trust, an investment firm may have researched and aggregated $60 million worth of tax-exempt securities. For example, the firm may have selected from a wide variety of state, city, school district, toll road, and other tax-exempt bonds and constructed a single portfolio. The firm would have subdivided this resultant fund or trust into units, roughly 60,000 of them, each with a par value of $1,000 plus accrued interest. To this they would add the cost of research and administration, say 3 percent, so that the unit might be priced to the public at $1,051.17 per unit. Somebody investing in ten such units would have invested $10,511.70 at the initial offering. As an added inducement, some of these units may pay monthly interest to the investor.

Figure 4.1 Closed-End Investment Company Fund Monitor

Company: ______________________________ Symbol: __________

No. of shares: _____ Cost/share: $______ Market value: $______ Total cost: $ ______

Reinvest dividend? Yes____ No____ Commission: $______ Date of purchase: ________

Objective: ____________ Stock %: ______ Bonds %: ______ Foreign %: ______

Year End								
NAV ($)								
Market value ($)								
Capital gains distribution ($)								
Dividend ($)								
Interest ($)								
Market-value change ($)								
Net change ($)								
Total return (%)								
Number of shares								
Value ($)								
Year End								
NAV ($)								
Market value ($)								
Capital gains distribution ($)								
Dividend ($)								
Interest ($)								
Market-value change ($)								
Net change ($)								
Total return (%)								
Number of shares								
Value ($)								
Year End								
NAV ($)								
Market value ($)								
Capital gains distribution ($)								
Dividend ($)								
Interest ($)								
Market-value change ($)								
Net change ($)								
Total return (%)								
Number of shares								
Value ($)								

Figure 4.2 Open-End Investment Company Fund Monitor

Company: ________________________________ Symbol: ____________

No. of shares: ______ Cost/share: $________ NAV: $________ Total cost: $ ________

Reinvest dividend? Yes_____ No_____ Load %________ Date of purchase: __________

Objective: ______________ Stock %: ______ Bonds %: ______ Foreign %: _______

Year End								
NAV ($)								
Capital gains distribution ($)								
Dividend ($)								
Interest ($)								
NAV change ($)								
Net change ($)								
Total return (%)								
Number of shares								
Value ($)								
Year End								
NAV ($)								
Capital gains distribution ($)								
Dividend ($)								
Interest ($)								
NAV change ($)								
Net change ($)								
Total return (%)								
Number of shares								
Value ($)								
Year End								
NAV ($)								
Capital gains distribution ($)								
Dividend ($)								
Interest ($)								
NAV change ($)								
Net change ($)								
Total return (%)								
Number of shares								
Value ($)								

As interest rates fluctuate and as the fortunes of the individual bonds rise or fall, the value of the unit will vary accordingly. Usually, because the resale or secondary market for such investments is small, you do not see their prices published in your local newspaper or even major financial dailies such as the *Wall Street Journal* or *Investor's Business Daily*. You must retrieve the up-to-date value from the originating brokerage house or from the values appearing in your monthly statement.

Most unit investment trusts issued during the twentieth century have enjoyed, at best, only brief upsurges and generally have decreased in value since issuance. This decrease occurs when bonds in the unit trust are prepaid and part of the original investment is returned to the owner. Consequently, we will not show specific examples of active monitoring or control. The principles are identical to those illustrated for the closed-end investment companies. Use the closed-end investment company monitor sheet.

Closed-End Investment Companies

The closed-end investment company arises from the aggregation of a body of stocks, bonds, mortgages, options, and possibly other investment vehicles into a single portfolio. For comparison, suppose we use $60 million again. The fund then sells its shares at a relatively salable price, say $10 per share at the time of its issuance. This results in six million shares outstanding. At this point no new investment vehicles or shares can be added to the portfolio, and it would be listed on an exchange or over the counter at a price above or below the net asset value.

To the extent that it is well managed and the aggregate investment improves over the initial $60 million, each share could change in value in two ways. The first is in its apparent value, that is, the value perceived by the market. If investors believe this is a hot fund, they may pay a premium to own it on the expectation of a much higher future increase. In addition, the value could change to reflect changes made by the underlying investments. Thus, if the fund increases its net asset value, for example, to $15 per share, the net results would be to push the price up to a premium over $15 due to expectations alone. If the demand were low, a fund share could be priced at a discount from the net asset value, say $9.50. The discounted value could indicate either that a real bargain exists or that there is a lack of confidence in its management, assets, and future.

Monitoring most closed-end investment companies in the United States and the Western world is relatively easy because the price of such funds is listed daily in major financial newspapers as well as in your brokerage firm's monthly statement. As an example of monitoring this type of fund, Figure 4.3 shows a Fund Monitor form for 300 shares of a well-known closed-end fund, Zenix Investment Fund, Inc. This chart shows clearly how the fund performed during the period from the start of January 1989 until the close of December 31, 1996. If you owned it from 1988

Figure 4.3 Closed-End Investment Company Fund Monitor: Zenix Example

Company: Zenix Income Fund, Inc. Symbol: ZIF

No. of shares: 300 Cost/share: $ 9.785 Market value: $ 9.50 Total cost: $ 2,935.50

Reinvest dividend? Yes X No ___ Commission: $ 85.50 Date of purchase: 04/31/90

Objective: Income Stock %: 0 Bonds %: 100 Foreign %: ___

Year End	1989	1990	1991	1992	1993	1994	1995	1996
NAV ($)	8.71	6.30	5.58	6.39	6.86	6.76	5.88	6.31
Market value ($)	9.50	5.88	5.50	6.63	7.25	7.13	6.63	7.00
Capital gains distribution ($)								
Dividend ($)	0	1.20	0.90	0.85	0.82	0.82	0.87	0.73
Interest ($)								
Market-value change ($)		(3.62)	(0.38)	1.13	0.62	(0.12)	(0.50)	0.37
Net change ($)		(2.42)	0.52	1.98	1.44	0.70	0.37	1.10
Total return (%)		(27.68)	10.58	39.12	24.02	10.02	6.41	20.01
Number of shares	300.00	350.53	414.40	478.25	542.40	606.80	694.39	789.29
Value ($)	2,850.00	2,061.12	2,279.19	3,170.80	3,932.43	4,326.46	4,603.79	5,525.01
Year End	1997							
NAV ($)	6.35							
Market value ($)	7.25							
Capital gains distribution ($)								
Dividend ($)	0.72							
Interest ($)								
Market-value change ($)	0.25							
Net change ($)	0.97							
Total return (%)	15.55							
Number of shares	880.57							
Value ($)	6,384.14							
Year End								
NAV ($)								
Market value ($)								
Capital gains distribution ($)								
Dividend ($)								
Interest ($)								
Market-value change ($)								
Net change ($)								
Total return (%)								
Number of shares								
Value ($)								

Note: Data based on fiscal year ending March 31. Negative numbers are shown in parentheses.
Source: Data from Smith Barney, Inc.

to the close of 1990, you might well have despaired over its performance. Happily, its results improved greatly since 1991; it showed negative returns in 1994, but the total returns for the remainder of the time ranged from 20 percent to 39 percent annually.

Open-End Investment Companies (Mutual Funds)

Finally, the open-end investment company is commonly called a mutual fund. In this type of vehicle, the fund *normally* stands ready to accept a constant supply of new cash from its current shareholders and from potential new ones desiring to participate. The currency flowing into the fund is invested in accordance with the fund's stated objectives and its current analysis of where the best investment values exist.

The reason for the caveat "normally" is that, on occasion, a perfectly sound mutual fund may elect to become "closed" for a while. During this period it will not accept any new investments. This is a rare occurrence and happens only when more cash has been contributed than the fund can place at that time. Another possibility is that a significant change in capabilities has occurred internally—loss of key management or analysis staff precluding normal activities. Also, occasionally, a fund's merger or acquisition may cause a temporary interruption of its open-end status.

All open-end mutual funds are valued once per day, and their closing values, always stated at net asset value (NAV), appear in many major-city newspapers and in the major financial dailies. A significant difference between the closed-end and open-end funds is that open-end funds are redeemed at net asset value, whereas closed-end funds are auctioned on the exchanges and may trade at prices above or below net asset value.

Such a plethora of funds is available, and the entire arena of fund activity has multiplied so rapidly lately, that it is imperative to be guided properly in fund selection. Monitoring, however, is easy for virtually all funds for current fund rating, payout, and net asset value.

Fund Rating

Over 8,000 funds exist today, and their objectives vary considerably. In general, Morningstar breaks the investment style of a fund into nine categories based on type of investment and median size of companies purchased. It separates the various proportions of stocks and bonds into three categories (value, growth, and blend), and categorizes the median size of companies in the fund portfolio into three levels (large, medium, and small).

The completed examples in Figures 4.4 to 4.7 illustrate the performance of four mutual funds in hypothetical portfolios. The mutual funds shown are Investment Company of America (ICA) (one of the oldest and most popular), Oppenheimer

Main Street, Income & Growth Fund A, Van Kampen American-Capital Emerging Growth A, and Merrill Lynch Capital Fund. These funds are all A shares.

Some brokerage funds that construct and administer mutual funds put together funds categorized as A, B, or C shares. The A shares carry full commission (load) up front but a lower annual expense, whereas B shares are "back-end" loaded, and C shares have no load but a higher annual expense. This means that for B and C shares you pay no sales charge or commission when purchasing them. If, however, you turn around and sell B shares within one year from purchase, you must pay the entire commission or load at the time of sale. If you hold the fund for a year, the sales charge decreases by 1 percent or so for each year that you retain your shares, reaching zero after four or five years. During those four or five years, your annual expenses are higher, but they drop to match those of the A funds. The annual expenses of the no-load funds (C shares) remain constant for as long as you hold them.

Payout

Naturally, each fund you have may produce periodic dividends or capital gains (or loss) resulting from managed trading within the fund. Usually the cash dividends are reported out and may be paid to you quarterly or semiannually. The capital gains, in contrast, are typically paid every half year or after each annual period of performance. The sum of dividend cash and capital gains represents your total payout. For income-tax purposes, the IRS considers mutual-fund capital gains as long term, regardless of how long you have held the fund. The true total return, however, should include not only your total payout amount or percentage but also the payout when added to your gain or loss in net asset value of the specific fund.

Net Asset Value

Fund managers derive NAV daily, and you need to track this value quarterly or at least annually in the Fund Monitor (Figure 4.2) where the performance is calculated. You can obtain these numbers from your newspaper or account statements from your broker or the fund manager.

Follow the NAV especially carefully. Another important indicator is the quarterly or semiannual cash dividend, whose relative size gives indications of the fund's performance enhancement or deterioration. You calculate the annual dividend per share by reviewing your monthly or quarterly statements. On each statement you will see a total dividend paid out. Divide this total dividend by the number of shares of the fund you own. Add each of these per-share values for the entire quarter or year.

The capital-gains distributions are likely to be the most volatile figures and the least predictable. Your overall total return, which is based on the combination of NAV premium (or discount), cash dividends (or interest), and capital-gains distributions, should show strength over time.

You can calculate the change in NAV by subtracting last year's NAV from this year's NAV. For example, consider the Oppenheimer fund, Main Street Income & Growth

Figure 4.4 Open-End Investment Company Fund Monitor: ICA Example

Company: Investment Company of America Symbol: AIVSX

No. of shares: 100 Cost/share: $ 16.12 NAV: $ 15.24 Total cost: $ 1,611.63

Reinvest dividend? Yes X No ___ Load %: 5.75 Date of purchase: 12/31/88

Objective: Growth and income Stock %: 86.6 Bonds %: 2.8 Foreign %: 11.6

Year End	1989	1990	1991	1992	1993	1994	1995	1996
NAV ($)	15.24	14.42	17.48	17.89	18.72	17.67	21.61	24.23
Capital gains distribution ($)	0.85	0.22	0.38	0.32	0.75	0.60	0.91	1.03
Dividend ($)	0.59	0.59	0.44	0.47	0.47	0.48	0.50	0.50
Interest ($)								
NAV change ($)	2.30	(0.82)	3.06	0.41	0.83	(1.05)	3.94	2.62
Net change ($)	3.74	(0.01)	3.88	1.20	2.05	0.03	5.35	4.15
Total return (%)	29.41	0.68	26.54	6.99	11.62	0.15	30.63	19.35
Number of shares	100.00	106.41	111.07	116.12	123.86	131.42	140.37	149.42
Value ($)	1,524.00	1,534.36	1,941.58	2,077.30	2,318.68	2,322.16	3,033.44	3,620.41
Year End								
NAV ($)								
Capital gains distribution ($)								
Dividend ($)								
Interest ($)								
NAV change ($)								
Net change ($)								
Total return (%)								
Number of shares								
Value ($)								
Year End								
NAV ($)								
Capital gains distribution ($)								
Dividend ($)								
Interest ($)								
NAV change ($)								
Net change ($)								
Total return (%)								
Number of shares								
Value ($)								

Note: Negative numbers are shown in parentheses.
Source: Data from Morningstar, Inc.

Figure 4.5 Open-End Investment Company Fund Monitor: Van Kampen Example

Company: Van Kampen American-Capital Emerging Growth A Symbol: ACEGX

No. of shares: 200 Cost/share: $ 15.69 NAV: $ 14.84 Total cost: $ 3,138.66

Reinvest dividend? Yes X No ___ Load %: 5.75 Date of purchase: 12/31/89

Objective: Income Stock %: 95.3 Bonds %: 0 Foreign %: 4.7

Year End	1989	1990	1991	1992	1993	1994	1995	1996
NAV ($)	14.84	14.67	21.41	22.27	25.85	23.37	30.49	34.36
Capital gains distribution ($)	—	0.37	1.91	1.16	1.66	0.62	3.19	1.55
Dividend ($)	0.26	0.08	0.03	0	0	0	0	0
Interest ($)								
NAV change ($)	3.14	(0.17)	6.74	0.86	3.58	(2.48)	7.12	3.87
Net change ($)	3.40	0.28	8.68	2.02	5.24	(1.86)	10.31	5.42
Total return (%)	29.06	1.97	60.43	9.73	23.92	(7.13)	44.63	17.91
Number of shares	200.00	206.30	226.78	239.24	255.40	262.36	290.85	304.31
Value ($)	2,968.00	3,026.47	4,855.37	5,327.79	6,602.20	6,131.46	8,867.94	10,456.09
Year End								
NAV ($)								
Capital gains distribution ($)								
Dividend ($)								
Interest ($)								
NAV change ($)								
Net change ($)								
Total return (%)								
Number of shares								
Value ($)								
Year End								
NAV ($)								
Capital gains distribution ($)								
Dividend ($)								
Interest ($)								
NAV change ($)								
Net change ($)								
Total return (%)								
Number of shares								
Value ($)								

Note: Negative numbers are shown in parentheses.
Source: Data from Morningstar, Inc.

Figure 4.6 Open-End Investment Company Fund Monitor: Oppenheimer Example

Company: Oppenheimer Main Street, Income & Growth Symbol: MSIGX

No. of shares: 200 Cost/share: $ 12.99 NAV: $ 12.29 Total cost: $ 2,599.34

Reinvest dividend? Yes X No ___ Load %: 5.75 Date of purchase: 12/31/89

Objective: Growth and income Stock %: 76.5 Bonds %: 3.6 Foreign %: 3.7

Year End	1989	1990	1991	1992	1993	1994	1995	1996
NAV ($)	12.29	11.14	15.52	17.85	21.76	20.98	26.89	28.74
Capital gains distribution ($)	0.15	—	2.51	2.20	1.99	—	0.08	1.98
Dividend ($)	0.20	0.40	0.22	0.19	0.28	0.44	0.43	0.40
Interest ($)								
NAV change ($)	2.18	(1.15)	4.38	2.33	3.91	(0.78)	5.91	1.85
Net change ($)	2.53	(0.75)	7.11	4.72	6.18	(0.34)	6.41	4.23
Total return (%)	25.18	(6.15)	66.37	31.08	35.39	(1.53)	30.77	15.70
Number of shares	200.00	207.08	247.29	281.83	313.01	319.68	326.16	353.08
Value ($)	2,458.00	2,306.83	3,837.88	5,030.69	6,811.05	6,706.84	8,770.54	10,148.00
Year End								
NAV ($)								
Capital gains distribution ($)								
Dividend ($)								
Interest ($)								
NAV change ($)								
Net change ($)								
Total return (%)								
Number of shares								
Value ($)								
Year End								
NAV ($)								
Capital gains distribution ($)								
Dividend ($)								
Interest ($)								
NAV change ($)								
Net change ($)								
Total return (%)								
Number of shares								
Value ($)								

Note: Negative numbers are shown in parentheses.
Source: Data from Morningstar, Inc.

Figure 4.7 Open-End Investment Company Fund Monitor: Merrill Lynch Example

Company: Merrill Lynch Capital Fund Symbol: MACPX

No. of shares: 200 Cost/share: $ 22.51 NAV: $ 21.39 Total cost: $ 4,502.60

Reinvest dividend? Yes X No ___ Load %: 5.25 Date of purchase: 12/31/88

Objective: Growth and income Stock %: 55 Bonds %: 45 Foreign %: 20

Year End	1988	1989	1990	1991	1992	1993	1994	1995
NAV ($)	21.39	24.43	24.38	26.92	26.33	27.97	27.46	30.55
Capital gains distribution ($)	—	0.72	0.39	0.26	0.95	0.70	0.93	1.42
Dividend ($)	—	1.10	1.30	1.36	0.92	1.20	1.07	2.04
Interest ($)								
NAV change ($)	—	3.04	(0.05)	2.54	(0.59)	1.64	(0.51)	3.09
Net change ($)	—	4.86	1.64	4.16	1.29	3.54	1.49	6.55
Total return (%)	—	22.98	1.08	24.69	5.03	13.71	0.91	32.87
Number of shares	200.00	215.35	218.13	246.32	264.51	283.13	291.02	347.56
Value ($)	4,278.00	5,261.00	5,318.00	6,631.00	6,964.00	7,919.00	7,991.00	10,618.00
Year End	1996							
NAV ($)	31.05							
Capital gains distribution ($)	1.46							
Dividend ($)	1.73							
Interest ($)								
NAV change ($)	0.50							
Net change ($)	3.69							
Total return (%)	12.67							
Number of shares	385.29							
Value ($)	11,963.00							
Year End								
NAV ($)								
Capital gains distribution ($)								
Dividend ($)								
Interest ($)								
NAV change ($)								
Net change ($)								
Total return (%)								
Number of shares								
Value ($)								

Note: Negative numbers are shown in parentheses.
Source: Data from Morningstar, Inc.

(Figure 4.6). On December 31, 1990, the NAV was $11.14, and on December 31, 1989, the NAV was $12.29. The change in NAV is therefore a drop of $1.15 per share.

To calculate the net change in NAV, add together the capital gains, dividends, interest, and the NAV change. Thus, on December 31, 1990, the net change is zero for capital gains plus $0.40 for dividends, plus zero for interest and minus $1.55 for the NAV change, producing a net change of negative $0.75 per share.

Other Performance Measures

The total return is the percentage gain or loss during the last year (or quarter). At the end of 1989, the value of one share of the fund was $12.29. By the end of 1990, the value had dropped to $11.14, although this drop was mitigated by the receipt of dividends.

Note that the number of shares is growing from year to year. From 1989 to 1990, the number of shares in the fund increased from 200 to 207.08. This is because this investor chose to reinvest all capital gains and dividend distributions. The number of shares acquired at each distribution depends on the NAV at the time of distribution, which is usually at or near the end of a quarter. Consequently, at the end of each quarter, the number of shares increases by a small amount.

For example, at the end of the first quarter, you owned 200 shares and received $0.05 per share as a dividend distribution. The total value of your distribution is 200 times 0.05, or $10. If at that time the value of one share of the fund was $10.69, the reinvestment of this dividend would give you 10/10.69 or 0.9355 new shares. If you repeat this each quarter for both dividend and capital-gains distributions, you will end up with 206 shares at the end of the year. You don't need to make these calculations yourself; your monthly or quarterly statement should indicate the total number of shares you own.

If you multiply the number of shares in the fund by the NAV, you arrive at the value of the fund. Both the number of shares and the total value are reported on your brokerage or fund statement. To calculate the percent total return for the year, subtract this year's value from last year's value, divide the result by last year's value and multiply by 100. In this case, you get [($2,306.83 – $2,458)/$2,458] × 100, or –6.15. (Negative numbers are shown in parentheses in Figure 4.6.)

If these returns meet your expectations, you may want to consider dollar-cost-averaging by continually adding more money to these funds. When you reinvest dividends, you are effectively dollar-cost-averaging. Over time you will find that you will buy new shares at a lower value than you would pay at the end of the year. This is because the market is continually in a state of fluctuation and is normally down more than it is up.

If you are especially heavily committed to mutual funds, you may wish to maintain surveillance over certain somewhat esoteric key performance indicators. These include the beta, alpha, Sharpe ratio, and others. A description of these indicators can be found in Morningstar and other fund review companies at your local library. These publications can be your source of information, but if you use full-service brokers, you should be able to request the data from them.

5 Monitoring and Controlling Options

Lawrence Lynn

TRADING IN STOCK options can be either a highly conservative and protective activity—that is, protecting your account against market declines—or a highly aggressive and, indeed, speculative activity, depending on how you use those options. Most investors, even today, a generation following the establishment of the so-called listed stock options exchanges in the United States, remain blissfully unaware of the diversity of what options activities might accomplish for them—or to them. In a way, options usage is somewhat akin to the ancient humans' use of fire. Fire, they learned, could do many wonderful things: cook one's catch of game; smelt copper ore for adornments; shape iron into tools or weapons. But fire could also bring death and destruction upon ancient people. It was all in how fire was used. The same is true for options, which offer a plethora of activities—pros and cons—from which to choose.

Although I assume that most readers or users of this chapter have developed more than a nodding acquaintance with options—after all, why be interested in monitoring or controlling something you have never been involved with?—it may also be that some readers have never used options but would like to try. Hence, we will start with a few definitions and a brief review of the several concepts familiar to regular options users. The subject and its rationale are treated in greater depth in recent general-investment books, such as *How to Invest Today* (which I edited in 1995).

Definitions and Basic Concepts

For purposes of buying, selling, and monitoring, stock values are measured in points and in fractions of dollars. One point equals $100; eight points equals $800. These points can be divided into halves, quarters, eighths, and the value is written 1 1/2 ($150), 7 1/4 ($725), 8 1/8 ($812.50), etc.

Options

An option is a right or privilege of a financial nature that can be bought or sold. Most options now traded are listed; unlisted options are quite scarce today. The listed exchanges in the United States include the Chicago Board Options Exchange (CBOE), which is the largest, three smaller exchanges, and the New York Stock Exchange (NYSE). Paradoxically, the NYSE is the largest stock exchange yet the smallest of the options exchanges.

The listed options exchanges identify two basic classes of options, calls and puts.

Calls

A **call option** gives the buyer of the option the right to purchase typically 100 shares of the specified (underlying) stock issue, e.g., General Motors or IBM, at a predetermined price, the strike price, up to a certain date termed the expiration date. For this right, the option buyer pays a price known as the premium.

For example, if you buy an option on General Motors stock, which currently has a market value of $50 per share, at a strike price of $55 and pay a premium of $2 per share, or $200 for the 100 shares, you would make a substantial profit if GM were to rise to $60. However, if the price remained below $55 during the period up to the expiration date, your option would end up worthless, costing you the entire $200. Therefore, when you buy a call, you want the underlying stock to rise in value, and you want this to happen within a definite time span.

Who receives the premium? The person who sells the call option receives it, less a commission. The option buyer also pays a commission.

Puts

Although it's not an exact analogy, a **put option** may be considered the mirror opposite of a call. If you buy a put, you are convinced that the underlying stock issue is about to plummet—precipitously, you hope. Hence, you buy a put that entitles you to the right to sell that stock at a predetermined strike price at any time up to its expiration date.

For example, if you thought that Sumerian Oil Company (SUME) stock, which was trading over the counter at $60, was headed for a fall, you might buy a put, as follows:

60 SUME MAY 55 @ 2

This is interpreted as an expiration date of the Friday preceding the third Saturday of May, a $55 strike price, and a premium of $200 per option.

What you now own is the right to sell (or put to someone else) 100 shares of Sumerian Oil at $55 per share, even if the price falls to, let's say, $45. Thus, for two points (or $200) plus commission, you can sell the stock for $55 and buy it right back for $45, for a nice $10-per-share profit. Of course, if Sumerian did not accommodate you and remained steady or actually increased, you would lose the $200. You could mitigate this loss by selling a lower-valued put to someone else, maybe for ½ or $50 per option, but you would still take a loss.

Exercise

One of the methods by which you may profit from an option is through **exercising** it, or buying or selling stock according to the terms of the option. For example, if you bought a call with a strike price of $50 and the stock climbed to $65, clearly you could exercise your option to buy the stock at $50. You would then simultaneously sell it for $65 for a gain of $15 per share, less your original option cost and commissions. Similarly, a put buyer would exercise an option when the underlying stock reached a price sufficiently lower than the strike price for a profit. The exercise of a put consists of selling the stock at the higher strike price (a momentary short sale) and simultaneously buying it at the lower market price.

Many option buyers use a method other than exercise. Instead of ever dealing with the underlying stock per se, you can simply recognize that the option for which you paid a lower price, e.g., $2 per share or $200 per option, has now escalated to possibly $15 or $16 ($1,500 or $1,600 per option). Thus, you can sell the option itself and generate your profit—say, $1,550 on an initial option premium (price) of $200, for a $1,350 short-term gain from your $200 investment. A quick 650 percent profit, not bad!

It is important to remember that the exercise date in any month is the Friday preceding the third Saturday of the month. For example, in November 1994, the last date during which a nonmember of the exchange could have exercised an option was November 18. Actually, the option continues its life until that Saturday, but only members of the exchange (floor traders) can transact business on that day. Furthermore, in my experience, a nonmember should not try to exercise or otherwise trade an option near the end of the day before expiration. Noon should probably be considered a practical deadline.

Premium

As previously stated, the price one pays for the call or put is called the premium. The buyer must add a commission to this, and a commission is deducted from the payment the seller receives.

The premium is actually determined by supply and demand. The actual bidding and offering prices reflect the same factors as those that determine the price of the underlying stock shares.

The premium (Pm) is a composite of two factors: the intrinsic value of the option (IV) and the so-called "time-value" (TV):

$$Pm = IV + TV$$

The intrinsic value is simply the degree in dollars to which the option is said to be "in the money." If the underlying issue were listed at $40 per share and the strike price were set at exactly $40, this option would be said to be neither in the money nor out of it; it's *at the money*. If you bought a call option with a strike price of $40 when the stock was at $42, the intrinsic value would be $2. It would stand to reason, therefore, that the premium would be something over $2. However, with a strike price of $40 and a current market of $34, there would be no intrinsic value; the call clearly is out of the money.

The amount of time value depends on the length of life that the option has before expiration. If it has only two weeks or so, the time value is small, perhaps 1/8 (meaning 100 x 0.125 = $12.50) per option. If the underlying stock is very active, the time value might be 1/4 ($25); for an inactive stock, it might be only 1/16 ($6.25). The time value could also be zero if no trading were occurring at all because of disinterest in the option or if its expiration date were close.

Writing (Selling)

For each option bought, there must be an option sold. Hence the world of option trading is inhabited by sellers as well as buyers. An option seller is also called an option maker or, more commonly, a **writer**.

The buyer purchases the right or privilege of holding and exercising or reselling as he or she wishes. The seller owns no such rights. The writer is the one who receives the option premiums paid by the buyer, less the broker commissions.

A seller who sells calls on stock he or she already owns is called a covered seller. If you write on stock you only partially own, you are considered a ratio writer. For example, you own 400 shares of General Electric but are convinced it is not moving up seriously, so you may sell six instead of four calls; hence, four are covered and two are "naked." If you sell naked options, or ratio write, you must maintain a margin account that contains enough collateral to be able to back up a situation in which you are called and hence must sell short.

It follows that if you are a writer of naked calls, you will avoid writing calls on stock you think is liable to make a dramatic move upward. By like token, if you write naked puts, you will do so only on stock you do not expect to plunge. Or, if the underlying stock is an exemplary growth stock, you will not object to having that stock put to you in the event it decreases in market value.

For example, considering the way Glaxo Wellcome, Ltd. stock declined in 1993 and through most of 1994 to below $20, an option writer who believes Glaxo Wellcome to be a great turnaround candidate might have sold a number of Glaxo Wellcome Feb. 15 puts. If the stock stayed above $15, the writer would pocket the premium with a smile. If it should actually drop below $15, he would pick up the shares, expecting them to rebound above $15 per share. In reality, his loss is mitigated by the value of the premium he received when he sold the puts. When he considers the premium he got for the sale of the put option, he could, in effect, have contrived to buy Glaxo Wellcome at a price below the point at which he expected it to turn around.

In actual practice, the number of transactions in calls usually significantly exceeds the trading in puts. This may reflect some degree of innate optimism, which seems to affect most market investors or traders.

Straddles

An option writer may elect to buy or sell both calls and puts at the same time. If she sells a true straddle, she is writing both a call and a put at the same strike price. Consider the following example:

Sell 1 SUME MAY 55 Call @ $6

Sell 1 SUME MAY 55 Put @ $2

Combinations

Consider a writer who is convinced that Eastman Kodak will increase only slightly over its current price of $45.25. He may sell puts with a strike price of $45 and calls at a substantially higher price, say, $55 or $60. Suppose he turned out to be correct. He would then collect the premium for both the call and the put. Furthermore, there is a maximum allowable number of options a trader can write. However, with a straddle you don't use vacancies for all puts and calls; a combination is only counted as a single option from the point of view of required collateral. In this instance the trader has therefore written both a put and a call using only one vacancy on his maximum.

Positions Allowable

Because of the inherently greater risk in buying and selling options rather than stocks or bonds, and especially the greater risk inherent in selling naked options, the federal government and most brokerages set strict limitations. Actually there are no risk limitations on the buying side, since it is obvious to the buyer that he or she may lose 100 percent of the premium paid for the options. The risks are far greater for the uncovered writer, since potential losses are theoretically limitless. If an option written naked is called, it is considered a short position and one with exposure. How high is up? The loss could be $1,000, $100,000, or many times these amounts if you are wrong.

Hence, limitations on number of positions are necessary, and dealings are closely supervised by the more responsible brokerage firms. Certain firms base their limit of puts sold on the total equity in an account. Under Regulation T of the Federal Reserve, accounts are restricted to using a maximum of 50 percent of the equity in the account in the case of puts.

For example, in writing McDonnell Douglas (MD) 130 puts, the seller must recognize that if one such put is exercised, the value of MD stock to be assigned (put) the account is 100 times $130, or $13,000. Consequently, a small account—say, with about $40,000 of equity—could not possibly absorb more than one or two puts being exercised before going afoul of Reg. T. This limits a writer's usage of MD puts, despite the temptation of the high premium and good chance for success.

Another limitation imposed by some firms includes reserving $10,000 of equity to collateralize the first uncovered call or put, followed by a minimum of $1,000 in equity for each added option sold naked. Thus a $40,000 account is permitted to write 1 + ($30,000/$1,000) or one plus thirty options naked for a total of thirty-one positions. Typically, however, an account is limited to a maximum of twenty-five positions until it has shown a good track record for handling uncovered option writing successfully. This generally means the account must demonstrate success for six months or perhaps a year to allow its positions to be increased.

A third and always-present requirement is the need to maintain an adequate reserve special miscellaneous account (SMA) and/or firm maintenance requirement (FMR) moneys in the account to back up the options. The SMA is the unused loan value in the margin account. Some of this SMA will be used up by the demand for collateral invoked for writing each option position. These demands are established through the following equations:

$$\text{SMA} = 0.3(\text{CMV}) \pm \text{O/M} + \text{Pm}$$

and:

$$\text{SMA} = 0.15(\text{CMV}) + \text{Pm}$$

where CMV is the current market value of 100 shares, O/M is the out-the-money part of the option, and Pm is the premium. If the option is in the money (I/M) instead of out the money(O/M), the I/M portion is added to the SMA requirement. The SMA used is the greater of the two expressions.

As an example of using these equations, consider a potential writer who considers U.S. Surgical (USS) to be in a weak position. With USS at $24.5 (its CMV) and an expiration date of, say, three months, he might have wanted to write USS Jan. 30 calls in October 1994. The premium (Pm) was ¾, or $75. The out-the-money portion (O/M) is 100($30 – $24.5) = $550. To find the SMA requirement, the potential writer enters these amounts into the two equations:

$$\text{SMA} = 0.3(\text{CMV}) - \text{O/M} + \text{Pm}$$

$$= 0.3(\$2{,}450) - \$550 + \$75 = \$260 \text{ per option}$$

$$\text{SMA} = 0.15(\text{CMV}) + \text{Pm}$$

$$= 0.15(\$2{,}450) + \$75 = \$443 \text{ per option}$$

The second equation yields the higher amount, so it dictates the SMA requirement.

To write five such positions, you would need an SMA of five times $443 or $2,215. If your strategy succeeds, you will generate five times $75, or $375, by your use of $2,215 collateral. That's a return of $375/$2,215: 16.9 percent for a three-month period. Not bad as a way to enhance account earnings! It may not present the vast possibilities of the option buyers, but this certainly is a worthwhile way to augment your account. Of course, if you are wrong, you could lose money at an equal or faster rate.

Reasons for Using Options

There are several quite sound reasons for using options, always with the caveat that the option writer must be constantly cautious and diligent in their use and avoid excesses at all times.

One sensible manner in which to utilize option trading was already alluded to—the use of short puts in a general margin account either to augment the ongoing total return (dividends and capital gains) from the account via added premiums, or alternatively to add healthy growth stocks at effectively lower purchase prices. If this is your purpose, you must do it cognizant of your account's ability to absorb put exercises with their attendant requirements for cash or margin.

Another prudent application for option writing develops from the use of covered calls wherein you own the underlying stock. Writing calls that are covered sacrifices some of the opportunity potential in growth-oriented accounts, but it is inherently very conservative and, indeed, can be considered like taking out insurance on the equity in the account. In fact, in a static or slightly declining market, it can insulate the account from declines to the extent at which it can generate premiums. Covered calls can even be written in a regular cash account, IRA, or pension trust to augment overall yield and provide an element of equity shelter.

More aggressive by far than use of covered options or put shorts to selectively augment account growth is the use of naked-call options. This is not a practice for the faint of heart, nor for an amateur. The rewards can be extremely high, however, as shown in an earlier example.

If the SMA is taken to be the unused loan value of a marginable equity account, it may be 50 percent of the current market value of the equity in the total account. Hence, a $100,000 equity account could have an SMA of $50,000. If uncovered options are used to generate a stream of premiums based on 20 percent to 40 percent of the SMA available, naked option writing could produce yields or returns of 10 percent to 20 percent per year. Thus, if the account is generating an average dividend yield of 4 percent and a capital appreciation of 9 percent per year, which is fairly typical for the overall market in the twentieth century, this account can increase its total return to 4 percent plus 9 percent plus another 10 percent in premiums, or 23 percent per year. This is a lofty gain if made repeatedly, but it demands a high degree of knowledge concerning the market, diligence in avoiding excesses or overwriting, close surveillance and monitoring, plus, probably, some degree of good fortune. But this result certainly is theoretically possible.

The reason for buying, rather than selling, options as the principal mechanism for using options is to take advantage of the tremendous leverage extended by option trading. Buying, however, is inherently quite speculative; historically, few (roughly 3 percent to 5 percent) of such options are successfully exercised compared to the total number bought. The blessing in buying, if there is one, is that the purchase of an option entails a lower level of capital than the buying of individual stock.

The completed examples of Figures 5.1 and 5.2 show the options written for an account that can be described as medium sized and conservatively aggressive. The underlying issue in Figure 5.1, Epitope Corp., a biopharmaceutical firm of medium size, was used repeatedly for option writing, in this case uncovered, to generate premiums for account expansion. Having successfully used Epitope options earlier in the year, this option writer elected to use the same underlying issue over and over during 1994. This writer had used it in like manner in 1993 (not shown), and it illustrates an old option writer slogan: "If you kick a dead horse, you ain't gonna be bit . . . just be sure that horse is dead." If there had been a combination of unsuccessful trades as well as successful trades, the writer would understandably become more shy about writing on such an underlying stock.

In contrast, Figure 5.2 recaps options written on McDonnell Douglas (MD) during 1994. Here, the monitor exhibits a combination of successes and failures. The first call written led to a loss of $1,005, whereas the second achieved a $607 profit. All the trading, thirty-two options in total, achieved a gain of $3,097, less than $100 per option. If you contrast this experience with Epitope in Figure 5.1, you

Figure 5.1 Options Monitor: Epitope Example

Company: Epitope Corp. (EPT) Account no.: 123-45678

Sold							Bought or Expired								
Date	Option	#	Premium	Gross	Commissions and Taxes	Net	Date	#	Premium	Gross	Commissions and Taxes	Net	Profit or Loss	Total
1/21/94	APR25C	5	$0.75	$375.00	$69.87	$305.13	4/22/94	5					$305.13	$305.13
3/22/94	JUL15P	2	$2.00	$400.00	$69.87	$330.13	7/16/94	2					$330.13	$635.26
3/30/94	JUL12.5P	2	$1.38	$275.00	$69.86	$205.14	7/16/94	2					$205.14	$840.40
7/15/94	OCT20C	4	$1.06	$425.00	$69.87	$355.13	10/22/94	4					$355.13	$1,195.53
7/15/94	OCT12.5P	4	$0.69	$275.00	$69.86	$205.14	10/22/94	4					$205.14	$1,400.67
Total													$1,400.67	

Options expiring in taxable 1994 reportable on Schedule D, Form 1040 IRS
Summation: EPT 1994 17 options
Short-term capital gain = $1,400.67

Figure 5.2 Options Monitor: McDonnell Douglas Example

Company: McDonnell Douglas (MD)

Account no.: 123-45678

Sold							Bought or Expired							
Date	Option	#	Premium	Gross	Commissions and Taxes	Net	Date	#	Premium	Gross	Commissions and Taxes	Net	Profit or Loss	Total
11/12/93	MAY100C	1	$15.00	$1,500.00	$34.97	$1,465.03	2/22/94	1	$24.00	$2,400.00	$69.85	$2,469.85	($1,004.82)	($1,004.82)
11/12/93	MAY90P	2	$4.25	$850.00	$69.88	$780.12	4/6/94	2	$0.56	$112.50	$61.10	$173.60	$606.52	$398.30)
11/11/93	MAY90P	2	$5.00	$1,000.00	$69.89	$930.11	5/20/94	2					$930.11	$531.81
11/12/93	MAY100C	2	$15.00	$3,000.00	$69.95	$2,930.05	5/20/94	2					$2,930.05	$3,461.86
2/22/94	AUG110C	1	$17.13	$1,712.50	$69.91	$1,642.59	4/6/94	1	$7.50	$750.00	$69.85	$819.85	$822.74	$4,284.60
2/22/94	AUG110P	1	$5.50	$550.00	$69.87	$480.13	8/19/94						$480.13	$4,764.73
3/1/94	AUG110P	1	$6.38	$637.50	$69.88	$567.62	8/19/94						$567.62	$5,332.35
3/28/94	MAY125C	4	$0.94	$375.00	$69.87	$305.13	5/20/94						$305.13	$5,637.48
3/31/94	AUG125C	1	$2.25	$225.00	$69.86	$155.14	4/6/94	1	$2.63	$262.50	$69.85	$332.35	($177.21)	$5,460.27
5/20/94	AUG125C	3	$0.50	$150.00	$69.86	$80.14	8/19/94						$80.14	$5,540.41
7/15/94	AUG110P	2	$1.50	$300.00	$69.86	$230.14	8/19/94						$230.14	$5,770.55
8/12/94	NOV110P	1	$2.75	$275.00	$69.86	$205.14	11/18/94						$205.14	$5,975.69
8/22/94	NOV105P	2	$1.94	$387.50	$69.87	$317.63	11/18/94						$317.63	$6,293.32
9/22/94	NOV125C	3	$1.25	$375.00	$69.87	$305.13	10/21/94	3	$3.75	$1,125.00	$69.85	$1,194.85	($889.72)	$5,403.60
10/21/94	FEB130C	3	$4.88	$1,462.50	$69.90	$1,392.60	11/4/94	3	$12.50	$3,750.00	$72.28	$3,822.28	($2,429.68)	$2,973.92
11/4/94	FEB140C	3	$6.50	$1,950.00	$69.92	$1,880.08	11/8/94	3	$5.63	$1,687.50	$69.85	$1,757.35	$122.73	$3,096.65
Total														$3,096.65

Note: Negative numbers are shown in parentheses.
Options expiring in taxable 1994 reportable on Schedule D, Form 1040 IRS
Summation: MD 1994 32 options
Short-term capital gain = $3,096.65

will clearly see that there is better control for the EPT options. There is less nail-biting for the writer and a fairly similar result. The monitor reveals that the prudent writer, all things being equal with the companies involved, should stress selling options on Epitope for 1995 and subsequent years.

Here's another approach: by adding a few options to their portfolios, money managers can dodge a bear market without excessively churning accounts. One practice is to buy at-the-money or near at-the-money put options on the key individual stocks. Thereafter, for every dollar these stocks decline, the value of the long put options, and hence of the portfolio, will increase roughly in equal amounts. If exchange-traded stock options are not available for these given stocks, one may take recourse to index options. A market index is made up of many traded issues and is considered to track the market closely. An example is the S&P 500 Index.

Normally, the province of trading index options should be reserved as the venue of only the most knowledgeable and capable investors and traders, but when used to protect a portfolio from declines, the application of index options falls within the bounds of conservative aggressive logic. Of course, such use of puts protects you only from small to moderate declines and may not protect you much from either a prolonged period of decline or a severe quick "crash," such as occurred in October 1987.

Monitoring Options

By studying your track record and recording the trades you have made, you learn which issues to accentuate and which to avoid. You can do this by using copies of the blank Options Monitor in Figure 5.3. If you are trading many options, be sure to keep each underlying issue to its own page.

The reason for using a separate page for each underlying issue is so you can review it at a glance and see how your options on each issue are progressing. In the case of Epitope Corp. (Figure 5.1), each option traded (sold in this case) generated a profit. This is a good signal that the investor has some understanding or perhaps financial empathy of sorts for the movement of this issue. Consequently, Epitope may be a good candidate for option trading in the future.

The options trading for McDonnell Douglas (Figure 5.2), in contrast, shows some losses despite an overall gain on options traded during 1994. The presence of some trades entailing losses is reason enough at a quick glance for the option writer either to eschew the selection of McDonnell Douglas in the future or at least to approach it with greater caution. Naturally, this warning posture for an underlying stock stands out most boldly if each issue has its own monitoring sheet.

An option, if sold, is not considered finished until either its expiration date arrives or the offsetting position is bought. Hence, in the two examples shown, the earlier dates apply to the date of short sale of puts or calls. If, instead, the options were bought, the earlier date would appear on the right-hand side of the page.

Figure 5.3 Options Monitor

Company: ____________________ Account no.: ____________

Sold							Bought or Expired							
Date	Option	#	Premium	Gross	Commissions and Taxes	Net	Date	#	Premium	Gross	Commissions and Taxes	Net	Profit or Loss	Total
Total														

Another reason for showing the date and issues sold on the left-hand side is that IRS Form 1040 calls for the issue and date *sold* to be on the left-hand side of Schedule D. Thus, after completing these pages for your monitoring, you can simply duplicate your own record, and you have the data for this portion of your annual IRS submission.

Because the date on which a position is closed is the time at which the option is finished, we may, by like token, show the gains and losses for each month as the year progresses, using the form in Figure 5.4. You would enter the net gain or loss for each month in which option positions ended. The final tally, of course, has to agree with the final tally for gains and losses on your individual option sheets, in the event that the IRS wants to use it to check your trades or your arithmetic. The IRS allows recording to the nearest dollar, so these may be completed without the cents portion of the trade. Thus, a gain of $257.19 would be reported as $257.

Figure 5.5 shows entries for the account that traded Epitope Corp. and Sumerian Oil Corporation options.

How to Select Options

Selecting options for either buying or selling is no simple matter. It requires careful research, and in general, the more experience you have, the better. Either you yourself must have the experience, or you must find a well-trained tutor or financial adviser to hold your hand when you start your options campaign. Or both, ideally. This is especially true for writing uncovered options or buying options.

The favorable results of some careful option selections appear in Figure 5.6, which presents some of the key indicators for options. For background on stock basics such as EPS (earnings per share) and P/E (price/earnings ratio), see Chapter 2. This chart illustrates two option candidates, and you can see why and how they were selected. Perhaps you can also discern why the results were successful for the writer and his account. Before trying to use this chart, however, you should become more than noddingly familiar with the concepts embodied in the column headings. To illustrate, let us examine how the investor used the results presented for Epitope in Figure 5.1, as well as a put option on stock in Chiron Corp.

Epitope Example

The first option in Figure 5.1 is Epitope Apr. 25 calls, of which five were written. The premium was 3/4 ($75) for each of four calls. After commissions, a residual gain of $305 remained. Why did this appear so attractive? First, consider that its P/E was infinite in view of its deficit in 1993 and 1994, hardly a factor that could motivate a significant upward move in price. Epitope's earnings trend showed that it had sustained several years of deficits, which seemed to worsen with the passing of time. Again, quite a negative indicator.

Figure 5.4 Annual Capital Gains and Losses from Option Trades

Year: ______

Security	Jan	Feb	Mar	Apr	May	Jun	Jul	Aug	Sep	Oct	Nov	Dec	Total

Figure 5.5 Annual Capital Gains and Losses from Option Trades: Completed Example

Year: 1994

Security	Jan	Feb	Mar	Apr	May	Jun	Jul	Aug	Sep	Oct	Nov	Dec	Total
Sumerian Oil Corp. (SUME)	$170.00	$541.00	$1,049.00	$299.00		$1,023.00	$432.00	$711.00	($255.00)	($42.00)	$2,523.00	$852.00	$7,303.00
Epitope Corp. (EPT)				$305.13			535.27			$560.27			$1,400.67
Total	$170.00	$541.00	$1,049.00	$604.13		$1,023.00	$969.27	$711.00	($255.00)	$518.27	$2,523.00	$852.00	$8,703.67

Note: Negative numbers are shown in parentheses.

Figure 5.6 Key Indicators for Options: Completed Example

Year: 1994

Date	Issue	Option	#	Premium (Pm)	Stock Price			P/E	EPS	EPS Relative Strength	EPS Trend	Beta	Alpha	Accumulation vs. Distribution Position	SMA	% Return on SMA	Annualized Return
					Minimum	Maximum	Present										
7/15/94	EPT	OCT20C	4	$1.06	$13.25	$24.25	$18.00	N/A	deficit	29	flat	1.67	-0.02	70	$446	20%	80%
5/28/94	CHIR	OCT55P	2	$3.00	$42.00	$79.00	$65.00	31.00	2.10	49	up	3.48	-0.21	79	$1,056	50%	120%

Beta is a measure of the fund's yield relative to the yield from the market in general. Beta is considered 1.0 for the market, and for stocks the benchmark is the S&P 500. A value of 1.1 indicates that the fund moves up 10 percent faster than the market when the market is rising. However, it also indicates that the fund goes down 10 percent faster than the market when the market declines. Thus, higher values of beta mean greater market risk. Higher beta is aggressive, and lower beta is defensive. Epitope's beta was 1.67, which meant that even in a slow-moving market, it could plunge faster than the Dow Jones and S&P averages.

Alpha is a measure of the difference between the actual and expected return based on the risks involved with the underlying investments. A positive value means that the fund performed better than expected, whereas a negative value means that the manager did not yield the returns justified by the risks taken. Epitope's alpha showed that it had not had average gains monthly during the past sixty months, assuming a static S&P 500 average, but actually had decreased slightly in price by 0.02 per month. Its price varied from a low of $13 1/2 to $24 1/2, the high coming early in 1994.

The **EPS relative strength**, an indicator found in the *Investor's Business Daily* newspaper, relates the entire universe of stocks to earnings-growth progress on a scale of 99 to 1, where 99 is the highest and 1 is the poorest. In the case of Epitope, the relative earnings strength was 29, hardly positive progress in earnings strength relative to the market.

The tendency for people to acquire this stock versus distribute it (get rid of it) is recorded under the heading **Accumulation vs. Distribution Position**. It, too, is measured on a 99 to 1 scale. Surprisingly, for Epitope, this measure stood at 79. A reading this high almost, but not quite, showed some favorable momentum.

All considerations made a strong case that Epitope's stock would not achieve or overachieve $22 1/2 or $25 during the three-month period following July 15. Hence, it was selected as a good naked write for a call.

In effect, the investor earned $305 on an SMA requirement of $446 per call. This means that the SMA or collateral used generated **a return on SMA** for the three-month period of $305/(4 x $446), or 17 percent. If this gain could actually be repeated for the full year by selecting comparable options following the expiration of this one, this would translate to an annualized return of $305/$446, or 68 percent. With U.S. Treasury long bonds generating 7.5 percent to 8.0 percent in this time frame, 68 percent is not half bad.

Chiron Example

The next option shown in Figure 5.6 is a put selected on Chiron Corp. (CHIR), based on favorable financial data of like nature. Chiron perched at about $60 during the May 1994 period. However, information was becoming public about Betaseron, Chiron's "breakthrough" pharmaceutical for the first real solution to multiple sclerosis. Based on that news, it seemed that Chiron's earnings would turn strongly positive. Many of the leading brokerage firms reported its progress in effectively marketing this wonder drug, and the future looked bright indeed. Besides considering the background of strong news, the investor reviewed key indicators such as EPS trend, P/E, and price range for the year, along with a motivating premium of 3 or $300, and elected to write two Chiron Oct. 55 puts. The investor also thought that if the account were actually put 200 shares of Chiron at $55 per share—less, of course, the $3 premium (net cost $52)—it would be a worthy addition to the account.

As it turned out, Chiron moved up smartly, and in November, after the expiration of this put, Ciba-Geigy, the massive Swiss pharmaceutical firm, announced plans to increase its stake in Chiron during 1995 at $117 per share. So it was a superb put selection with an SMA requirement of $1,056 per option. It generated a postcommission premium of $4,530 for the five-month option life, for a 50 percent yield. If you project this yield over twelve months, the total expected yield would be 120 percent per year.

Other Considerations

Although the examples in Figure 5.6 are of well-written options, bear in mind that for every option thus selected there probably were ten or twenty that did not have these appeals. The investor had to review all candidates intensively to establish such calls as Epitope Oct. 20 and the Chiron Oct. 55 puts. Many had to be discarded based on too small a potential gain, too risky an EPS trend, too high or too low a P/E, too much momentum in relative strength to chance selling a call, or too abysmal an accumulation-distribution posture to countenance writing naked puts.

In selecting calls or puts to buy rather than to write, the mental process is almost exactly the opposite as for selling calls or puts. To buy puts, you want a fairly convincing picture of a potential precipitous loser. To consider buying calls, you are looking for fairly convincing potential of a strong upmover. But the mental process you use is generally identical to that of writing, and you can amass the same data to help weed out your puts and calls.

When you are ready to tackle this type of analysis, make photocopies of the blank form in Figure 5.7. You can record your own data on these.

Figure 5.7 Key Indicators for Options

Date	Issue	Option	#	Premium (Pm)	Stock Price			P/E	EPS	EPS Relative Strength	EPS Trend	Beta	Alpha	Accumulation vs. Distribution Position	SMA	% Return on SMA	Annualized Return
					Minimum	Maximum	Present										

6 Technical Analysis for Monitoring Investments

John R. Markle

AN EXPERIENCED INVESTOR realizes that successful investing is a result of three primary components: formulating a plan, implementing the plan, and monitoring that plan. Technical analysis is a tool used in conjunction with fundamental analysis to help implement, monitor, and control the course of a financial plan. It incorporates mathematical tools such as charts to determine which stocks, industries, indices, and averages have the greatest probability of rising or falling in value.

Basics of Bar Charting

The most basic tool of technical analysis is the bar chart, such as the one in Figure 6.1. At the bottom is a bar chart graph showing trading volume over time (the horizontal axis). Above this, the vertical axis is a scale of price. The lines graphed show the stock's trading range for the day. As in this example, there is often a faint dotted line that represents the fifty-day (ten-week) moving average. It is computed each day by adding the last fifty days of prices and dividing by 50. The calculated average is then plotted each day to form the moving line. Some services plot a 150-day or 200-day moving average as well. Figure 6.1 shows both the 50-day (dotted) and 200-day (dashes) moving averages.

Bar charting requires daily posting to the graph, such as the blank form in Figure 6.2. You can use this form to record and monitor the performance of one or more of your own securities. However, bar charting is extremely labor intensive. Given the time and diligence needed to keep the data up to date, many investors and advisers rely on charting services or computer programs to prepare their charts.

Figure 6.1 Sample Bar Chart

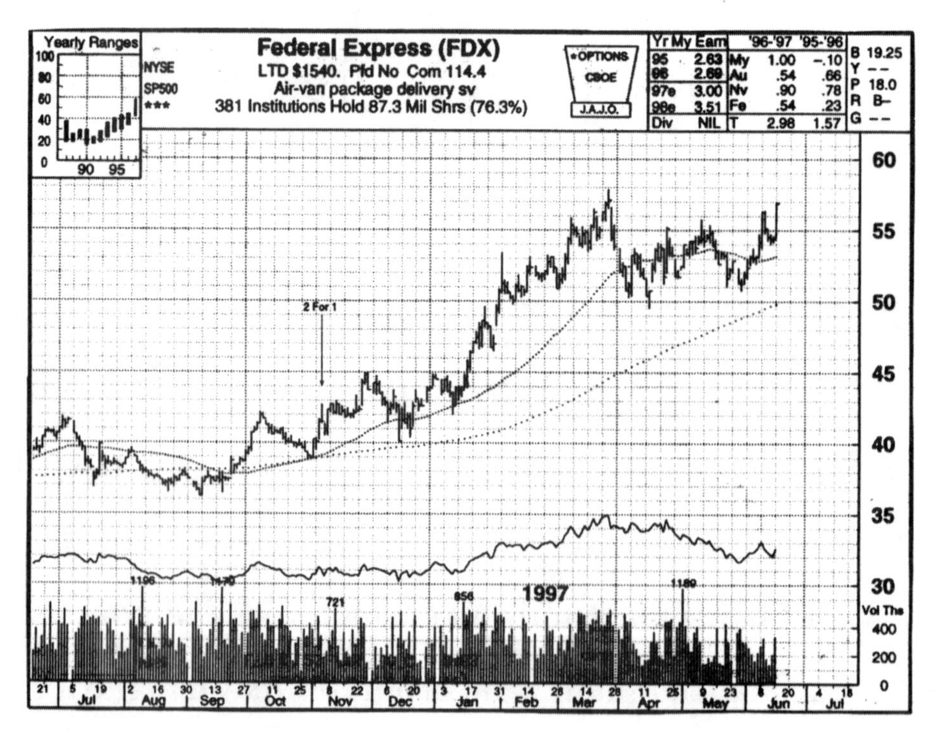

Source: Courtesy of Standard & Poor's—Trendline, New York, NY.

Figure 6.2 Bar Chart Form

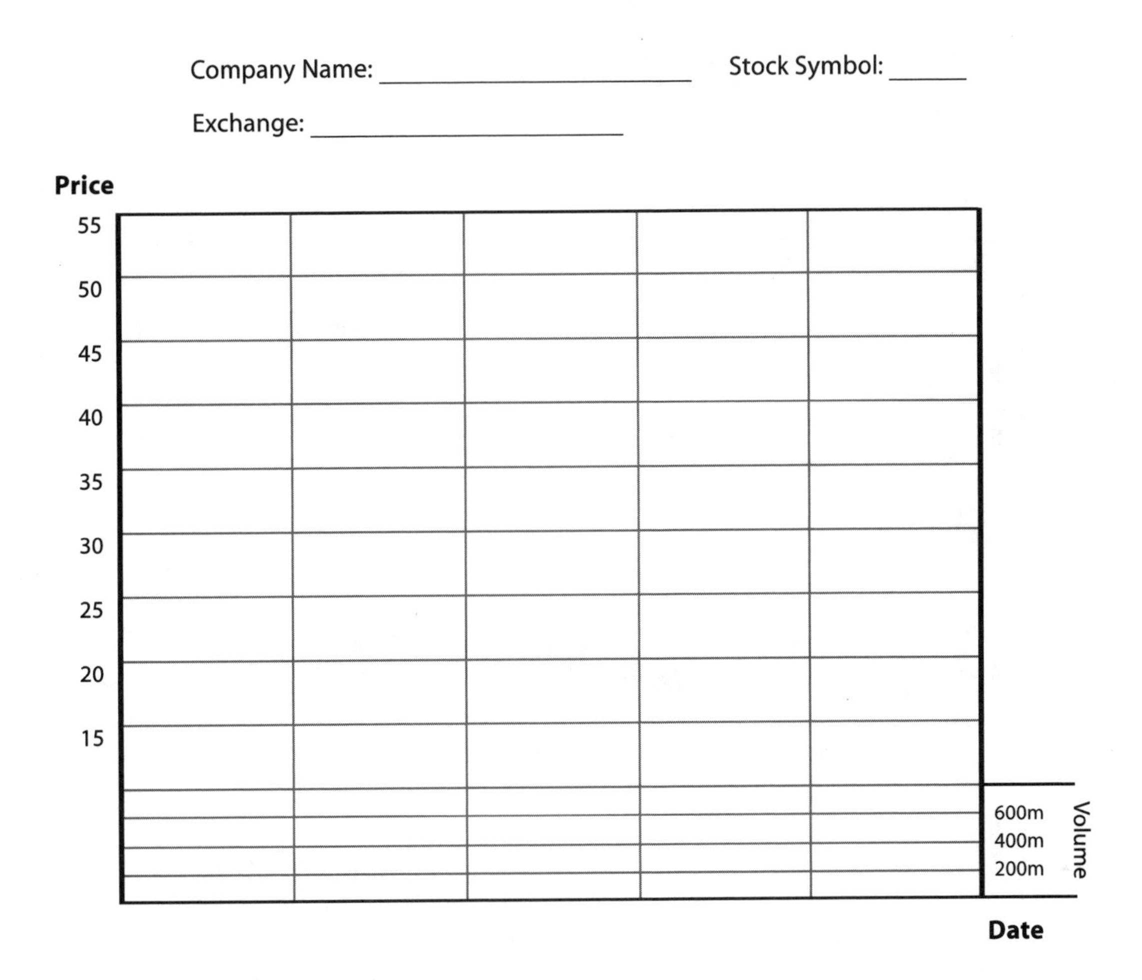

Chart Patterns

As bar charts develop, certain patterns emerge that signify changes in supply and demand. One of the favorite patterns of William O'Neill, author of *How to Make Money in Stocks* (1991) and publisher of *Investor's Business Daily*, is the cup-and-handle formation (see Figure 6.3). A stock with this formation declines gently in value, then rises at about the same rate, forming a cuplike figure. From top to bottom, the stock generally falls 15 percent to 30 percent. The stock then trades sideways, forming a handle on the graph, as seen in the center of Figure 6.3. What is occurring is that the company is being traded from weak hands to strong hands to form the cup and then a period of "accumulation" occurs to form the handle. The term *accumulation* refers to investors buying stock slowly and steadily so as not to cause the stock to rise much in value, creating a small trading range on a chart pattern. With no significant supply hanging overhead, the stock has a high probability for a large advance in price, which follows a formation of this pattern.

Figure 6.3 Cup-and-Handle Formation

Source: Courtesy of Standard & Poor's—Trendline, New York, NY.

The W pattern is another bar chart formation that offers a high degree of predictability. As in the example in Figure 6.4, the stock falls in value, then rises to form a V. The trading then falls again to near the previous bottom. As the graph rises a second time, the pattern forms a W. When the price breaks above the midpoint of the W, it often is beginning a new uptrend. This type of pattern occurs less often than the cup and handle, but it becomes easy to spot with practice and offers excellent potential for gains.

The most widely recognized and followed of the bar chart patterns is the head-and-shoulders formation. Such formations appear at major tops and bottoms of stock prices, indices, and averages. This pattern has a large hump in the middle to form the head and two smaller humps on each side of the head to form the shoulders (see Figure 6.5). The shoulders do not have to be duplicates of one another, just generally similar. A line should be drawn connecting the bottoms of the two shoulders to form what is referred to as the "neckline."

The key factor in determining whether the pattern is a head-and-shoulders formation is volume (see Figure 6.6). Trading volume should be higher at the left shoul-

Figure 6.4 W Formation

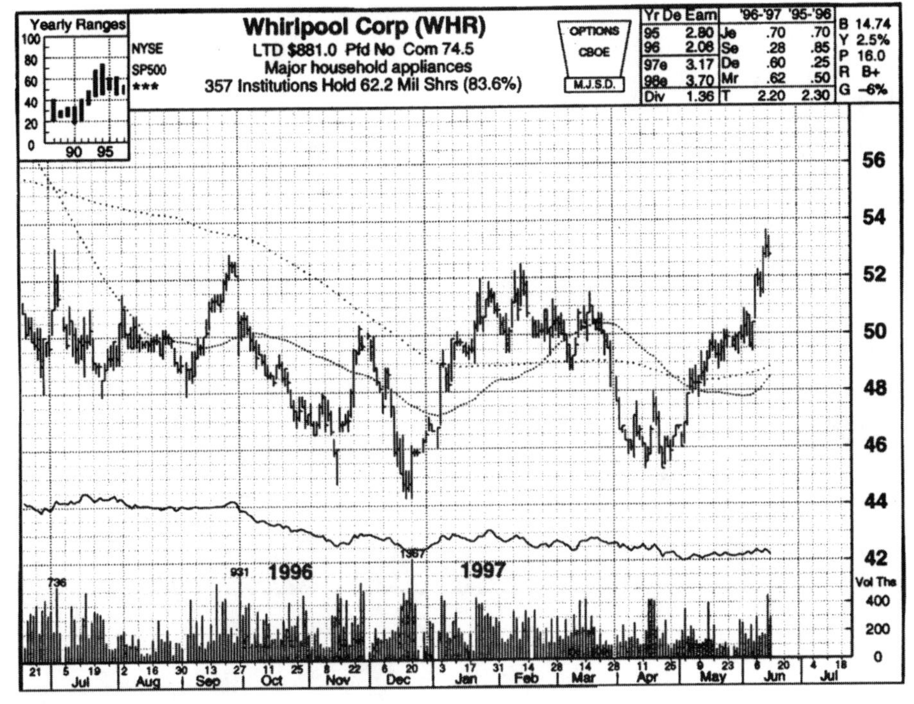

Source: Courtesy of Standard & Poor's—Trendline, New York, NY.

der than the right shoulder. Also, the volume at the head should be slightly lower than at the left shoulder. When the right shoulder breaks the neckline, volume must accelerate dramatically. Price and trading activity are working together to strongly indicate a change in trend.

The inverse head-and-shoulders pattern (shown in Figure 6.7) often marks the bottom of a trend. Once the right shoulder breaks above the neckline, it is a strong buy signal for the investor.

Trading Channels

To make it easier for you to identify patterns, notice breakouts, and recognize changes in trends, **trading channels** are added to bar charts. To add trading channels, simply draw one line connecting tops and another connecting bottoms (see Figure 6.8). Once a channel is broken, wait for another period in time when the stock forms a recognizable pattern or period of accumulation before inserting channel lines on the graph.

Figure 6.5 Head-and-Shoulders Formation

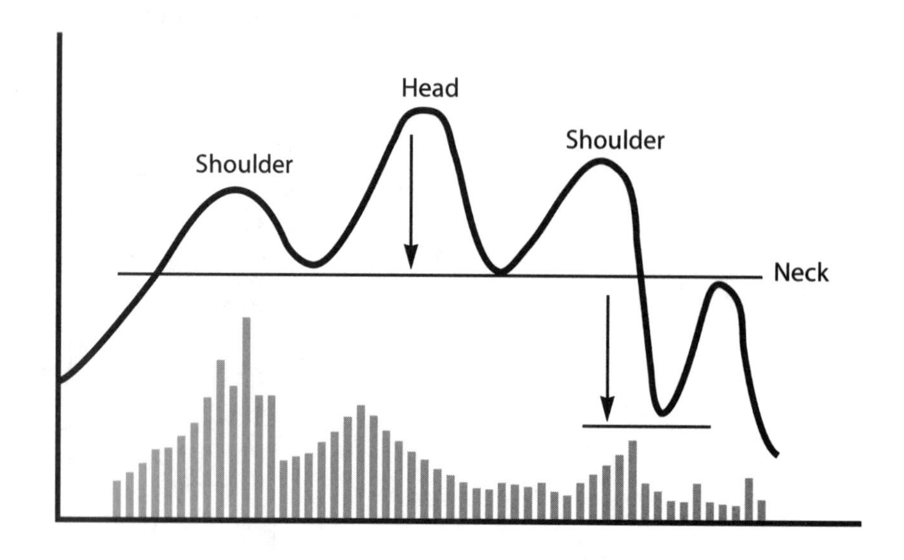

Figure 6.6 Chart with Head-and-Shoulders Formation

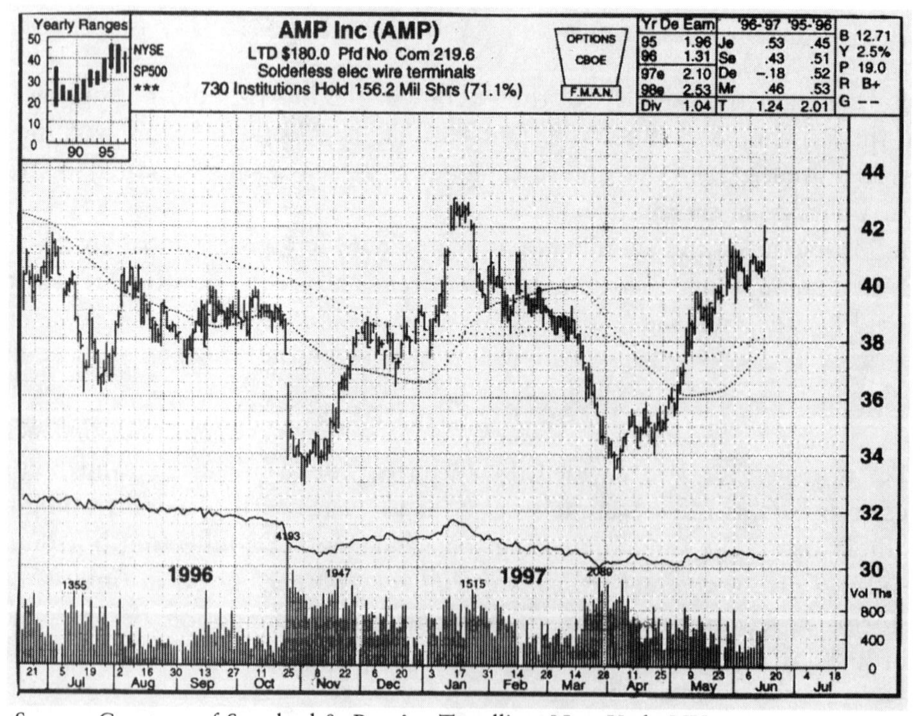

Source: Courtesy of Standard & Poor's—Trendline, New York, NY.

Figure 6.7 Inverse Head-and-Shoulders Formation

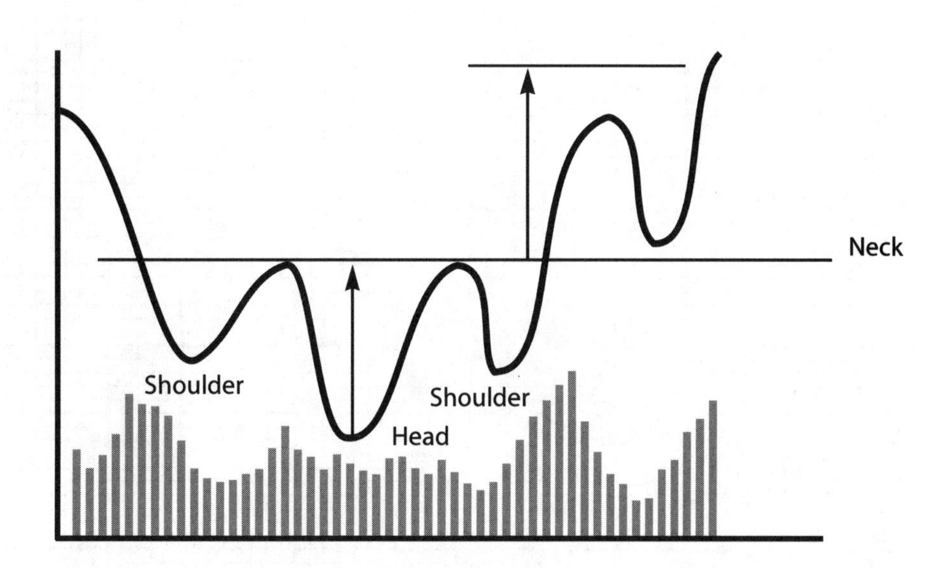

Chartbooks

Chartbooks that are published weekly are a tremendously helpful tool for investors as they monitor the performance of their stock portfolios. Here are the names, addresses, and phone numbers for two of the most popular weekly chartbooks:

Daily Graphs
P.O. Box 66919
Los Angeles, CA 90066-0919
800-472-7479

Standard & Poor's/Trendline
25 Broadway
New York, NY 10004
212-208-8000

Besides providing individual charts for most companies listed on the New York, American, and NASDAQ exchanges, the chartbooks contain additional useful information. Frequently they supply data such as a description of the company's basic business, annual price ranges for the past several years, earnings per share for the latest and prior fiscal years, price/earnings ratio, relative strength, stock dividends, institutional holdings, earnings estimates, availability of options, stocks in similar industries, average daily volume, daily trading volume, and much more.

Figure 6.8 Chart with Trading Channels

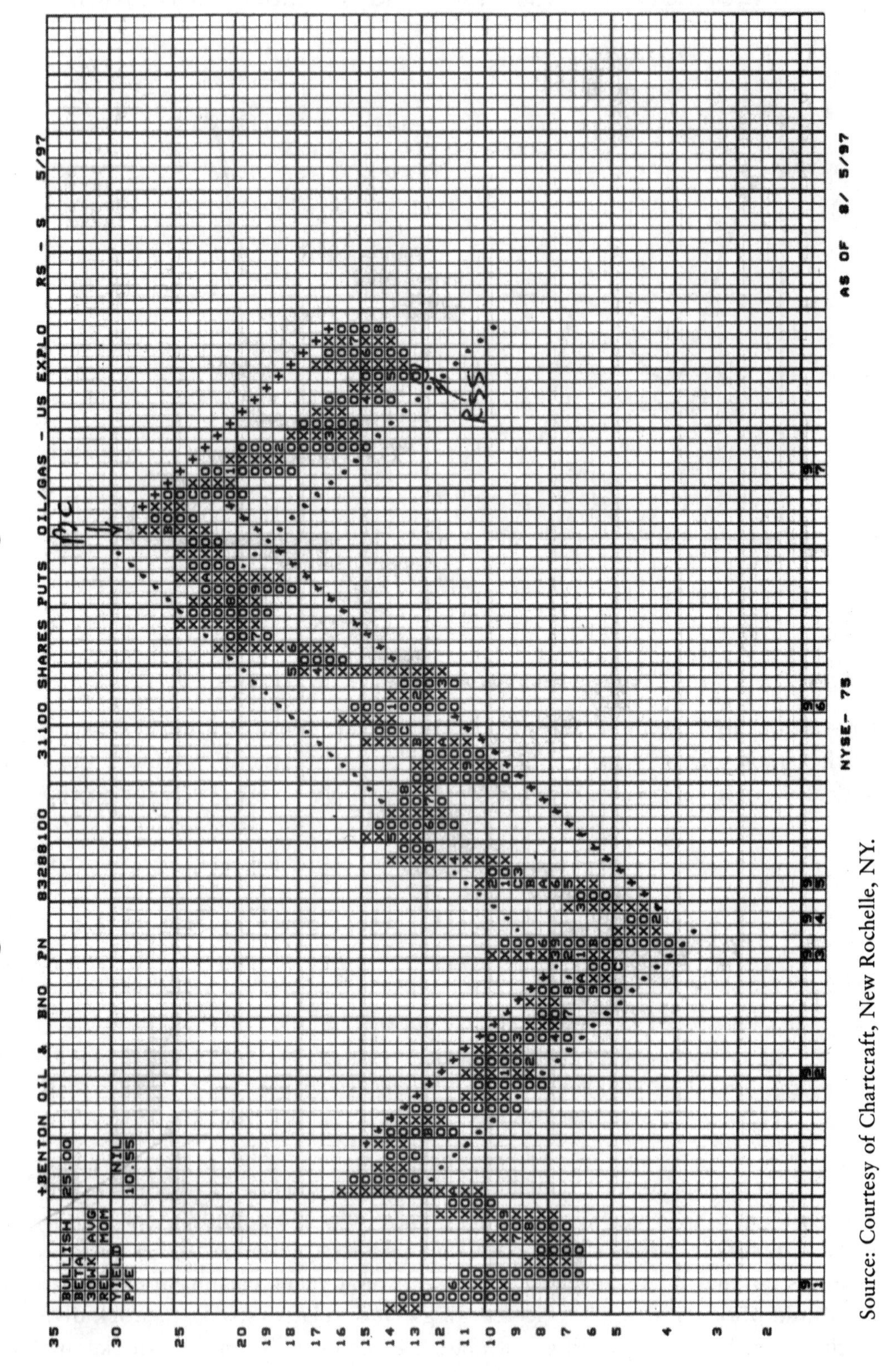

Source: Courtesy of Chartcraft, New Rochelle, NY.

Advantages of Bar Charts

Bar charts offer several advantages over other forms of charting. First, they are the most widely used in newspapers and stock reports. They not only look at price action but take volume into consideration as well. Computer programs for investors usually include bar charts. They are easy to find in most libraries and brokerage offices.

Although time-consuming, they are very easy to plot. It is the follow-through that sometimes may prove tedious. When you begin to plot stocks, don' t start with too many. It quickly becomes very difficult and complex. As a monitoring tool, however, bar charts are hard to beat.

Basics of Point & Figure Charting

The second most popular form of charting is **point & figure (P&F) charting** (see Figure 6.9). This type of graph uses Xs to represent rising prices and Os to indicate falling prices. Like bar charts, P&F charts show time on the horizontal axis and stock price on the vertical axis. P&F charts assign the following values for each box on the price scale of the graph: under 5, 1/4 point; between 5 and 20, 1/2 point; between 20 and 100, 1 point; and above 100, 2 points.

Most investors purchase point & figure (P&F) charts from a charting service and keep them updated by hand or use a computer to have updated charts readily available. The most widely used P&F charting service is: Chartcraft, P.O. Box 2046, New Rochelle, NY 10801 (914-632-0422).

Here's how to keep P&F charts current by hand. First, you look up trading data in a newspaper such as the *Wall Street Journal*, *Investor's Business Daily*, or the business section of a major newspaper. Make a list of the daily high and low for each stock that you follow. Next, examine the chart to see if the last column is a column of Xs or Os. Keep the column going in the same direction until the stock reverses by three or more boxes. If the last entry is an X, look at the high for the day to see if you need to add one or more Xs onto the column. If not, look at the low for the day to see if the stock price has reversed by three boxes or more to start a column of Os. If the price action on the downside has dropped three or more boxes, then enter them all at once to start a new column. This is called the three-point reversal method, explained by Michael Burke in his 1990 book, *The All New Guide to the Three Point Reversal Method.*

Perhaps you would like to do some P&F charting for a stock you want to follow closely, especially after learning to chart some of the interesting forecasting formations. It should be less tedious than bar charting and make monitoring your stocks easier. A blank graph is included as Figure 6.10 to help you get started. Make copies for your own P&F charting. There is a more detailed discussion about doing such charting in Lawrence Lynn's book, *How to Invest Today*.

Figure 6.9 Point & Figure Chart: Completed Example

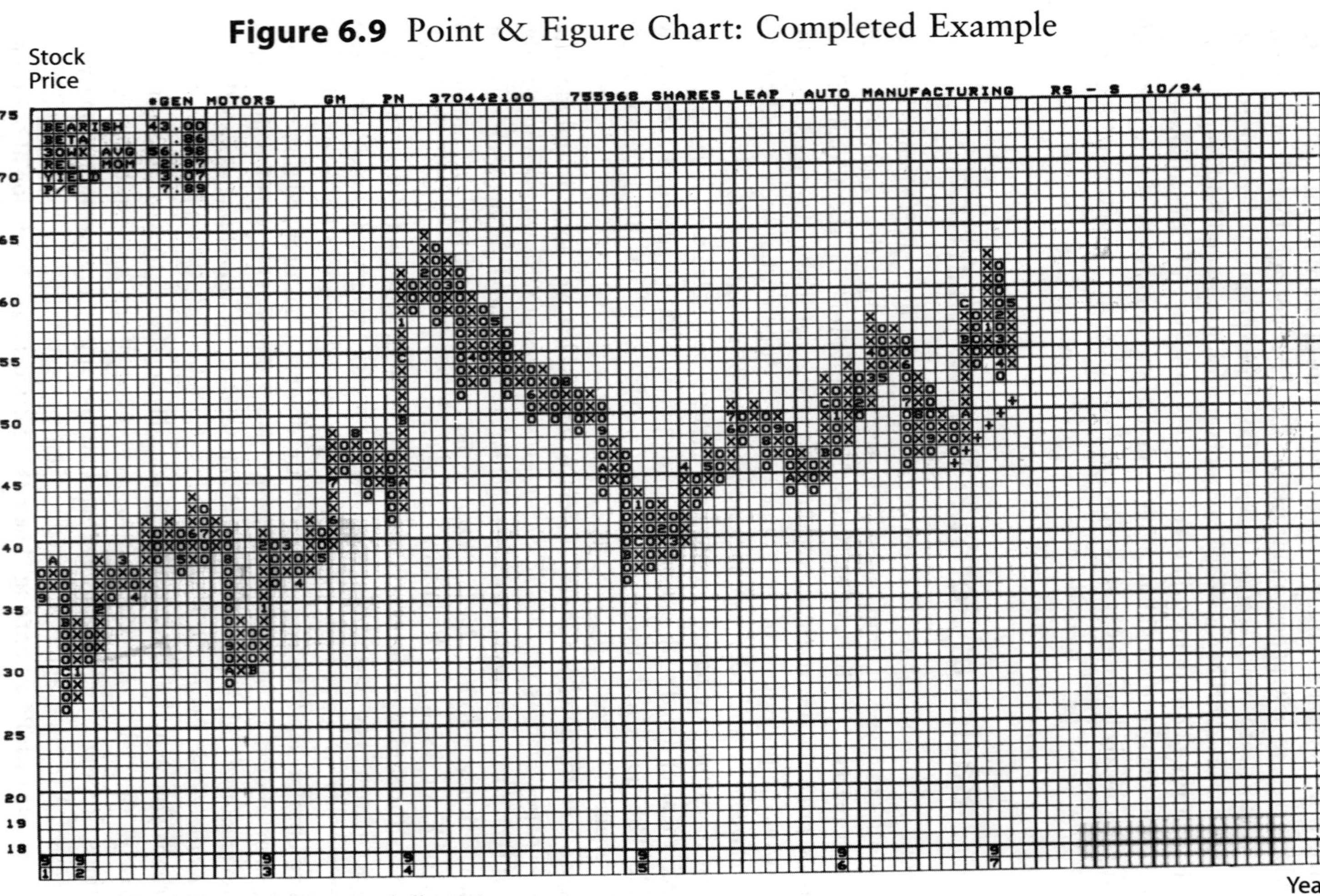

Source: Courtesy of Chartcraft, New Rochelle, NY.

Figure 6.10 Blank Graph for P&F Charting

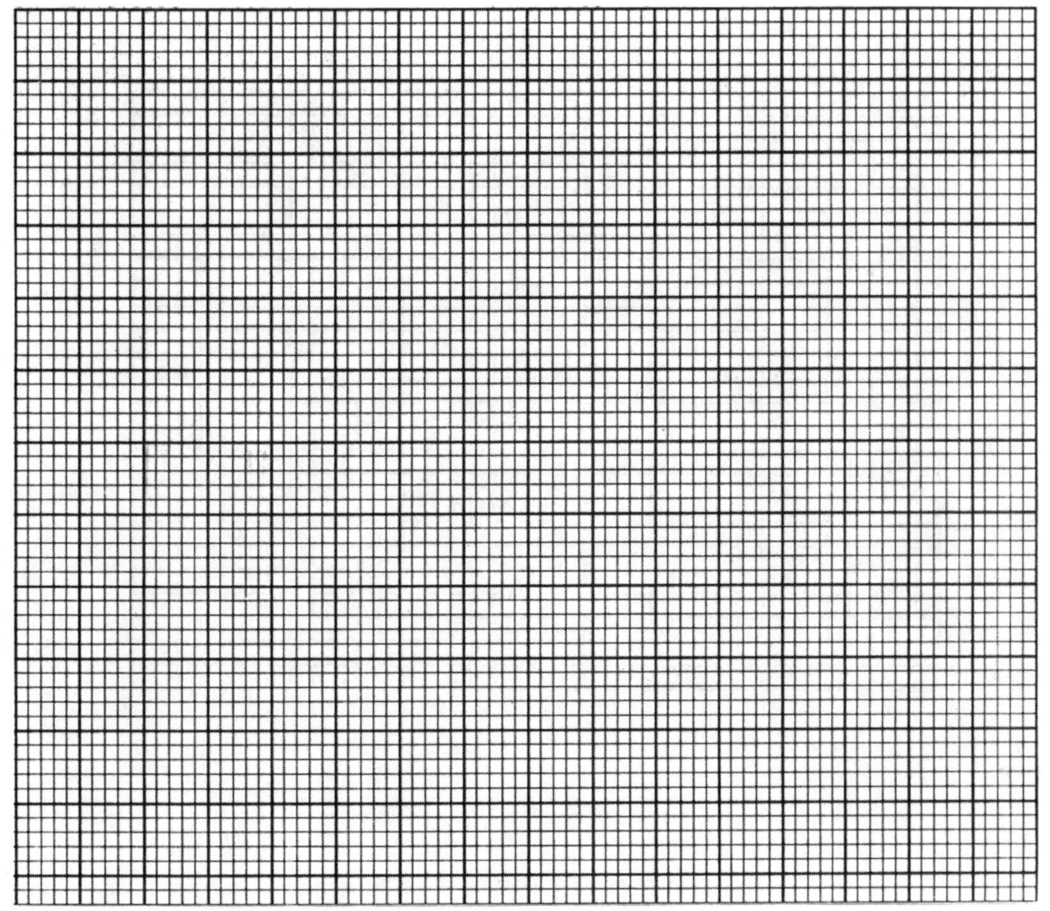

Chart Patterns

The columns of Xs and Os entered on the charts form certain patterns, some of which are useful as buy and sell signals. The most common buy-signal patterns (illustrated in Figure 6.11) are the flat triple top, V-triple top, angle triple top, double top. All of these are bullish signal formations. These patterns, especially triple tops, suggest a change in trend or continuation of a trend on the upside. When a stock price rises two or three times to a particular price level and then exceeds it, an existing equilibrium has been just broken, and the stock has a high probability of rising in value. During a bull market, you may set a price-rise objective of 25 percent to 35 percent for the stock over the next six-month period.

Figure 6.11 Common P&F Buy-Signal Patterns

Triple-Top Formation

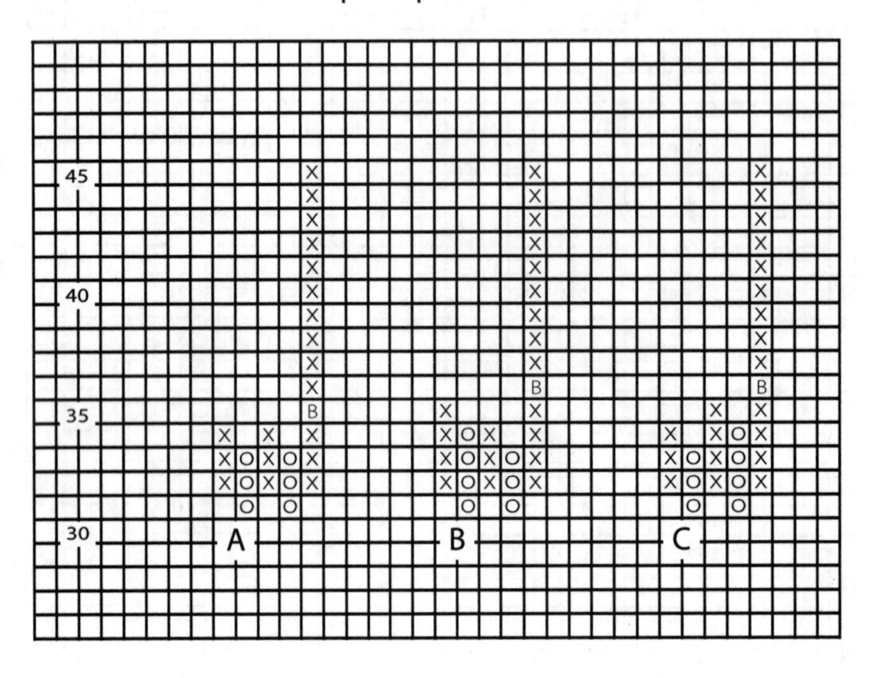

Double-Top Formation

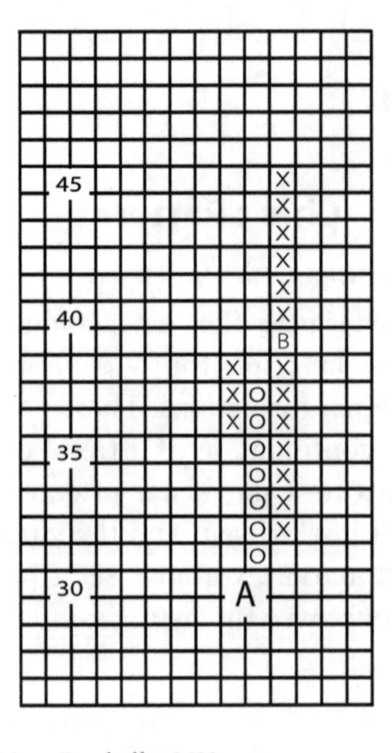

Source: Courtesy of Chartcraft, New Rochelle, NY.

You can use sell-signal patterns (pictured in Figure 6.12) to dispose of an owned stock position or to sell short. The most common patterns are the flat triple bottom, V-triple bottom, angle triple bottom, double bottom, and bearish signal formation. They are just the reverse of the buy signals, for obvious reasons. When stocks fall out of favor, the prices start to fall due to lack of demand. Normal points where buyers would usually enter the marketplace begin to deteriorate, causing bottoms of the columns to be lower and lower. When a bear market is occurring or a major correction is taking place, you should set a price-decline objective move for that security of 30 percent to 40 percent over a four-month period.

Stocks usually move further and faster in a bear market than a bull market. One reason is that investors who bought on margin and then receive margin calls are forced to liquidate stock. The other is that persons tend to panic-sell in a bear market but do not panic as drastically to buy in a bull market.

Trading Channels

You can establish trading channels on P&F charts by drawing parallel forty-five-degree lines. When a graph depicts a rising trend, the bottom line is the **bullish support line**. Once the stock gives a buy signal, go to the bottom of the pattern and place a plus mark (+) under the lowest O in the formation. Then come up one box and over one box, repeating to form a forty-five-degree line, as shown in Figure 6.13.

The top line of the trading channel is called the **bullish resistance line**. Find a wall of Os consisting of seven or more Os to the left of the buy-signal formation, and draw a forty-five-degree line parallel to the bullish support line.

Most investors who own a stock in a trading channel will continue to hold the position until the bullish support line is broken twice, thereby decisively breaking the uptrend. At this point the stock is said to have the highest probability of declining in value for an extended period of time.

Bearish channels are constructed in a similar manner. The top line is called the **bearish resistance line,** and the lower line is the **bearish support line**. They are parallel forty-five-degree lines. From the top X in a bearish-signal formation, put a plus mark, then come down one box and over one box to continue the line.

The bearish support line is drawn from a wall of Xs to the left of the sell-signal pattern. Unless you are shorting a stock, it is best to stay away from investing in a company that is in a bearish channel. The chart probably will continue to fall until there is an accumulation of stock based on a projection of good news ahead, causing a base of several buy signals to occur.

The support and resistance lines that form the trading channels are essential data for traders of put and call options. Investors in options are looking for short-term moves, which is exactly what the channels attempt to forecast. Short-term supply and demand can change quickly in the market without a significant change in a company's fundamentals. When trading puts and calls, try to find a chart pattern that has a well-defined channel. Buy calls or sell puts near the bottom of the channel, and sell calls or buy puts near the top of the channel. These areas of support and resistance can also be used as tools for timing short-term trades of stocks.

Figure 6.12 Common P&F Sell-Signal Patterns

Triple-Bottom Formation

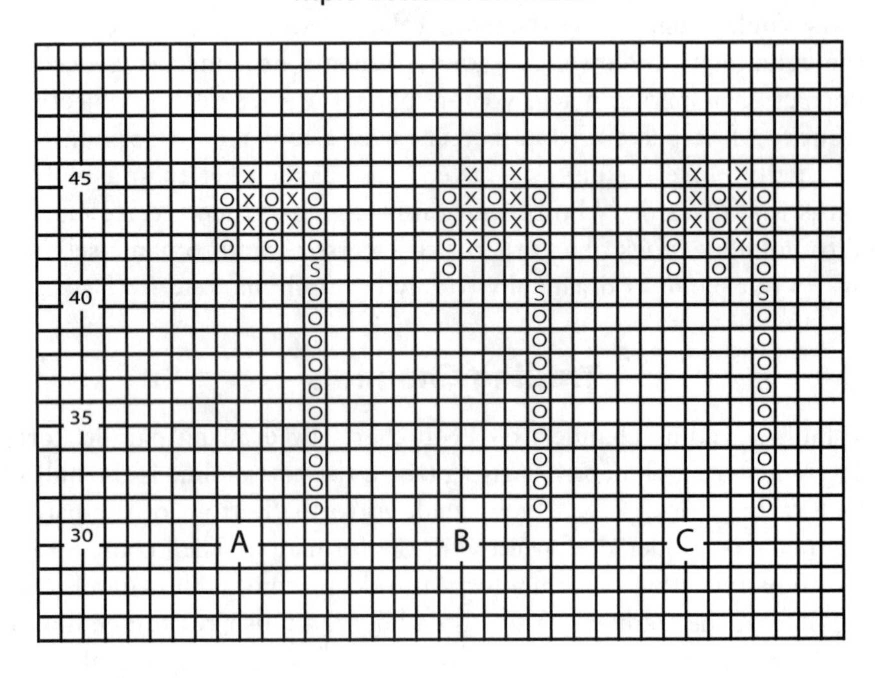

Double-Bottom Formation

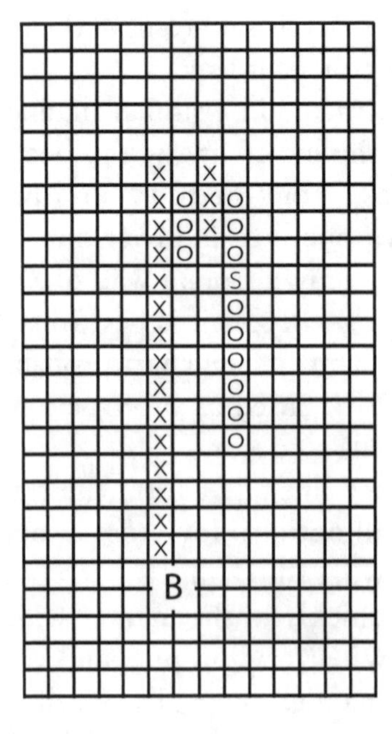

Source: Courtesy of Chartcraft, New Rochelle, NY.

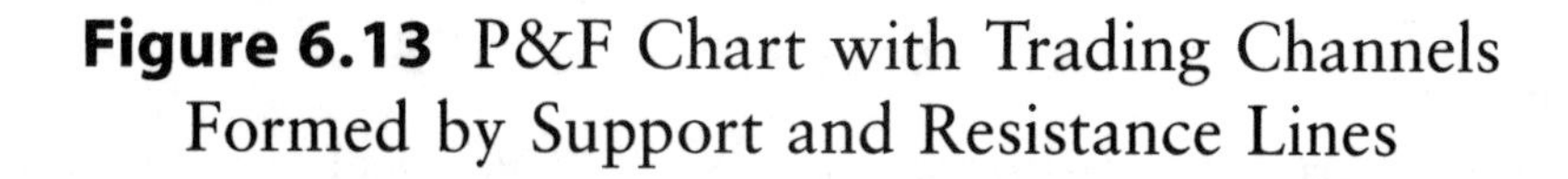

Figure 6.13 P&F Chart with Trading Channels Formed by Support and Resistance Lines

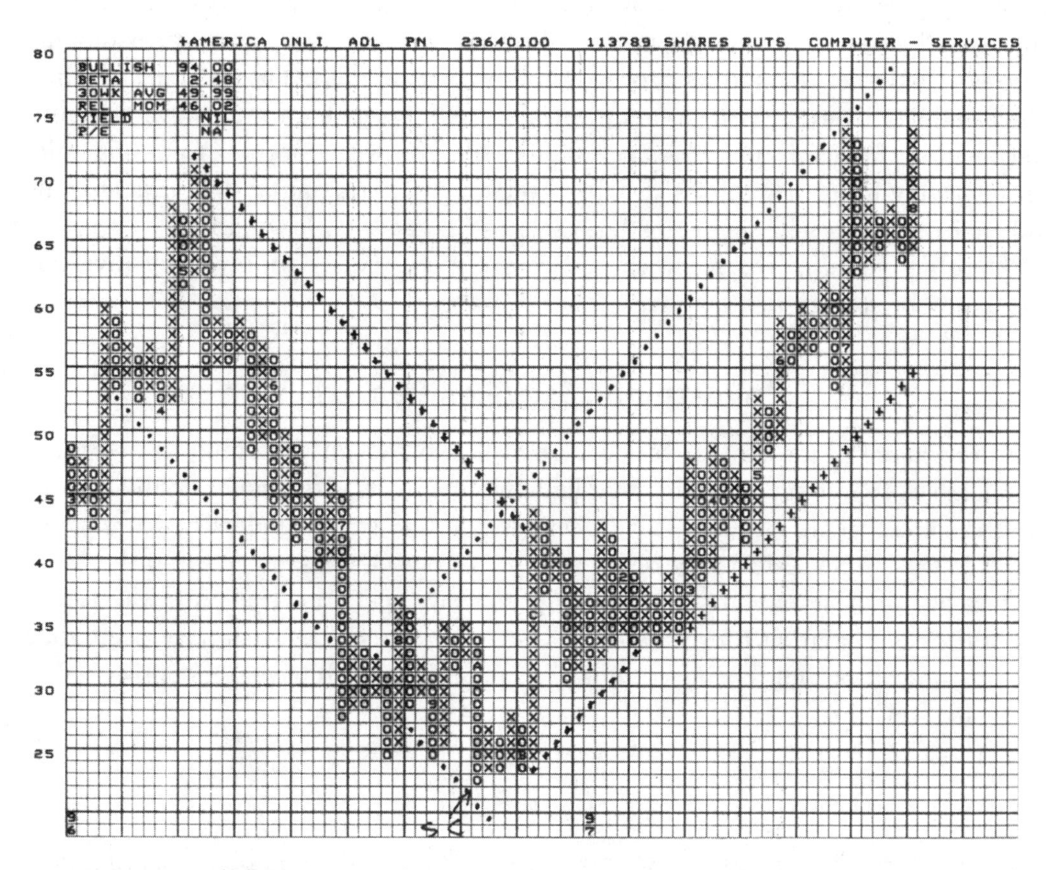

3-point reversal chart; move to the next column when the price changes $3 in the opposite direction. Numbers in columns represent months; the number is entered the first time stock trading causes an entry to occur that month.

x stock price moves up;
o stock price moves down.

Source: Courtesy of Chartcraft, New Rochelle, NY.

Advantages of P&F Charts

P&F charts offer several advantages over bar charts. They are less time-consuming to update, since you can record data if a specific high or low price occurs during the day. In this way P&F charts attempt to record only significant price movement, not all price movement. Buy and sell signals are easier to spot from the P&F chartbooks or computer charts. The technical departments of most major brokerage firms rely heavily on P&F charts for selection of individual stocks and for support and resistance targets.

Sentiment Indicators

Besides using chart patterns of individual stocks, technical analysts also study charts of various averages, indices, and ratios. Some of these are the Dow Jones Industrial Average, the S&P 500 advance-decline line, percent of NYSE stocks bullish, Russell 2000, and industry group bullish ratio. These charts help provide indications of whether the markets are in a bull or a bear trend. They give insight into which industries are bullish. In addition, these graphs give an indication of public sentiment in the marketplace. Some investors like to invest contrary to public opinion, believing that the public is usually too late in recognizing an investment trend and that the trend will change or has already changed its direction.

Here are some of the technical indicators more widely followed by investors and major brokerage firms.

Investment Services Bearish

The percentage of investment services bearish is based on the opinions of professional advisory services and is compiled by *Investors Intelligence*, published by Chartcraft. Extreme readings have been useful "contrary" indicators at turning points in the market. Most services tend to be trend followers, so you find the greatest number of bears when the market approaches major bottoms and the fewest bears at or near market tops. Readings of over 60 percent bearish have been good bottom indicators, and readings of under 20 percent bearish have frequently marked major market tops.

Put/Call Ratio

The put/call ratio is the ratio of total put option buying divided by call option buying. When the ratio reaches 1.20, there is heavy buying of puts over calls, which usually indicates the bottom of a market sell-off. A ratio of 0.80 usually accompanies the peak of a market rally. Since this is generally a measure of the public speculating in options contracts, it is a good contrary indicator.

Industry-Group Percent Bullish

Charts are published of the percentage of stocks bullish in each industry group. When looking at the Computer Group percent bullish, you would expect the stocks in that group to be overbought when the percentage reaches 70 percent and oversold when it reaches 30 percent. "Overbought" refers to a condition that occurs when large amounts of stock are purchased over months or years. The stock price has risen to a point where buyers are less likely to drive it significantly higher. After a stock reaches an oversold level, watch for its chart to give a buy signal to indicate that the trend for the industry is getting ready to reverse and start a new upward movement. Then examine charts of competitive stocks in its particular industry to make an investment decision.

Foreign Buy/Sell Ratio

The foreign buy/sell ratio is total foreign buying divided by foreign selling, indicating sentiment abroad regarding the U.S. market. Ten-day ratios above 1.40 often accompany market peaks, an excessively bullish situation that could accompany a rapid decline in U.S. stocks.

NYSE Percentage Bullish

To find the NYSE percentage bullish, the number of stocks with a bullish pattern is divided by the total number of all NYSE stocks. The resulting fraction or percentage is graphed weekly. A 70 percent reading shows an overbought condition, and a 30 percent reading means the market is oversold.

Institutional Buy/Sell Ratio

The institutional buying divided by institutional selling measures the level of enthusiasm or pessimism of the largest source of demand for, or supply of, equities. The trend relative to the market action is important. High ratios (1.40) occur during stampedes and tops, and low ratios (0.60) occur during sharp declines and at climax bottoms.

Advance/Decline Ratio (Seven-Day)

The seven-day advance/decline ratio is calculated by adding the number of advancing issues on the NYSE in the last seven days and the number of declining issues in the last seven days and dividing the larger total by the smaller. If the advances total is the larger of the two, the ratio is preceded by a plus. If the declines total is the larger, the ratio is preceded by a minus notation. Readings around or above +1.75 represent a short-term overbought market, whereas readings of −1.75 or less represent a short-term oversold market, which may reverse direction in the near future.

Using Technical Analysis with Fundamental Analysis

Combining technical analysis with fundamental analysis can be tricky. Both disciplines attempt to determine which stocks, industries, and markets are likely to rise or fall in value. They generally will work in concert with one another during a steadily rising or falling trend in the market, but they usually disagree as to outcome, while major tops and bottoms are being formed.

Think about it logically. When is news on a stock the most exciting? At the top. This often occurs during a period known as distribution on a chart pattern, preceding a sell-signal formation. The converse is also true. After a stock has been declining for some time, it stands to reason that fundamentals are generally poor. When the last sellers, accompanied by bad news, have driven the stock to a major low, a period of accumulation will begin as some future forecasters see prospects for improvement. A buy signal will occur long before massive positive news appears in print. Other than these two extremes, the two approaches tend to complement each other.

Many investors view charts as a timing tool. As persons implement a plan for building a stock portfolio, they often first choose industries, then which specific stocks to buy. Technical analysis can provide insight for deciding when to buy and at what price. It is advantageous to base buying decisions on both sound fundamental and technical analysis, i.e., a solid uptrend on the charts. Charts can therefore be viewed as an additional filter or screen in making decisions.

Timing a Sale

The two hardest decisions most investors make are not when to buy and when to sell. They are when to sell and when to sell. Deciding when to take a profit and when to take a loss are the hardest choices you will ever have to make.

Here are some guidelines you can use to determine the time to sell a stock from your portfolio. You can use any one of the following scenarios or a combination of them to trigger a sell decision.

- Sell when a stock has broken through the bullish support line on a P&F chart and has given a triple-bottom sell signal or two other sell signals.
- Sell after a stock has made a long advance on a P&F chart followed by a period of sideways movements and then appears to be "curling over" as it gives multiple sell signals.
- Sell when a stock breaks the neckline of a head-and-shoulders formation on a bar chart.
- When you acquire a stock, set a price objective that you wish to achieve. Discipline yourself to sell when you reach that target.
- Determine how much loss you are willing to stand should the stock not work out as you had planned. Try not to take more than a 20 percent loss on any one position. Should you cut your losses at this level and invest the proceeds, you need to find a stock that will rise 25 percent just to break even. If you take a loss greater than 20 percent, a recovery to break even will be much more difficult.

Using Your Computer for Technical Analysis

Computers are revolutionizing both charting and technical analysis. They can record and analyze data with lightning speed. Many data services exist that will enable an investor to download data such as the high, low, closing price, and volume on daily stock activity. Ten- to twenty-five-year price and trading histories are available for purchase on CD-ROM. Companies that supply this type of information can be found in ads placed in the *Wall Street Journal*, *Investor's Business Daily*, and investment trade magazines. Consult your financial adviser for help in finding such firms.

You can use a variety of computer software programs to analyze the data by plotting bar charts or P&F charts. Two of the most popular are Supercharts and Metastock. A lesser-known, but very effective, program is Savant Technical Investor. Supercharts' forte is bar charts. A person can go back and forth between daily, weekly, and monthly bar charts. P&F charts are available on the software also, but the spacing varies on the Xs and Os making it difficult to create forty-five-degree trading channels. Metastock does both bar charts and P&F charts well. The resolution of P&F charts is especially clear. Savant Technical Investor does the best of the three with P&F charts. The graphs come closest to the ones in chartbooks from Chartcraft. The bar charts are also easy to read. All three software programs have various additional features, such as split-screen capability, stoichastics, moving average lines, Japanese candlestick charts, trendlines, and many more sophisticated tools for building and analyzing charts.

Computer stores carry these and other programs in their software area. Investment magazines, newspapers, and financial consultants' trade magazines carry ads for software that can be purchased by mail or over the phone. New programs are coming out all the time to make charting easier and faster for you.

Although computer-generated charts are making great strides, their usefulness is limited. The charts are relatively small compared to those in chartbooks. Often the chart of a stock and stock average contain data covering only a few years or a few months. It is helpful to have at least six to ten years of trading history to understand the long-term trend. It can be advantageous to purchase a long-term chartbook several times a year to be able to check the long-term chart pattern of a stock you find through computer analysis.

Besides creating your own charts with software programs, you can find many chart patterns on the Internet. Several Web sites containing stock market information, include bar charts along with the fundamental data. Most major brokerage firms have Web sites that you can browse as well. Some firms offer on-line services so that you can obtain information on your brokerage account as well as research information on companies they follow. You can often pull up charts and other technical information on the stocks their analysts cover. As computers get faster and monitors get bigger, it will become easier and easier to do technical analysis and charting on a personal computer.

7 Life Insurance and Annuities

Lynn E. Marx and
George S. Eckhardt, Jr.

THE CONCEPT OF life insurance, the sharing of an assumed risk of unknown timing among many persons, is simple. Actually understanding and monitoring the enigmatic assortment of insurance options and policies available today is not. First, some basics.

Life insurance is a legal contract involving the insurance company, the owner, and the beneficiary. The contract is essentially a promissory note whereby the company promises to pay an agreed-upon sum of money to the party or parties designated by the owner at the insured's death. The owner has to pay the insurance company a given sum of money each year. The company promises to pay the beneficiaries the full amount of the contract, regardless of how many payments the owner has made.

A number of additional benefits can be added as extras, or "riders," to a basic life insurance policy. For example, a disability waiver of premium provides for the automatic continuation of premiums by the insurance company in the event the insured becomes disabled. All riders have specific limitations and restrictions, and each rider adds to the cost of the insurance policy.

How Do You Know How Much You Need?

Begin by determining whether you need life insurance at all. If you have no dependents, you may not need it. If you rely on work income to provide your standard of living or have a lot of debt such as a mortgage or business loan, insurance is probably a good idea.

Next, evaluate how much insurance you and your family need and how long you need it. Determine who should be insured. If you live in a two-wage-earner household, both of you may need to be insured. As you become more financially secure and reduce debt, your need for life insurance to provide survivor benefits may decrease. As your assets grow over time, however, your life insurance policy may become a powerful estate-planning tool that can provide the opportunity to get more of your assets to your heirs at your death.

Monitoring the performance of your life insurance policies along with your investment portfolio is essential to your long-term financial and emotional well-being. Start with a thorough review of all life insurance you currently own to see if your policies are still in sync with your objectives, risk tolerance, and time frame. Inventory your policies, using the information from this chapter and the Policy Review Worksheets provided later in the chapter. Then track each policy annually on a copy of the Life Insurance Policy Monitor (Figure 7.1). To guide you, Figure 7.2 is a completed example of this form.

Compare your calculated need with the amount of life insurance you currently have in place. With that information and an understanding of the basic concepts, you will be in a position to make informed decisions about whether your current life insurance coverage is meeting your objectives. You can also make adjustments on a timely basis as your lifestyle changes.

Types of Life Insurance

To facilitate your initial inventory and ongoing tracking, you need to have a basic understanding of the sometimes overwhelming maze of insurance choices. Figure 7.3 diagrams primary types of life insurance.

Figure 7.1 Life Insurance Policy Monitor

Company name: ______________________ Phone no.: __________

Agent name: ______________________ Phone no.: __________

Policy type: ______________________ Policy no.: __________

Policy owner: ______________________ Date issued: __________

Insured: ______________________ Age at issue: __________

Beneficiary: ______________________ Face amount: __________

Date	Premium Payment	Withdrawals/ Loans	Death Benefit	Cash Value/ Account Value	Credited Rate/ Rate of Return*	Company Ratings Best's	S&P

*For a variable-life investment account, the net rate of return = 100 × (current contract value – last year's contract value) / last year's contract value. For universal- and whole-life policies, track the current "credited" interest rate.

Figure 7.2 Life Insurance Policy Monitor: Completed Example

Company name: General Life Insurance Company of Texas
Phone no.: 222-999-9999

Agent name: Matt Wilson
Phone no.: 999-222-2222

Policy type: Whole Life Survivorship
Policy no.: 123456789

Policy owner: Jim & Ann Jones 1987 Trust, Amy Jones, Trustee
Date issued: 1/15/87

Insured: Jim & Ann joint insureds
Age at issue: 41 & 39

Beneficiary: Jim & Ann Jones 1987 Trust, Amy Jones, Trustee
Face amount: $1,885,874

Date	Premium Payment	Withdrawals/ Loans	Death Benefit	Cash Value/ Account Value	Credited Rate/ Rate of Return*	Company Ratings Best's	S&P
1/1/87	25,000	0	1,885,874	475	8.50%	A++	AAA
1/1/88	25,000	0	1,885,874	6,296	8.25%	A++	AAA
1/1/89	25,000	0	1,885,874	37,537	8.25%	A++	AAA
1/1/90	25,000	0	1,885,874	71,168	7.80%	A++	AAA
1/1/91	25,000	0	1,885,874	107,303	7.50%	A++	AAA
1/1/92	25,000	0	1,885,874	146,078	7.00%	A++	AA
1/1/93	25,000	0	1,885,874	187,622	7.00%	A++	AA
1/1/94	25,000	0	1,885,874	232,069	7.00%	A+	AA
1/1/95	25,000	0	1,885,874	279,583	7.25%	A+	AA
1/1/96	25,000	0	1,885,874	330,336	7.50%	A+	AAA

Note: Company name, contract terms, and performance data are for illustration purposes only and do not represent a specific life insurance company.

*For a variable-life investment account, the net rate of return = 100 × (current contract value – last year's contract value) / last year's contract value. For universal- and whole-life policies, track the current "credited" interest rate.

Figure 7.3 Categories of Life Insurance

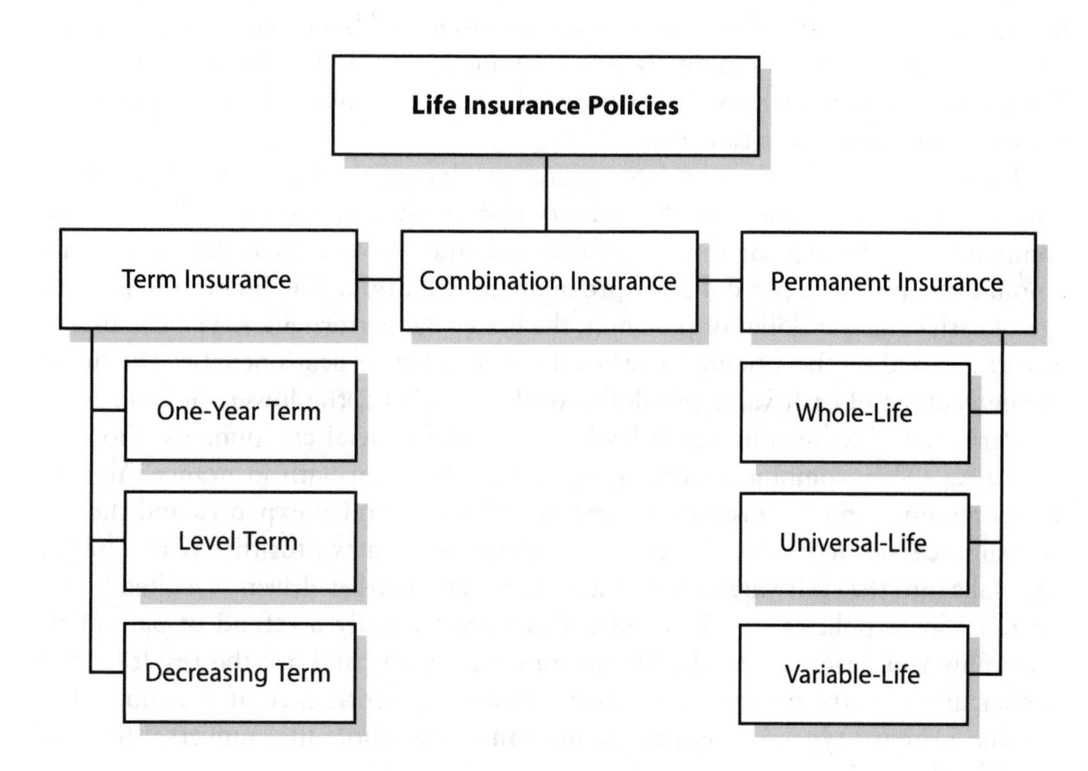

Term Life Insurance

Term insurance is the most basic of all life insurance coverage. It is temporary insurance provided under an agreement to pay a death benefit if your death occurs during a specified period of time. Term insurance provides pure insurance protection and has no cash accumulation or investment component. The sole function is protection. If you die while the contract is in force, the death benefit is distributed to your beneficiary. If you live to the end of the term, the policy expires without value, and insurance coverage will terminate unless the policy includes a provision permitting it to be continued. A term insurance policy never develops any equity for the owner; its cash value in the estate is always zero. For this reason, we do not provide a Policy Review Worksheet for term insurance.

Term insurance comes in a variety of forms. The differences among policies relate to three items: length of time for coverage, level or decreasing death benefit, and premium duration. Term insurance may be nonrenewable or renewable. If the policy is renewable, you have the option of extending the protection without proof of good health or "evidence of insurability." Usually, term policies are renewable to a certain age, such as 75, or for a certain duration. Term insurance costs more as you get older and may become prohibitively expensive beyond retirement.

Permanent Life Insurance

In addition to the pure insurance protection provided by a term policy, permanent insurance has a "cash value" reserve account that builds up within the contract. This cash value increases annually as premiums are paid. The owner can borrow from it or take it as cash-surrender proceeds (taxable above cost basis if you have a gain) if the contract is canceled.

Performance and risk of policy failure, or "lapse," in a permanent life insurance contract are functions of the stability and investment results of the insurance company and the size of the cash-value account. Performance depends on the amount of cash value per dollar of premium contribution. The higher the percentage of cash value per dollar of premium, the better the performance. The net amount at risk is based on the amount of cash value per dollar of death benefit. The higher the percentage of cash value per dollar of death benefit, the lower the risk.

Permanent life insurance policies have several financial components, shown in Figure 7.4. They combine a savings account (cash value) with insurance. You pay your premium, and the insurance company takes out policy expenses and the cost of insurance, or "mortality charges" (essentially term rates), for that year. The balance falls into the cash-value account and grows at a market-driven "credited" interest rate. Some policies pay dividends, which are basically a refund of part of the premiums you have paid to the life insurance company and are the result of your participation, as the policy owner, in the business performance of the company.

The primary types of permanent insurance are whole-life, universal-life, and variable-life.

Whole-life insurance offers lifetime insurance coverage and an investment account managed by the insurance company. In the early years of a whole-life policy, the annual level premium is more than enough to pay the policy expenses and

Figure 7.4 Financial Components of Permanent Life Insurance

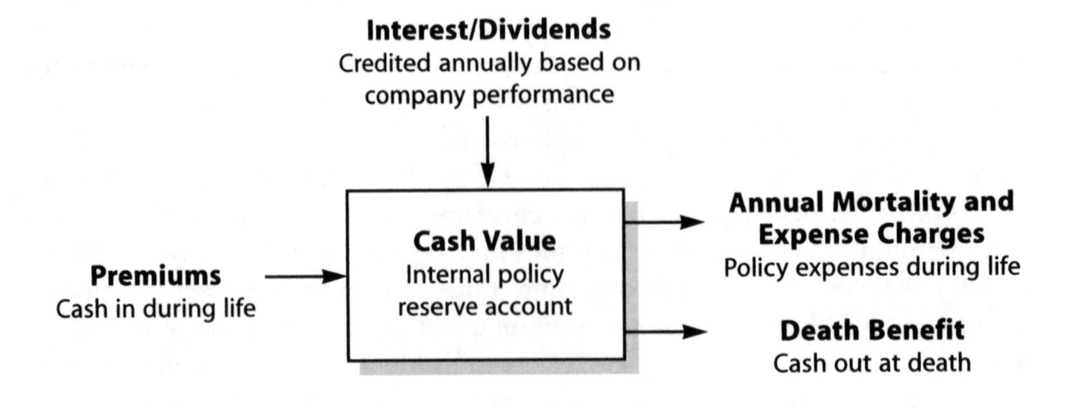

cost of insurance coverage. The excess premiums, growing at interest, make up for the deficiency of premiums in later years, when the annual level premium is no longer sufficient to pay the increased cost of insurance protection at your older ages.

Whole-life policies have limited flexibility to adjust premiums, cash values, and level of protection during the policy term. The good news, though, is that for traditional whole-life insurance, the insurance company bears most of the risk of loss. If the company's assumptions about its investments are not accurate and earnings on investments are not adequate to provide the benefits promised, the insurance company must still pay the guaranteed benefits and make up the difference elsewhere. The annual premium amount can never be raised for the life of the contract.

The investment part of the whole-life premium is generally composed of medium- to long-term bonds and mortgages with some common stock. Investment decisions are made by the insurer, and credited interest rates can change annually.

Many hybrids of traditional whole-life policies have evolved over the years. In general all fall into one of three categories:

1. *Guaranteed-cost whole-life policies*—These require the highest premium payments per dollar of death benefit and involve no risk to the policyholder. All risk is borne by the insurance company. Premium amount, cash values, death benefit, mortality costs, and operating expenses are all guaranteed. Fully guaranteed policies are rare because of the high premium requirement and low interest rates.
2. *Participating or interest-sensitive whole-life policies*—These require the policy owner to share the market-driven interest risk with the insurance company. Fluctuations in investment performance directly affect dividends and cash-value growth. The insurance company guarantees that it will credit a minimum rate of dividends and/or interest to the policy. In most cases, the guaranteed rate will be exceeded, with the policy owner participating in the spread.
3. *Blended whole-life policies*—These add a term rider to a base whole-life policy. The more term insurance, the lower the premium and the more risk of lapse the policy owner incurs. A blend of 25 percent term decreasing to zero over a limited number of years can provide more protection in the early years at a reduced premium cost without your assuming much risk. Be careful, however, of "whole-life" policies that have more than half term; the additional risk assumed may become substantial. One way to tell if your current whole-life policy is blended is by tracking the increase in death benefit each year since issue. Traditional whole-life has an increasing death benefit when not blended with term. The death benefit in a blended policy is generally level until any term is gone. A whole-life death benefit projected to stay level forever may indicate a large percentage of term (for example, 20 percent base

whole-life blended with 80 percent term) that does not ever decrease. Guarantees inherent in standard whole-life policies do not apply to the term portion. Determine the actual coverage provided by reviewing your contract and/or calling the insurance company.

If you have whole-life policies, inventory them on copies of Figure 7.5. For a completed example of this worksheet, see Figure 7.6.

Universal-life insurance offers flexible premiums and, in return, flexible death benefits. Universal-life performance is sensitive to changing interest rates. Fund earnings are generally based on short- to medium-term bonds and money instruments, are guaranteed for one year, and can change monthly thereafter. Because the policyholder's return is based on shorter-term interest rates, more risk of market volatility is shifted from the insurance company to the policyholder. The flexible nature of the contract stems from the fact that you are not required to pay premiums every year as you are for whole-life contracts. To receive the death benefit, you just need to pay enough to maintain a positive cash-surrender value. If you skip a premium or don't pay enough into the contract to cover policy expenses and mortality charges, those costs will be funded from cash value. For universal-life, it is critical to maintain cash value to keep the policy in force. Investment of excess premium is, as in whole-life, controlled by the insurance company. Surrender charges are levied on termination, or "surrender," of universal-life policies during the first ten to twenty years.

You, as the policyholder, may set your own pattern of premium payments based on future needs. The universal-life contract gives you the ability to increase (within limits) or decrease the face amount without having a new policy issued. Ongoing monitoring of the performance of your policies will position you to take full advantage of universal-life's flexibility to meet your changing insurance needs.

If you own universal- or whole-life, the insurance company decides the interest rate you get paid, or "credited," on the cash value that is building up in the policy. You can't determine a company's investment expertise by looking at the "illustrations" projecting future performance. Given the importance of maintaining a healthy cash-value account, it makes sense to research the track record and monitor the ongoing performance of your company's investment portfolio. One good source of information is *Best's Review*, a monthly magazine published by the A. M. Best Company. Every year the editors create a table that shows which companies have had the highest interest "crediting rates."

Inventory any universal-life policies you own on copies of Figure 7.7. For a completed example of this worksheet, see Figure 7.8.

Variable-life insurance policies amount to mutual funds with a wrapper of life insurance. They typically offer a wide range of separate accounts, similar to a family of mutual funds, which are available within the contract. The investment accounts are legally separate from the insurance company's own portfolio and generally are not affected by the company's investment returns or subject to its creditors. The policyholder defers paying taxes on investment gains realized inside these accounts.

Figure 7.5 Whole-Life Policy Review Worksheet

Company name: ____________________ Phone no.: ______________

Agent name: ____________________ Phone no.: ______________

Policy type: ____________________ Policy no.: ______________

Objective: ____________________ Target year: ______________

Policy owner: ____________________ Issue date: ______________

Insured: ____________________ Age at issue: ______________

Beneficiary: ____________________ Contingent: ______________

Policy riders: ____________________ Rider cost: ______________

Death benefit: ____________________ Death benefit option: ________

Blended policy? ❑ Yes ❑ No % Term: ______________

Scheduled premium: ____________ No. of years: ______________

Premium mode: ❑ Monthly ❑ Quarterly ❑ Annually

Company Ratings

Standard & Poor's: ____________________

Moody's: ____________________

A. M. Best: ____________________

Current credited rate: ____________________

Benefit Paid at Maturity

Death benefit: ______________

Cash value: ______________

Other: ______________

Contract maturity age: ________

	Policy Projections at Current Rates			Policy Projections at 1% Below Current		
	10 Years	25 Years	Maturity	10 Years	25 Years	Maturity
Cash value:	______	______	______	______	______	______
Death benefit:	______	______	______	______	______	______

Number of years premium is projected to be paid out of pocket at current credited rate: ________; if rate drops 1%: ________

Figure 7.6 Whole-Life Policy Review Worksheet: Completed Example

Company name: Great Life of Texas — Phone no.: 222-999-9999

Agent name: Matthew A. Wilson, CLU — Phone no.: 999-222-2222

Policy type: Whole-Life Survivorship — Policy no.: 123456789

Objective: Estate tax payment — Target year: Life expectancy

Policy owner: Jim & Ann Jones 1987 Trust — Issue date: 01/15/87

Insured: Jim & Ann — Age at issue: 41 & 39

Beneficiary: Jim & Ann Jones 1987 Trust — Contingent: None

Policy riders: None — Rider cost: $0.00

Death benefit: $2,145,584 — Death benefit option: Increasing

Blended policy? ❑ Yes ☑ No — % Term: 0

Scheduled premium: $25,000 — No. of years: 12

Premium mode: ❑ Monthly ❑ Quarterly ☑ Annually

Company Ratings

Standard & Poor's: AAA

Moody's: Aaa

A. M. Best: A+

Current credited rate: 7.50%

Benefit Paid at Maturity

Death benefit: Face amount – loans

Cash value: Held as death benefit

Other:

Contract maturity age: 99

	Policy Projections at Current Rates			Policy Projections at 1% Below Current		
	10 Years	25 Years	Maturity	10 Years	25 Years	Maturity
Cash value:	330,336	1,054,189	2,087,542	330,336	875,988	1,898,000
Death benefit:	2,145,584	2,304,876	2,788,979	2,145,584	2,007,890	2,309,888

Number of years premium is projected to be paid out of pocket at current credited rate: 11 ; if rate drops 1%: 13.5

Note: Company name, contract terms, and performance data are for illustration purposes only and do not represent a specific life insurance company.

Figure 7.7 Universal-Life Policy Review Worksheet

Company name: ____________________ Phone no.: ______________

Agent name: ____________________ Phone no.: ______________

Policy type: ____________________ Policy no.: ______________

Objective: ____________________ Target year: ______________

Policy owner: ____________________ Issue date: ______________

Insured: ____________________ Age at issue: ______________

Beneficiary: ____________________ Contingent: ______________

Policy riders: ____________________ Rider cost: ______________

Death benefit: ____________________ Level ❑ Increasing ❑

Surrender penalties: ____________________ No. of years: ______________

Scheduled premium: ____________________ No. of years: ______________

Premium mode: ❑ Monthly ❑ Quarterly ❑ Annually ❑ Variable

Company Ratings

Standard & Poor's: ____________________

Moody's: ____________________

A. M. Best: ____________________

Current credited rate: ____________________

Benefit Paid at Maturity

Death benefit: ______________

Cash value: ______________

Other: ______________

Contract maturity age: __________

	Policy Projections at Current Rates			Policy Projections at 1% Below Current		
	10 Years	25 Years	Maturity	10 Years	25 Years	Maturity
Cash value:	______	______	______	______	______	______
Death benefit:	______	______	______	______	______	______

Number of years premium is projected to be paid out of pocket
at current credited rate: ________; if rate drops 1%: ________

Figure 7.8 Universal-Life Policy Review Worksheet: Completed Example

Company name: Westfield Life Insurance Co. Phone no.: 777-333-4444

Agent name: Matthew A. Wilson, CLU Phone no.: 999-222-2222

Policy type: Universal Life Policy no.: 98989898

Objective: Survivor benefit Target year: Lifetime

Policy owner: Bill Thompson Issue date: 01/10/76

Insured: Bill Thompson Age at issue: 30

Beneficiary: Amy Thompson Contingent: Children

Policy riders: Disability waiver Rider cost: $25.00

Death benefit: $150,000 Level ☑ Increasing ❑

Surrender penalties: 10% decreasing No. of years: 10

Scheduled premium: $248.25 No. of years: 10

Premium mode: ❑ Monthly ☑ Quarterly ❑ Annually ❑ Variable

Company Ratings

Standard & Poor's: AA–

Moody's: Aa2

A. M. Best: A

Current credited rate: 6.50%

Benefit Paid at Maturity

Death benefit: Face amount

Cash value: if $1.00 in CV

Other:

Contract maturity age: 100

	Policy Projections at Current Rates			Policy Projections at 1% Below Current		
	10 Years	25 Years	Maturity	10 Years	25 Years	Maturity
Cash value:	10,506	20,493	36,676	9,928	15,783	0
Death benefit:	150,000	150,000	150,000	150,000	150,000	0

Number of years premium is projected to be paid out of pocket at current credited rate: 10 ; if rate drops 1%: 18

Note: Company name, contract terms, and performance data are for illustration purposes only and do not represent a specific life insurance company.

Variable-life is treated as a registered security and must be sold through a broker-dealer. Nevertheless, like other insurance products, it requires health qualification, or **underwriting**. The purchase of a variable-life insurance product must be accompanied by, or preceded by, a prospectus approved by the Securities and Exchange Commission.

Variable-life policies charge annual fees, calculated as a percentage of your premium and/or invested dollars, on top of the normal management fees charged by any mutual fund. As part of your insurance review and monitoring process, check your variable-life prospectus for mortality and expense fee (M&E) charges and fees deducted from premiums paid. Consult the *Morningstar Variable Annuity/Life Insurance Performance Report*, published monthly, for a description of the cost components; fee averages; one-, three-, five- and ten-year fund performance summaries; and just about anything else you'd like to know about specific variable-life policies. The monthly report can be purchased by subscription or for $45 a single issue. For information about available performance reports and database software, call Morningstar at 800-735-0700.

As in traditional universal-life contracts, variable-universal-life premiums and death benefits can vary within limitations. Differing from whole-life and universal-life contracts, you, the policy owner (not the insurance company), have total management responsibility over the mix of investments you choose and the total investment risk based on your choices. In return for accepting investment risk, you have the potential for earning higher returns than in traditional life products. Depending on the policy's design, if investment returns are good, the death benefit may also increase. If investment returns are bad, however, the policy may lapse.

Be aware that, unlike traditional cash-value insurance ledgers, which project values based on recent performance, variable-life projections are allowed to use an arbitrary rate of investment return based on past performance. The maximum rate that can legally be used currently is 12 percent. Don't make decisions regarding a variable-life policy based on an attractive projection of future performance assuming a 12 percent rate of return over the life of the policy, often thirty years or more. Make your decisions, instead, on the basis of suitable separate account choices, adequate funding, and conservative investment assumptions. Your risk will be minimized in the long run.

If your asset-allocation plan, based on your personal time frame and risk tolerance, does not include growth investments, stick to more traditional insurance products. Variable-life expenses will eat up any gains you realize in a conservative portfolio. If, however, you have the time to withstand the ups and downs of the stock market for ten years or more and can handle the risk therein, variable-life offers an attractive package of death-benefit protection, creditor protection in many states, investment choices with potentially high returns, and tax-deferred accumulation. Many life insurance buyers, particularly baby boomers, like variable-life because they are interested in cash accumulation for retirement in addition to the death benefit. The cash values in these policies can be withdrawn to basis or borrowed, usually tax free, to provide supplemental retirement income.

Figure 7.9 Variable-Life Policy Review Worksheet

Company name: ______________________ Phone no.: ______________

Agent name: ______________________ Phone no.: ______________

Policy type: ______________________ Policy no.: ______________

Objective: ______________________ Target year: ______________

Policy owner: ______________________ Issue date: ______________

Insured: ______________________ Age at issue: ______________

Beneficiary: ______________________ Contingent: ______________

Policy riders: ______________________ Rider cost: ______________

Specified amount: ______________________ Level ☑ Increasing ☐

Surrender penalties: ______________________ No. of years: ______________

Scheduled premium: ______________________ No. of years: ______________

Premium mode: ☐ Monthly ☐ Quarterly ☐ Annually ☐ Variable Loan rate: ______________

Company Ratings

Standard & Poor's: ______________________

Moody's: ______________________

A. M. Best: ______________________

Policy Charges

M&E expense: ______________

Administrative fees: ______________

Premium deductions: ______________

Investment Accounts in Variable Universal-Life Policy	Account Expenses	Account Performance		
		1 Year	3 Years	5 Years

Figure 7.10 Variable-Life Policy Review Worksheet: Completed Example

Company name:	General Life of Texas	Phone no.:	777-333-4444
Agent name:	Matthew A. Wilson, CLU	Phone no.:	999-222-2222
Policy type:	Variable Universal Life	Policy no.:	23456789
Objective:	Survivor needs/retirement	Target year:	65
Policy owner:	Alexander M. Morningstar	Issue date:	01/10/90
Insured:	Alexander M. Morningstar	Age at issue:	43
Beneficiary:	Elizabeth S. Morningstar	Contingent:	Testamentary trust
Policy riders:	None	Rider cost:	0
Specified amount:	$250,000	Level ☑ Increasing ☐	
Surrender penalties:	15% decreasing each year	No. of years:	10
Scheduled premium:	$3,400	No. of years:	13
Premium mode:	☐ Monthly ☐ Quarterly ☑ Annually ☐ Variable	Loan rate:	.9% yrs 2–14, then 0
Company Ratings		**Policy Charges**	
Standard & Poor's:	AA–	M&E expense:	8% yrs. 1–11, then .5%
Moody's:	A1	Administrative fees:	$12.50 yr. 1, then $5
A. M. Best:	A+	Premium deductions:	4%–6%

Investment Accounts in Variable Universal-Life Policy	Account Expenses	Account Performance 1 Year	3 Years	5 Years
Capital appreciation fund	1.00%	–0.06%	6.57%	5.33%
Global securities fund	0.81%	16.86%	3.49%	11.53%
Stock index fund	0.25%	21.56%	18.18%	13.72%
Money-market fund	0.50%	4.27%	4.04%	3.32%
Asset manager fund	0.74%	13.69%	7.11%	10.37%
Equity-income fund	0.58%	13.37%	17.30%	17.04%

Note: Company name, contract terms, and performance data are for illustration purposes only and do not represent a specific life insurance company.

If you have any variable-life policies, inventory them on copies of Figure 7.9. For a completed example of this worksheet, see Figure 7.10.

Second-to-die/survivorship insurance policies are whole-life, universal-life, or variable-life policies that insure two people. The death benefit under this type of policy is not paid until the last of the two insureds dies. Generally, survivorship policies have the same attributes as the comparable single-life versions. Used typically for insuring husbands and wives, this kind of policy can be very effective in providing liquidity to pay estate tax for couples who choose to defer estate taxes until the second death. It may also be used to create an estate to leave to your children and grandchildren. Structured properly, survivorship insurance can provide cash for your family that will not be income- or estate-taxed at your death.

Potential Pitfalls with Life Insurance

Turning Your Insurance into a Taxable Investment

If you put too much premium in too fast, withdrawals or loans will be taxed. In 1986 Congress realized that life insurance offers unique tax advantages over other investments and set limits on the maximum amount of premiums allowed relative to the death benefit. All policies must now meet specific tests to qualify them for favorable income tax treatment as life insurance. If there is too much cash value relative to the death benefit, the proceeds will be income-taxed as an investment.

If you intend to maximum-fund a permanent contract, be sure it will not become a Modified Endowment Contract (MEC) under the tax code. Your life insurance company should alert you if overfunding will create an MEC problem.

Setting Yourself Up for a Future Cash Call

Consistently funding your contract with the minimum premium or regularly skipping out-of-pocket premium payments may create a "thinly funded"contract, one with minimal cash value, which will be in danger of lapsing with even small decreases in current interest rates or increases in expenses. Even worse, to keep your policy in force, you may be subjected to future "cash calls" of larger premiums.

You can control the amount of risk by the level of funding. Paying the "cheapest" premium for permanent life insurance may sound like a good idea, but will not be in your best interest over the long term if you plan to keep the policy.

Outliving Your Insurance Contract

Each permanent-life contract defines the "maturity" year of a contract as a specific age of the insured between ninety-five and one-hundred. At maturity, premiums are no longer accepted, and the policy cash-surrender value in most contracts will be returned to the policy owner. With longer and longer life expectancies, a thinly funded contract could mean the benefit may be very small if you're still around at ninety-seven. A policy funded to "endow"at maturity has a cash value equal to the death benefit at that time. Some universal-life contracts provide for payment of the full death benefit as long as one dollar remains in the cash-value account. Review the maturity age and the terms of your contract beyond maturity.

The Nonvanishing Premium

Vanish is a term used over the last twenty years to define a permanent insurance contract that does not need to have any additional out-of-pocket premiums paid after a specified number of years. Unfortunately, many policyholders assumed that the policy was "paid up" at that time. Actually, changes for policy expenses and mortality are paid throughout the life of the insured in permanent policies. At some point, when the cash value is adequate, the policyholder can choose to have the premium paid from the policy values, as illustrated in Figure 7.11.

Clearly, if the policy is thinly funded or interest rates drop, the option to pay premiums from the cash-value account may not be available. Permanent insurance contracts sold in the 1980s are a good example of what can happen. Policies that were projected using 11 percent and 12 percent interest rates are now crediting 6.5 percent to 7.5 percent. Interest rates on quality bond investments crested at 14 percent in 1981 but since then have declined to around 7 percent. Those policy owners are paying more premiums to keep their contracts in force than were projected at the time the policies were purchased because their cash-value accounts have not grown as projected.

Figure 7.11 Payment of Premium from Policy Values

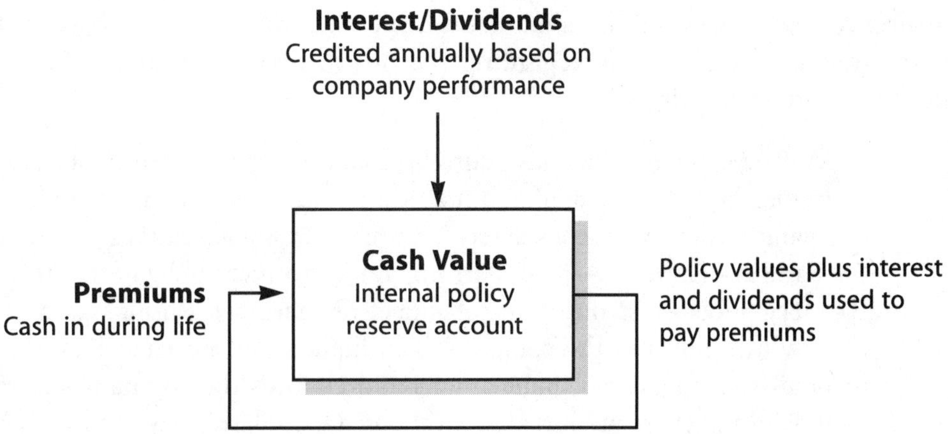

Interest/Dividends
Credited annually based on company performance

Premiums
Cash in during life

Cash Value
Internal policy reserve account

Policy values plus interest and dividends used to pay premiums

Plan to fund your policy with sufficient premiums, generally for a minimum of ten to twelve years, to build cash value. Don't assume, however, that ceasing out-of-pocket premiums will always be the best decision, even if your cash values will support doing so. Funding permanent policies beyond the required years can significantly increase the death benefit.

Projections Are Just Projections

Due to the myriad assumptions and designs from different companies, it's almost impossible to evaluate fully or to compare accurately life insurance illustrations. Fortunately, the National Association of Insurance Commisssioners has recently adopted a model Life Insurance Illustrations Regulation, requiring much more forthright creation of proposals. As this change is made across the insurance industry, review and monitoring projections will become easier.

It is important to monitor your interest-sensitive policies annually to be sure your cash value is maintained at a safe level. Call your life insurance carrier and request an "in-force" projection of values based on current credited rates, assuming premiums are paid each year. Also ask for one ledger projecting the earliest year your policy is likely to be self-sustaining based on current rates, and another at one percent below current. If projected values are decreasing at current rates, you must either put more premium dollars into the policy or drop the death benefit to a sustainable level at current premiums. Track premiums paid and changes in credited rate, cash value, and death benefit each year on copies of the Life Insurance Policy Monitor (Figure 7.1).

Your Insurance Company Should Outlive You

When you buy permanent insurance, you are giving a company your money on the assumption that it will be around to give it back with interest sometime in the future. The good news is that at least five different services rate the solvency of insurance companies on today's market. Independent third-party ratings are the primary source of information regarding the health of your insurer. These are the major private rating firms:

- *A. M. Best Company* measures current financial strength, lapse rates, expenses, and mortality experience of about 4,000 domestic and international insurance companies. Companies considered "secure" are assigned ratings that range from A++ and A+ (superior—a very strong ability to meet obligations) to B++ and B+ (very good—a strong ability to meet obligations). Ratings go all the way to F, which indicates the company is in liquidation. Best receives most of its income from the sale of publications and chooses the companies it wants to include. Ratings are published monthly on a cumulative basis in *Best's Review*.

You can also confirm current ratings through the BestLine Service by calling 800-424-BEST. A recorded listing of available reports and corresponding charges is provided.

- *Moody's Investors Service Inc.* measures the degree of financial security and risk in each company's investment and asset portfolio. Moody's charges the company being rated a substantial fee. As might be expected, not all companies choose to be rated. While it makes sense that strong companies go to Moody's to get a stamp of approval, other companies may not want to pay the required fee and receive a report showing a low rating. The highest rating given by Moody's is Aaa, "exceptional security," unlikely to be affected by change. To obtain insurance company credit ratings without charge from Moody's Corporate Ratings Desk, call 212-553-0377.
- *Standard and Poor's Ratings Group* measures financial strength and claims-paying ability of insurance companies and evaluates the adequacy of each company's surplus to meet future financial obligations and claims. Superior financial security with highest safety receives a grade of AAA from S&P. As with Moody's, companies select into S&P's rating service at a fee. Not every company elects to do so. Solvency reports are available by subscription from S&P, and customized ratings research is available for a fee. You can obtain up to three ratings without charge through the Information Desk Ratings Line by calling 212-208-1527.

Most astute insurance buyers insist that their insurance company carry either an A+ or an A++ rating from A. M. Best and one of the top three ratings from Standard & Poor's or Moody's. Public libraries generally have copies of the annually published reviews of the rating services for your review, and copies of those reports should be available from your agent and/or insurance company. Track the ratings each year on the Life Insurance Policy Monitor (Figure 7.1).

Bail-Out Options for Insurance

What if you determine you no longer need a permanent insurance policy or that it is underperforming? Suppose you bought a policy from a company that was solid at the time but now seems shaky. Depending on how long you have had the policy, several alternatives may be available:

- Cash the policy in and buy a new one from another company on a tax-free basis under an IRS-sanctioned 1035 exchange. You may have surrender charges, but your cash value will be transferred to the new policy. This does require a new medical exam in most cases, and you pay new acquisition or "sales" charges.

- Instead of discarding a policy, take the "reduced-paid-up" option. This stops the premiums in exchange for a lower death benefit.
- Cash in the policy. If the cash surrender value exceeds your cost basis (the sum of all the premiums you've paid), you'll owe tax on the gain.
- Exchange the policy for an annuity. Depending on your objectives, you can roll over the cash value of an insurance policy to any kind of annuity, variable or fixed, deferred or immediate.
- Give the policy to a charity. You'll get a tax deduction equal to your cost basis or the cash value.

If you would like help analyzing your insurance company's statements, you can send your cash-value policy information to the Insurance Group of the Consumer Federation of America (CFA) for an analysis of the investment rate of return. The service costs $40 for the first illustration and $30 for each additional one. Call CFA at 202-387-0087 for more information

One word of caution, however: Do not cancel even a poorly performing policy before finding out by taking an insurance medical exam whether you can qualify for a new policy. Evaluate all options carefully before discontinuing an insurance policy. If you want coverage later, it might not be available, and it will almost certainly be more expensive.

Fundamentals of Annuity Contracts

Annuities, generally sold by insurance companies, offer a way to assure an income stream until your death and to defer taxes in the process. You pay a lump sum up front or pay into the contract on a regular schedule over a number of years to buy a fixed or variable annuity. The company invests the after-tax money for you, often in the mutual-fund-like accounts of your choice, and your money grows tax-deferred as a retirement plan until you withdraw it. Payments can begin immediately or can be deferred until a future date. Withdrawals can be in a lump sum or in a series of payments over a specified period of time.

Annuity income is treated as ordinary income, and all gains are taxed before you get your principal back unless you elect to receive a fixed monthly, quarterly, or annual payment for life. Each "annuitized" payment is considered part gain and part return of principal as received. Annuity principal payments do not count as income when you're figuring out what part of your Social Security payment is taxable, and annuity contracts generally enjoy protection from creditors.

Figure 7.12 diagrams primary types of annuities. The broad categories are immediate and deferred annuities.

Figure 7.12 Categories of Annuities

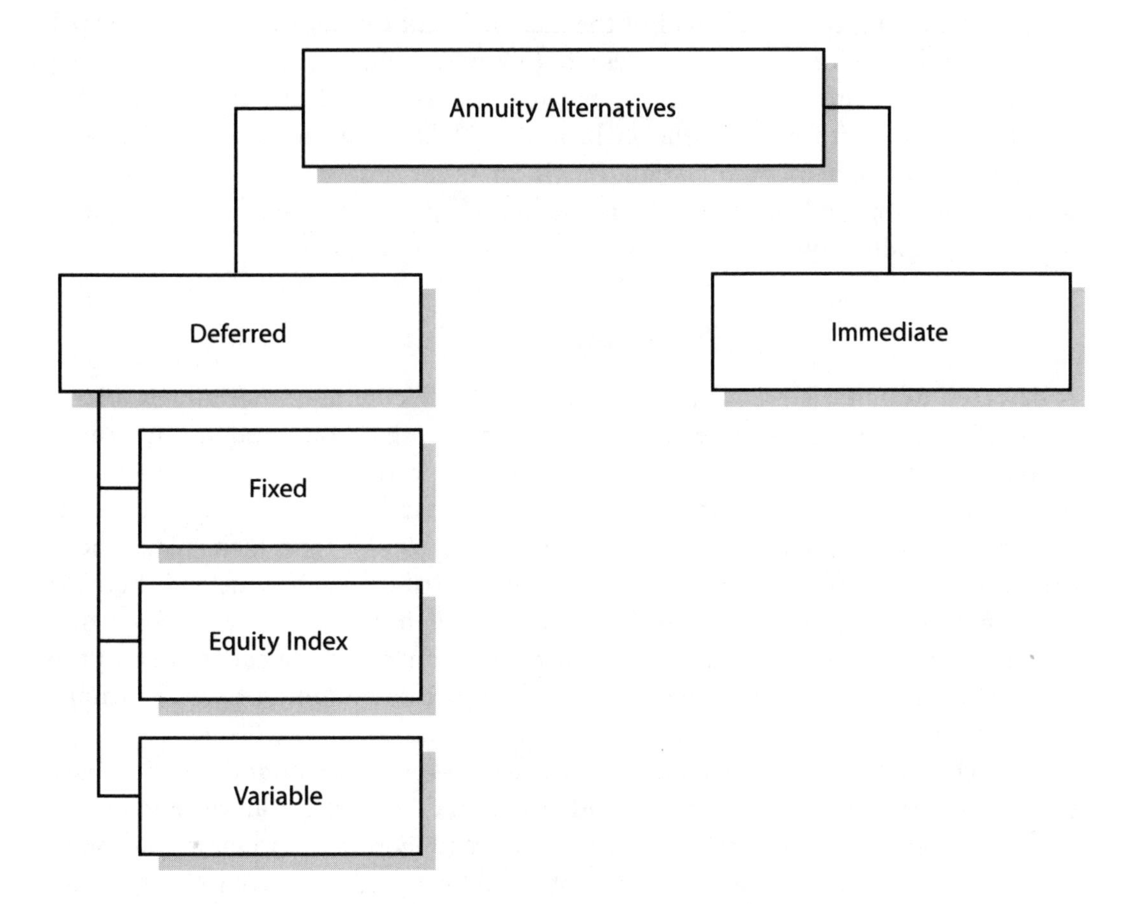

Immediate Annuities

An **immediate annuity** provides a regular monthly income the way a pension plan does. You buy the annuity with a lump-sum investment and begin collecting payments right away. Insurance companies invest your money and administer your contract. The amount of your monthly check depends on your age, the amount of investment, the expected return estimated by the insurance company, and the terms of the payout.

The varieties of immediate annuities are defined by the pattern of payments. **Joint annuities** are paid over your lifetime and the lifetime of your beneficiary, usually your spouse. **Life-or-period-certain annuities** are paid for the longer of your lifetime or for a fixed period of time, such as ten years. **Period-certain annuities** are paid to the annuitant or the annuitant's beneficiary just for the specified fixed number of years. **Single-life annuities** are paid each month for the duration of your lifetime.

One major advantage of an immediate life annuity is the security of a guaranteed income that can't be outlived. If investment returns go down, your payments remain steady. Approximately half of the income is tax free as a return of principal.

On the down side, if interest rates are low when you buy, your payments may not keep up with inflation, and there may not be anything left for your family after you're gone. As with a true pension benefit, you have an income stream but no account balance after annuitization. Also, an immediate annuity is irrevocable, which means you can't change your mind. Choosing a highly rated insurance company is especially important, since you're making a lifetime deal.

Deferred Annuities

A **deferred annuity** is a contract with an insurance company that allows you to invest money, either as a lump sum or over time, so that you build an investment account for your retirement. Because annuities are retirement plans, your investment grows tax deferred but also carries with that benefit the 10 percent tax penalty for making withdrawals before age 59½. Unlike retirement plans, however, there is no limit on the amount you may contribute each year, and there are no mandatory withdrawals after age 70½. You can choose either a fixed or a variable annuity. After the accumulation phase, you may take the money out as regular payments, use the money to buy an immediate annuity, or take a lump-sum withdrawal.

Drawbacks of deferred annuities are the penalties for early withdrawals and potentially large surrender charges and fees. All earnings distributed from the annuity are taxed as ordinary income with no capital-gain treatment. In addition, if you should die with funds in the annuity that had not yet been withdrawn, your family would owe income tax on the appreciation. The same gain in a mutual fund or other security would enjoy a stepped-up cost basis at your death, freeing it from income taxes.

Deferred annuities may be fixed, equity-index, or variable annuities. A **fixed annuity** is a contract whereby the insurance company invests your money in its general account and guarantees a fixed rate of return, usually for a year. After that, the rate is adjusted annually, based loosely on market-driven interest rates, with a guaranteed minimum floor of about 3.5 percent to 4.0 percent. The initial rate is usually higher than the rate at which your investment will grow. Fixed annuities don't have fund managers, annual administration fees, or a life insurance component; therefore, overall fees are generally substantially lower than fees for variable annuities.

An **equity-index annuity** combines the traditional guarantees of a fixed annuity with an excess-interest feature pegged to a market measure like Standard & Poor's 500-stock index. Index contracts return a percent of the price gains, or **participation rate**, in the index they are tied to. For example, an index annuity may have an annual gain of 10 percent, which is then multiplied by the contract participation rate. Assuming an 80 percent participation rate, the yield for the year would be 8 percent.

The substantial variations among equity-indexed annuities are the result of differences in index calculation terms, gains treatment, and other features and benefits. Despite the maze of contract alternatives and design complexities, the performance results of equity-index annuities over a broad range of economic scenarios tend to be highly similar. Be aware, however, that the "automatic rollover" provision present in some contracts allows you little time, usually thirty to sixty days, to decide whether to recommit to the next term before defaulting to another equity-index term with new rates and surrender penalties.

Variable annuities typically offer a choice of mutual-fund-like "subaccounts" with different investment objectives. Mutual fund performance and investment discretion plus the tax deferral afforded by an annuity contract has an undeniable appeal. With a variable annuity, the value of the account will change with the performance of the underlying investments. You can put your money into more aggressive investments and should, in fact, invest in high-return assets like equities or high-yield bonds. It's not advisable to put a 4.5 percent money-market fund into an annuity contract with high annual costs. You are responsible for deciding how your retirement savings will be invested. Variable annuities generally offer protection against loss if your death should occur during a market downturn, with a guarantee that your heirs will get back at least what was put in. In most contracts this floor is adjusted as the investment portfolio grows.

Investment Issues for Annuities

The major benefit of tax-deferred investing comes from the annual compounding on money that would have otherwise gone to pay income taxes. For long-term investors, tax deferral can make a big difference in the amount available at retirement.

Like mutual funds, variable annuities assess annual fees for investment management and administrative costs. Fees to cover the insurance costs average about 1.3 percent a year. Contract expenses vary greatly from company to company, and they can have a major effect on whether you benefit from investing in a tax-deferred annuity.

Annuities are just complex enough to make it hard for most people to weigh costs and benefits, and annuity companies are unveiling new options every day. The usual way to compare variable annuities is to determine which one has the best selection of funds available, and fund-performance data are easy to find. More difficult to research is the cost of insurance and other fees and the bottom-line effect of these charges, which are generally not part of traditional mutual-fund investing. Evaluating variable-annuity contracts is far more complex than simply comparing the performance of mutual funds.

An excellent resource for analysis and monitoring of variable annuities is A. M. Best Company. For many years A. M. Best has published life-insurance and fixed-annuity histories that reflect their cost structures. In 1996 Best added reports featuring accumulation and surrender values for variable-life and annuities. Comprehensive information can also be found in the *Morningstar Variable Annuity/Life Insurance Performance Report.* It lists almost all annuities on the market and should be available through your broker and/or insurance company. Published monthly, the report can be ordered by subscription or single issue from Morningstar.

Bail-Out Options for Annuities

If you no longer wish to maintain your annuity contract, owing to poor performance or because your objectives have changed, and you have not annuitized payments, you have several options:

- Roll the account balance into a new annuity contract via a 1035 exchange. You may have to pay new acquisition charges and surrender penalties.
- Cash in the policy. If the account value minus any remaining surrender charges exceeds your cost basis (the sum of all the deposits you've made), you'll owe tax on the gain. Distributions taken before age 59$^1/_2$ may be subject to 10 percent additional income tax.
- Annuitize the contract over your lifetime or the lifetimes of yourself and your spouse.
- Annuitize the contract over a set number of years. If you don't need the extra money, make gifts to your children and/or grandchildren or to your favorite charity. If you have assets that will be subject to estate tax at your death, your children or a trust for their benefit can use the cash gifts to buy life insurance on your life that will be available to pay estate tax at your death. You thus avoid the estate and income taxes that would have been due on the annuity contract at your death, and the children receive the insurance benefits with no tax.

Keeping Track of Performance

Read your prospectus and each annual performance report carefully, and use copies of the Annuity Contract Review worksheet (Figure 7.13) to inventory each of your annuities. (For an example of how to complete this form, see Figure 7.14.) An initial review of all life insurance and annuity contracts you have in force is the first step in controlling what happens with those contracts in the future.

Record the changes in your annuity contract annually using copies of the Annuity Contract Monitor (Figure 7.15). You can follow the example in Figure 7.16. This annual monitoring will keep you on track. Knowing the danger signs to watch out for and the options available at contract termination will allow you to make timely adjustments based on your objectives and changes in tax law so that you remain in control of your financial future.

Figure 7.13 Annuity Contract Review Worksheet

Company name: ____________________ Phone no.: ________________

Agent name: ____________________ Phone no.: ________________

Contract type: ____________________ Contract no.: ________________

Objective: ____________________ Target year: ________________

Payment mode: ❑ One Time ❑ Monthly ❑ Quarterly ❑ Annually ❑ Variable

Scheduled deposit: ____________________ No. of years: ________________

Fixed rate? ❑ Yes ❑ No Initial rate: ________________

Death benefit: ____________________ Death benefit step-up: ________________

Annuity owner: ____________________ Issue date: ________________

Annuitant: ____________________ Beneficiary: ________________

Surrender penalties: ____________________ No. of years: ________________

Withdrawal terms: ____________________ Cumulative? ❑ Yes ❑ No

Company Ratings

Standard & Poor's: ____________________

Moody's: ____________________

A. M. Best: ____________________

Contract Charges

M&E: ________________

Administrative: ________________

Maintenance: ________________

Investment Accounts in Variable-Annuity Contract	Account Expenses	Account Performance		
		1 Year	3 Years	5 Years

Figure 7.14 Annuity Contract Review Worksheet: Completed Example

Company name: Horizon Life of Canada | Phone no.: 777-609-9999

Agent name: Matt Wilson | Phone no.: 699-789-8888

Contract type: Variable | Contract no.: 123456789

Objective: Retirement income | Target year: 65

Payment mode: ☐ One Time ☐ Monthly ☐ Quarterly ☐ Annually ☑ Variable

Scheduled deposit: $10,000 | No. of years: N/A

Fixed rate? ☐ Yes ☑ No | Initial rate: 7.50%

Death benefit: Principal | Death benefit step-up: On anniversary

Annuity owner: Jennifer Williamson | Issue date: 01/01/90

Annuitant: Jennifer Williamson | Beneficiary: Todd Williamson

Surrender penalties: 7% decreasing to 0 | No. of years: 8

Withdrawal terms: 10%/year | Cumulative? ☑ Yes ☐ No

Company Ratings

Standard & Poor's: AA

Moody's: Aa

A. M. Best: A+

Contract Charges

M&E: 1.25%

Administrative: 0.05%

Maintenance: $30.00/yr.

Investment Accounts in Variable-Annuity Contract	Account Expenses	Account Performance 1 Year	3 Years	5 Years
Capital appreciation fund	1.00%	–0.06%	6.57%	5.33%
Global securities fund	0.81%	16.86%	3.49%	11.53%
Stock index fund	0.25%	21.56%	18.18%	13.72%
Money-market fund	0.50%	4.27%	4.04%	3.32%
Asset manager fund	0.74%	13.69%	7.11%	10.37%

Note: Company name, contract terms, and performance data are for illustration purposes only and do not represent a specific life insurance company.

Figure 7.15 Annuity Contract Monitor

Company name: ______________________ Phone no.: ____________________

Agent name: ______________________ Phone no.: ____________________

Annuity type: ______________________ Annuity type: ____________________

Owner: ______________________ Contract no.: ____________________

Annuitant: ______________________ Contract date: ____________________

Beneficiary: ______________________ Initial rate: ____________________

Date	Deposit/ Payment	Year-to-Date Payments	Account Value	Fixed Rate/ Rate of Return*	Withdrawal/ Payment	Company Ratings	
						Best's	S&P

*For a variable-annuity investment account, net rate of return = 100 × (current contract value – last year's contract value) / last year's contract value. For fixed annuities, record interest rate.

Figure 7.16 Annuity Contract Monitor: Completed Example

Company name: Horizon Life of Canada
Phone no.: 879-786-9999

Agent name: Matt Wilson
Phone no.: 222-786-9999

Annuity type: Horizon Gold Secure
Annuity type: Variable

Owner: Jennifer Williamson
Contract no.: 10088888

Annuitant: Jennifer Williamson
Contract date: 01/01/95

Beneficiary: Todd Williamson
Initial rate: N/A

Date	Deposit/ Payment	Year-to-Date Payments	Account Value	Fixed Rate/ Rate of Return*	Withdrawal/ Payment	Company Ratings Best's	S&P
1/1/90	10,000	10,000	10,900	9.00%	0	A+	AA
1/1/91	10,000	20,000	23,513	10.25%	0	A+	AA
1/1/92	5,000	25,000	31,506	10.50%	0	A+	AA
1/1/93	0	25,000	34,184	8.50%	0	A+	AA
1/1/94	15,000	40,000	53,955	9.70%	0	A–	AA–
1/1/95	10,000	50,000	71,950	12.50%	0	A–	AA–
1/1/96	0	50,000	81,303	13.00%	0	A–	AA–

*For a variable-life investment account, net rate of return = 100 × (current contract value – last year's contract value) / last year's contract value. For fixed annuities, record interest rate.

Note: Company name, contract terms, and performance data are for illustration purposes only and do not represent a specific life insurance company.

8 Retirement Plans, Reports, and Withdrawals

Kenneth Altvater

YOUR RETIREMENT YEARS are supposed to be your happy golden years in life. Assuming both a healthy body and attitude, what remains are the assets you have accumulated—healthy too, we hope—to be liquidated during your retirement.

Keeping track of what assets you have is difficult and can be a tedious job. The process is addressed in all the chapters in this book, since the whole is equal to the sum of its parts! The questions are how much you need, what you have now, and what you will need to accumulate during your preretirement years. Table 8.1 shows what is necessary, at various ages and assuming an interest rate of 7 percent, to fund $1 of monthly income for the balance of your life. This table is for both men and women, and the underlying mortality assumption is UP-84, which is a published government table.

Table 8.1

Cost to Fund $1 of Monthly Income

Age	Cost per $1	Age	Cost per $1
50	$139.44	60	$117.78
51	137.55	61	115.28
52	135.60	62	112.73
53	133.59	63	110.13
54	131.52	64	107.50
55	129.39	65	104.83
56	127.19	66	102.14
57	124.93	67	99.44
58	122.60	68	96.73
59	120.22	69	94.00

Note: Data based on mortality assumptions from government table, UP-84, 7 percent interest. Data are for men and women.

For example, if you retire at age sixty-five, the cost of a dollar of monthly income is $104.83. So, if you require a monthly income of $3,000, you will need a sum of $3,000 times $104.83, or $314,490, to fund your monthly income. Remember, this table assumes you will continue to earn 7 percent on the balance of your funds until they are all paid out.

But $314,490 is a lot of money! And you'll need even more if more than one person is retiring, or if you need an income higher than $3,000, or if your money earns less than 7 percent.

Some circumstances will change when you retire. Instead of funding Social Security, Social Security may be paying for part of your retirement needs. Your spending habits at retirement should be more conservative than your current spending. All extra expenses you had while you were working, such as work clothes, gas, parking, and eating lunches out will probably be lower. You may be in a lower tax bracket than you are while you are working. If you are lucky, you will be finished with the expenses of children and their education.

Many things will change. So, when you are estimating what you will need at retirement, try to project future expenses liberally. Inflation, even if low in 1997, is a significant factor. It is unrealistic to assume that 1997 dollars will buy as much in 2017.

About the best you can do is to approximate what you expect you will need twenty or thirty years from now. The best way to do this is to determine what you are spending on various items now, assume future expenditure increases or decreases in certain categories, and then project the amount of your current expenditures to see what will be necessary in terms of absolute dollars in the future. When you do these calculations, you will need to assume an inflation rate and compound this to retirement.

Once you have determined what you will need, you must determine what you now have. Finally, estimate what additional dollars you must accumulate to reach your goals.

Say, for example, you are age forty-two, make a salary of $50,000, have accumulated $23,000 in assets, and determine that you will need the equivalent of $3,000 per month at age sixty-five and for the balance of your life. If you spend nearly $3,000 per month now, at age forty-two, then how many dollars will you be spending per month twenty-three years from now? If your salary goes up by 4 percent per year, then it is fairly safe to assume that your expenditures will go up by 4 percent, too. That means you will be spending $7,394 per month twenty-three years from now.

At a cost of $104.83 per dollar of income, $7,394 per month means you will be required to have $775,113 on deposit at age sixty-five. If you have a spouse, add another 80 percent to the $7,394 per month required for your lifetime and that of your spouse. Furthermore, you may want to add extra if your spouse is significantly younger. (Remember, at this point you are simply trying to make your best estimate of what you will need twenty-three years from now. This almost sounds like science fiction now—but it will come true.)

So, you need $1,395,203, after adding 80 percent for your spouse! And right now you have only $23,000. But, remember, you need to compound that $23,000 at 7 percent interest for twenty-three years. At age sixty-five you'll have $124,830, so you'll only need to accumulate $1,270,373. How do you get that?

You get there through periodic savings, made to your personal investments and to a 401(k) retirement plan, if you are lucky enough to have one. The time to learn this fact is *now*, and not fifteen years from now. The sooner you establish a regimented retirement savings program, the less it will cost.

401(k) Plans

If your company has a 401(k) plan, join it. Nothing beats tax-deferred accumulation, and employers frequently match some or all of employee contributions. Even at a low match, or no match at all, tax-deferred income is still better than taxable income.

Accumulating $1,270,373 in twenty-three years (earning 7 percent annually on your deposits) would require an annual contribution of $9,272.70. This may be much more than you can afford to save monthly. Remember, however, that your salary will probably increase with inflation during the next twenty-three years, so as time passes, your annual salary may be $75,000 or $100,000. If your salary goes up by 6 percent per year, in twenty-three years your $50,000 salary will become $190,987! Thus, it is reasonable to expect you will be contributing larger dollar amounts in the future.

Let's say you make the decision to save 6 percent of your salary, or $3,000 per year, through your employer's 401(k) plan. Assume, further, that your employer matches twenty-five cents on the dollar. That's another thousand dollars, or $4,000, deposited annually. That's almost half of the $9,272.70 deposit you need. Your employer may contribute to a profit-sharing plan. Or your employer may provide a defined-benefit plan, which promises you a pension benefit at age sixty-five.

Accounting for Retirement

You should also have other assets accumulating for use during your retirement. Start accounting for them, and for your retirement.

First, think long and hard about what you will need at age sixty-five, in terms of monthly income. Remember inflation, and that it is better to overestimate than to underestimate. The example in Figure 8.1 illustrates how to calculate what you will need. The sources for line 10 (what needs to be accumulated) are your current and future personal assets, any inheritance you may receive, and what you will receive in retirement plan benefits.

You may also predict when your funds will run out—if you are spending more than you should! To determine what you need, use the blank worksheet in Figure 8.2.

Figure 8.1 Assets Needed at Retirement: Completed Example

Retirement year: 2029

Asset	Value
1. Estimated monthly income needed	$7,500
2. Estimated Social Security payment	500
3. Payment from employer pension	1,500
4. Net monthly income needed (line 1 – line 2 – line 3)	5,500
5. Cost of $1.00	104.83
6. Dollars needed for one person (line 4 × line 5)	576,565
7. Multiple for extra if needed for spouse (1.80 or 1.00)	1.80
8. Dollars needed at retirement with spouse (line 6 × line 7)	1,037,817
9. Current net worth accumulated (at 7% until retirement)	125,527
10. Amount that needs to be accumulated (line 8 – line 9)	912,290

Figure 8.2 Assets Needed at Retirement: Worksheet

Retirement year: _______

Asset	Value
1. Estimated monthly income needed	
2. Estimated Social Security payment	
3. Payment from employer pension	
4. Net monthly income needed (line 1 – line 2 – line 3)	
5. Cost of $1.00	
6. Dollars needed for one person (line 4 × line 5)	
7. Multiple for extra if needed for spouse (1.80 or 1.00)	
8. Total dollars needed at retirement (line 6 × line 7)	
9. Current net worth accumulated (at 7% until retirement)	
10. Amount that needs to be accumulated (line 8 – line 9)	

Enter your monthly expenses in line 1. Be fair and count gifts, vacations, special expenses, and unwelcome surprises—like a broken air-conditioning system. Once you've determined that number, subtract lines 2 and 3 to determine the net monthly income you need. If your employer has a defined-benefit pension plan, you should receive an annual statement listing your projected pension; use this value for line 3. (That statement may change annually, so plan to adjust the number in line 3 annually.) In Table 8.1, look up the cost to fund $1 at your current age. Multiply by the net monthly income (line 4) to get the dollars needed. This is the amount you should have on hand now, in order to maintain your lifestyle when you retire. If you are funding for your spouse as well as yourself, multiply by 1.8 to get the total dollars needed at retirement (line 8).

Monitoring a Defined-Contribution Plan

If your employer offers a defined-contribution plan (as opposed to, or in conjunction with, a defined-benefit plan), then you will receive statements annually (or sometimes as frequently as quarterly), listing the assets and value in your account. This is true whether the plan is a profit-sharing plan, a money purchase pension plan, or a 401(k) plan. You will receive the ending balance in your account on the plan's accounting dates. To keep track of these balances, enter them in a copy of the Defined-Contribution Plan Record (Figure 8.3).

Use a separate form to track *each money source* and *each type of plan*. For example, if your employer has a 401(k) profit-sharing plan and a money purchase pension plan, then you will need three sheets for the 401(k): one sheet for the employee 401(k) account, one for the employer 401(k) account, and one for the profit-sharing account. The money purchase plan will require only one sheet, since there is only an employer account in that type of plan.

Be sure to list *vested* balances, not total balances. As time passes, you will become 100 percent vested in any employer account, but until you have completed the required years of service, you may not be 100 percent vested. There is always time to add more money once the account becomes vested.

Figure 8.4 is an example of how to fill out the Defined-Contribution Plan Record.

Summarizing All Retirement and Personal Assets

Each chapter of this book tells you how to monitor and value different assets independently. Now it is time to add them together to see if they meet your current retirement goals. For this, follow the example in Figure 8.5.

Figure 8.3 Defined-Contribution Plan Record

Plan type: ____________ [e.g., money purchase, profit sharing, 401(k)] Account source: ____________ (e.g., employee or employer)

Date	Beginning Balance	Contribution Made	Income Earned	Forfeiture Received	Ending Balance	Percent Vested	Dollars Vested

Figure 8.4 Defined-Contribution Plan Record: Completed Example

Plan type: ____________ [e.g., money purchase, profit sharing, 401(k)] Account source: ____________ (e.g., employee or employer)

Date	Beginning Balance	Contribution Made	Income Earned	Forfeiture Received	Ending Balance	Percent Vested	Dollars Vested
12/31/93				0	0	$100	
3/31/94	0	$333	$7	0	$340	$100	$340
6/30/94	$340	$333	$7	0	$680	$100	$680
9/30/94	$680	$333	$13	0	$1,026	$100	$1,026
12/31/94	$1,026	$333	$19	0	$1,378	$100	$1,378
3/31/95	$1,378	$350	$23	0	$1,751	$100	$1,751
6/30/95	$1,751	$350	$17	0	$2,118	$100	$2,118
9/30/95	$2,118	$350	$37	0	$2,505	$100	$2,505
12/31/95	$2,505	$350	$43	0	$2,898	$100	$2,898
3/31/96	$2,898	$425	$130	0	$3,453	$100	$3,453
6/30/96	$3,453	$425	$129	0	$4,007	$100	$4,007
9/30/96	$4,007	$425	$148	0	$4,480	$100	$4,580
12/31/96	$4,580	$425	$168	0	$5,173	$100	$5,173
3/31/97	$5,173	$433	$279	0	$5,885	$100	$5,885
6/30/97	$5,885	$433	$219	0	$6,537	$100	$6,537
9/30/97							
12/31/97							
3/31/98							
6/30/98							
9/30/98							
12/31/98							

Figure 8.5 Summation of Retirement and Personal Assets: Completed Example

(Income-producing assets only)

	Retirement Plan Balances									
Calendar Year	Employee 401(k)	Vested Employer 401(k)	Vested Profit-Sharing Plan	Vested Money Purchase Pension	Vested Other Plan	IRA	Total of Retirement Plans	Other Non-retirement Funds	Total Assets Available	Expected Income (Total Assets Available x 7%)
1993	$2,692	$1,654	$2,537	0	0	0	$6,883	$33,129	$40,012	$2,801
1994	$5,917	$3,412	$4,700	0	0	0	$14,029	$37,153	$51,182	$3,583
1995	$7,912	$5,619	$6,210	0	0	0	$19,741	$36,295	$56,036	$3,923
1996	$11,129	$9,012	$9,915	0	0	0	$30,056	$48,727	$78,783	$5,515
1997	$14,918	$12,712	$11,575	0	0	0	$39,205	$53,187	$92,392	$6,467

Each year transfer your retirement plan balances to a copy of the annual summary sheet (Figure 8.6). Add your total nonretirement funds as well, under the column called Other (Nonretirement) Funds, to give you an idea of how you are coming along in meeting your retirement goals.

Although non-income-producing assets may prove quite valuable in the long run, you omit them from this summary. This entire analysis is based on the premise that you will be generating 7 percent income, from which you will live. When you sell non-income-producing assets, then it is time to add them, because then they can produce income.

At any point in time, you may determine your total worth from Figure 8.6 and project it at 7 percent from then until retirement. If your current assets come close to generating what you will need, congratulations! If not, you should hear a little voice in the background saying, "You must save more for retirement, or you will have a horrible one."

If You Are Already Retired

This chapter has discussed accumulating assets for retirement. But what if you are retired now? You know your present worth, and you are budgeting your current monthly expenditures within your known investments.

If you are retired, your retirement funds are probably in an IRA rollover. You may also be receiving a company pension and Social Security payments. You should know precisely what you have and whether it is sufficient to provide what you want.

Determine what you have in both retirement and nonretirement funds. See if you are on target, ahead, or behind. To find out, use the example in Figure 8.7 to guide you in filling out a copy of the worksheet in Figure 8.8. Subtract the income needed from the income produced to find your shortage or excess.

Address any shortages now, and determine your needed lifestyle changes now, or you may soon be out of funds. There is no magic here, just plain old common sense. Search for your weakness in saving money, or spending money, and then try to correct it.

Figure 8.6 Summation of Retirement and Personal Assets

(Income-producing assets only)

Calendar Year	Employee 401(k)	Vested Employer 401(k)	Vested Profit-Sharing Plan	Vested Money Purchase Pension	Vested Other Plan	IRA	Total of Retirement Plans	Other Non-retirement Funds	Total Assets Available	Expected Income (Total Assets Available x 7%)
	Retirement Plan Balances									

Figure 8.7 Distribution of Assets Accumulated vs. Distribution of Assets Planned: Completed Example

Calendar Year	Income-Producing Assets: Retirement Assets	IRA Rollover	Total Other Personal Assets	Total Income-Producing Assets	Income Produced	Income Needed	Shortages or Excess
1993	$122,067	$329,852	$196,522	$648,441	$45,391	$37,821	$7,570
1994	0	$462,817	$192,767	$655,584	$45,891	$40,468	$5,423
1995	0	$512,918	$175,827	$688,745	$48,212	$43,301	$4,911
1996	0	$522,066	$147,952	$670,018	$46,901	$46,332	$569
1997	0	$563,817	$153,822	$717,639	$50,235	$49,575	$660

Figure 8.8 Distribution of Assets Accumulated vs. Distribution of Assets Planned

	Income-Producing Assets						
Calendar Year	Retirement Assets	IRA Rollover	Total Other Personal Assets	Total Income-Producing Assets	Income Produced	Income Needed	Shortages or Excess

9 The Registered Investment Adviser

Lawrence Lynn

THE SECURITIES INDUSTRY is continuing its evolution from the "good old days" when individuals invested through a locally owned brokerage firm. Many years ago brokers were known as "customers men." It was not unusual to know the owners of the firm; they were a part of the local community.

Over time, these regional firms disappeared as the industry consolidated into a few large national wire houses. These megagiants have thrived on their ability to distribute financial products, and the broker has become the firm's marketing representative, essentially a salesperson.

This evolution, although good for the large firms, has not always been good for the investor. There has been an increasing need for unbiased research and investment advice without conflict of interest. Beginning in the late 1970s and early 1980s with the advent of individual retirement accounts, many investors put their small annual IRA contributions into mutual funds. In hindsight, this has proved to have been a successful and satisfactory move; mutual funds have shown the advantages of a professional money manager.

Today, individual investors want and need the services of an independent professional adviser. Mutual funds have shown them the benefits of professional management, but they miss having their own "customers man" with whom they can meet, talk, and have their own individual needs addressed. In the past this type of service was only available to the large trust funds or very wealthy individuals.

Now, investors with as little as $100,000 can have their account professionally managed by skilled advisers, whose sole interest is the client. Many of these firms work for a fee only; that is, the only compensation they receive is the predetermined fee paid by the client directly to them. It is important that such a professional, usually a registered investment adviser (RIA), does not sell any product or receive compensation from any other source so that he or she can be independent.

Many RIAs place their clients' accounts with major, well-regarded firms such as Charles Schwab & Co., Inc. These firms provide Security Investors Protection Corporation–insured custody, very low commissions, and regular client statements. In turn, the RIA is able to do independent research and is under no pressure to generate commissions or distribute any broker's financial merchandise. Today an investor can have an RIA whose only interest is the client's best interest.

Management Methods

Owners can select from among a wide variety of styles of management for their investment account(s) or estate. The options range from self-management to investment-company management. As we will show, use of an RIA lies somewhere between these extremes.

Self-Management

The simplest, most immediate, and easiest-to-comprehend system is self-management of the account. In this system the owner personally makes decisions on when and what to buy, when and what to sell, and all other key aspects. Therefore, this method may seem to be the least expensive, and some investors are swayed by this aspect rather than by actual performance or the bottom line.

An investor who is well educated, intelligent, business wise, and also adequately self-disciplined may achieve great success via self-management. If the Dow Jones or Standard and Poor's (S&P) 500 is improving 15 percent for the year and the investor has accomplished returns of 20 percent or 25 percent, he or she may well deserve accolades for that performance and have earned the right to continue self-management, at least for the near future. Unhappily, this is not the most usual result. Most investors find out, just like the "experts," that beating the averages, Dow Jones or other, is no easy task. Frequently, despite great efforts, investors wind up with lower performance than the popular indices or even with an absolute negative result. In this case we can only conclude that self-management, even carefully monitored and controlled as described in Chapter 1, was an unrewarding experience.

Investment Companies

To avoid management by yourself, you can transfer that burden to an investment company. For example, you can select from many so-called closed-end funds frequently trading on the major exchanges. In this case the fund is bought like a regular common stock from a previous owner, since the closed-end fund is normally "closed" to new monies and can only be owned by dealing with someone who is a present owner but wants to sell all or part of his or her present position. In this instance, you can invest in a fund like Zenix on the New York Stock Exchange, a fund with a higher dividend payment (over 9 percent in early 1997), good liquidity, and good diversification.

Having made an initial decision, however, the purchaser of these shares leaves future investment decisions to the investment company. The investor can't dictate or influence its decisions any more than an investor in General Motors can influence the auto design or sales policy of GM's Cadillac Division.

Investors also may select an open-end investment company, usually called a mutual fund, which accepts and invests all monies coming in. As in the case of a closed-end fund, investors hope to get good management skills working for them. However, they have little or nothing to say about what the fund managers should or should not do with their money. Furthermore, the fund managers usually report at no more than quarterly intervals to explain their gains and losses for the previous period. No real communication takes place between the investor and the fund, whether it's a small, new one or an established giant like Fidelity Magellan or Investment Company of America.

Other variations of the investment company exist, if by other names, such as the unit investment trust formed by major brokerage houses. In these, a large variety of bonds or stocks are compiled into one trust, totaling perhaps $25 to $100 million. This trust then is subdivided into units, usually approximately $1,000 plus a small amount of interest per unit; thus, a $50 million composite becomes 50,000 units. These are fixed as to composition, which is made known to the investor as soon as the units are offered for sale. Following the inception of the trust, again investors cannot influence its progress or activities; these are set in concrete. The investors can only earn income or, they hope, capital gains from choices made before their entry into ownership.

It is important to note that brokers ultimately depend for their own earnings on the volume of trading in an account. In contrast, a mutual fund or investment company actually benefits from less trading.

Registered Investment Advisers

This same independence of trading should also exist if one elects to use the third method of management and control, the RIA. Ideally the RIA should be totally independent of and divorced from trading commissions. His or her only interest should be the bottom line of the account; his or her only compensation should be based on performance. Most money managers charge a fee of 1 to 3 percent of the assets in the account; some also charge an additional minimum, such as $500 to $1,000 per year. Many subdivide the 1 percent or annual fee by quarters, thereby benefiting from gains they have generated.

Whereas the difference between self-management and investment-company management is obvious, the differences are not so clear between investment-company management and the RIA regime. In the instance of recently successful money managers, the clients have much more access and control than with the more nebulous and impersonal management of an investment company. They can call or, on occasion, visit. Investors receive monthly statements of their accounts plus the RIA's current economic thinking about the market. Clients cannot, of course, try to steer the manager's actions except for imparting a general sense of how aggressively or conservatively they would like the RIA to guide their account. Since clients can provide such guidance, the RIA stands at an intermediate position between self-management and the much more distant, impersonal investment-company management.

Choosing Your Registered Investment Adviser

The choice of an excellent RIA frequently is, but should not be, a matter of luck. The adage that the squeaky wheel gets the grease applies to marketing investment advice. The result of incessant telephone cold calls and mailings can bring new clients for the aggressive money manager. This frequently works for the adviser who is average or worse in generating good results. Such an adviser cannot earn good referrals based on little demonstrated success. Consequently, the worst way to choose an RIA, broker, or mutual fund is by falling for a particularly persuasive well-rehearsed pitch by a cold caller from some sweatshop or "office," usually in New York or Los Angeles, using a hot list of phone numbers.

Perhaps the best place to start to collect RIA suggestions for consideration is from your close friends, business associates, or relatives. Listen, but do your own follow-up investigation. Another source might be your broker, but brokers typically will respond by trying to route you into a "wrap" account with a 3 percent fee inclusive of commissions and RIA fees, the trading to be done via their brokerage firm . . . naturally. What did you expect? This frequently means only 1 percent for the RIA but 2 percent of the account's principal annually for the brokerage firm.

A largely accepted firm for rating money managers is Nelson Publications (Port Chester, New York), which, on a quarterly and annual basis, reports the "World's Best Money Managers." The Nelson firm receives performance data with details from over 2,000 money managers and subdivides them into several categories. One of the most important categories is what it calls "U.S. Balanced/Multi Asset," which numbers about 400 performers. Figure 9.1 shows Nelson's ranking of the top twenty for the one-year period ending June 30, 1996. For each ranking, the report gives the name of the fund, the volume and page number where Nelson published details, its composite return for the manager annualized for the period, and the amount of assets in the composite. The Nelson rating of the RIA is an excellent piece of data.

Also helpful is how the fund has done for the given period when compared to the Dow Jones Industrial Average (DJIA), the S&P 500, and passbook and certificate-of-deposit investments. This relative performance as well as the RIA's performance when compared to the results of other money managers is a helpful guide. Evaluate how the RIA has done over several years, not only a single year. One good year does not support a high level of confidence, whereas three, five, or ten years could do so.

But wait, there's more. Do you want an RIA with a huge amount of assets under control, $500 million, $700 million, billions, with a correspondingly large number of clients like yourself? Or do you want a medium-sized or small firm with relatively few accounts and within which you will be more important? Such a firm might permit or encourage more personal contact between you and the RIA. Do you want one in New York or on Wall Street with access to its many "experts," or would you prefer one near your home? If the RIA's offices are located in or near the city where you reside, it's feasible to actually meet the RIA personally, meet people associated with him or her, and talk directly about what you want to achieve. Do you get the impression the RIA is interested in your desires, in respecting them, in achieving them? Is he or she someone you can level with in a face-to-face meeting?

This may be as important as performance in selecting an RIA. If you think there is little chance of a good human relationship or little basis for confidence, perhaps you should look elsewhere to find an RIA with whom you would feel secure. Are you not confident or highly confident? Only by comparing the RIA and his or her firm can you determine these things.

I hope you have selected the right RIA to help you control and monitor your account to reach or surpass your desired targets!

Figure 9.1 Sample from Nelson's Ranking of Money Managers

Nelson's "Top 40" Money Managers—1 year returns

Product/Style Category: **U. S. Balanced/Multi-Asset (All Styles)**
Performance Measurement Period: **4 Quarters ending 9/30/96**
Ranking (Universe Size): **Top 40 (out of 360 composites/funds)**

Lists the top rates of return reported by the managers for this category and time period. All results are reported net of fees and inclusive of cash, as described in the introduction. For complete profiles of these managers, as well as performance footnotes and composite descriptions, please refer to the indicated page in Nelson's Directory of Investment Managers - 1996. Note: U. S. Equity products which are single-industry "Sector Funds" appear only in the "U. S. Dedicated Sector/Industry Equity" rankings and are not included in the "All Style" or other U. S. Equity rankings.

Rank	Firm Name (Profile Page Number) • Product Name	4 Qtr. Anlzd % Return	$Assets in Composite
1	**Richard J. Fruth & Associates** (Vol. I, Pg. 1776) • Balanced Accounts *Composite represents 100.0% of assets under management in this style*	**25.91%**	35.8 mil
2	**First Austin Capital Management** (Vol. I, Pg. 1595) • Balanced TAA *Composite represents 99.6% of assets under management in this style*	**25.22%**	23.1 mil
3	**Sunvest Asset Mgmt.** (Vol. II, Pg. 4304) • Balanced Accounts *Composite represents 100.0% of assets under management in this style*	**25.04%**	10.0 mil
4	**Corinthian Capital Company** (Vol. I, Pg. 1061) • Balanced *Composite represents 85.4% of assets under management in this style*	**24.64%**	91.0 mil
5	**Conseco Capital Management** (Vol. I, Pg. 1034) • Asset Allocation Portfolio *Composite represents 100.0% of assets under management in this style*	**24.18%**	14.9 mil
6	**Robertson, Stephens Investment Mgmt.*** (Vol. II, Pg. 3802) • Growth & Income Fund *Composite represents 100.0% of assets under management in this style*	**23.98%**	298.8 mil
7	**Sands Capital Management** (Vol. II, Pg. 3901) • Balanced Accounts *Composite represents 33.0% of assets under management in this style*	**23.44%**	15.4 mil
8	**Montag & Caldwell** (Vol. II, Pg. 2992) • Balanced Accounts *Composite represents 58.2% of assets under management in this style*	**21.53%**	1045.0 mil
9	**Estabrook Capital Management** (Vol. I, Pg. 1446) • U. S. Balanced Accounts *Composite represents 40.0% of assets under management in this style*	**20.39%**	282.0 mil
10	**Piper Jaffray Group** (Vol. II, Pg. 3522) • Piper Jaffray Growth & Income Fund *Composite represents 100.0% of assets under management in this style*	**20.36%**	97.4 mil
10	**Founders Asset Management** (Vol. I, Pg. 1724) • Founders Balanced Fund *Composite represents 100.0% of assets under management in this style*	**20.36%**	222.8 mil
12	**Vanguard Group** (Vol. II, Pg. 4567) • Vanguard Growth & Income Portfolio *Composite represents 100.0% of assets under management in this style*	**20.30%**	192.0 mil
13	**Geneva Capital Mgmt.** (Vol. I, Pg. 1854) • Balanced–Aggressive *Composite represents 100.0% of assets under management in this style*	**20.20%**	112.0 mil
14	**Weiss Peck & Greer Mutual Funds** (Vol. II, Pg. 4849) • WPG Growth and Income Fund *Composite represents 100.0% of assets under management in this style*	**20.19%**	76.0 mil
15	**A I M Advisors, Inc.*** (Vol. I, Pg. 71) • AIM Balanced Fund *Composite represents 100.0% of assets under management in this style*	**20.11%**	451.6 mil
16	**Edgewood Management Company** (Vol. I, Pg. 1380) • Tax-Free Balanced Accounts *Composite represents 100.0% of assets under management in this style*	**19.40%**	65.6 mil
17	**Janus Capital Corp.** (Vol. I, Pg. 2376) • Janus Balanced *Composite represents 100.0% of assets under management in this style*	**19.20%**	192.5 mil
18	**Westwood Management** (Vol. I, Pg. 4776) • Westwood Balanced Institutional *Composite represents 100.0% of assets under management in this style*	**19.15%**	34.6 mil
19	**Mentor Investment Group** (Vol. II, Pg. 2866) • Mentor Income & Growth *Composite represents 26.0% of assets under management in this style*	**19.13%**	23.6 mil
19	**McDonald Capital Investors** (Vol. II, Pg. 2812) • Balanced: Value Philosophy *Composite represents 99.8% of assets under management in this style*	**19.13%**	57.5 mil

* Reporting firm is not in compliance with AIMR Performance Presentation Standards

+ Reporting firm did not indicate whether or not they are in compliance with AIMR PPS

Source: Nelson's Investment Manager Database; © 1996 Nelson Publications, Inc., Port Chester, NY 10573

What Is "Good" for an RIA?

The performance of the RIA in planning, executing, and controlling the portion of your estate under his or her aegis must be "good." That is, it should be rewarding for you, the client, else why have an RIA involved? But what is "good"? Fortunately, monitoring will determine the answer for you. There are several valid criteria against which you might want to monitor the performance of your RIA, some of which have already been cited.

It could be valid to weigh the RIA's results when compared to the DJIA or the S&P 500. In point of fact, most of the time very few RIAs or mutual funds can match these popular averages, let alone beat them. Typically they fall short, which is why some mutual funds are so designed to mirror and mimic the DJIA and S&P 500. If the RIA can constantly outperform the DJIA or S&P 500, he or she is turning in an outstanding job.

You can also measure RIA results against what you yourself achieved with your account before you engaged the RIA. If his or her results, quarter to quarter or year to year, are well ahead of what you achieved, clearly your money manager is doing well. For example, in your years on your own, you generated 8 percent a year with a $200,000 investment, or $16,000 per year. After the RIA entered the picture, the same money ($200,000) generated $30,000 a year, almost twice the earlier gain. Even with a fee of, say, 1 percent ($2,000 per year), the performance is obviously worthwhile. And let us hope it will improve further.

You can monitor the RIA's results against such criteria as the rate of inflation, or the Consumer Price Index (CPI) plus estimated IRS tax burden. Or against the prime rate of U.S. Treasury thirty-year bonds. If, for example, your managed account gained 17 percent when the prime rate stayed at 7 percent, your account and your RIA have been quite successful. If, however, the U.S. Treasury thirty-year bond yielded 7 percent annually, but your account has been almost flat at 0 percent, your RIA's performance is at best questionable. Should such activity continue, it's clearly time for you to exert control, probably via a new RIA.

An Anecdote: The Choice of an RIA

What follows now is an inevitably personalized and biased account of my choice of a good RIA, to whom in confidence I referred several of the students in my investment and money-management classes. These classes are taught in local (Houston) adult-education curricula, as well as in industrial venues such as British Petroleum, Schlumberger, and various other local companies.

I first met Richard J. Fruth in 1973 when I joined Merrill Lynch at the Houston/Galleria office. Dick had been there a little over a year at the time. By coincidence we learned that we had each served as a chemical engineer at the Celanese Chemical Division years before, so, like me, he had a solid engineering foundation. I noted quickly how methodical he was in his individual research at Merrill Lynch, not typical for a branch-office broker, who was supposed to be more of a salesman than a financial researcher. It was also apparent that his clients were almost fanatically loyal to him. Six years later, Dick Fruth resigned to join Drexel Burnham Lambert as assistant manager, Texas.

Dick decided thereafter to persuade me to join his new firm. After several interviews, I relented. I was elected vice president and later senior vice president of Drexel Burnham Lambert. Fruth did well too; I noted that some of his clients and frequent visitors included people that I remembered from my earlier days at Merrill, still loyal to him after over a dozen years, loyalty apparently fathered by Fruth's performance for them.

Most financial analysts follow one of two widely differing schools of thought regarding proper analysis. Some belong to the fundamental school and are disciples of Benjamin Graham and Sir John Templeton. They believe one must dissect a company, or indeed a market, and examine a number of well-known fundamental key indicators such as current price, current ratio, price/earnings ratio (P/E), interest coverage, and earnings-per-share trend to determine whether a corporation's stock is going to move up, down, or sideways. Others belong to the school of technical analysis, studying charts of price versus time or trading volume versus time, so-called point-and-figure charts (see Chapter 6) with Xs and Os indicating significant price trends. They believe the past is preface to the future, and "the tape tells all tales." The charts alone, according to "true technicians," show the future for the corporation's stock, at least in the technician's opinion.

During our acquaintance at Merrill and subsequently, I learned that Dick Fruth was neither a true fundamentalist nor a pure technical analyst. In fact, he was a good blend of both, as his modus operandi described later will show you. He was diligently spending three to four hours per day, each and every day, studying both charts and fundamental data to make his choices. He relied on the firm's research data extensively, but not on its conclusions nor its recommendations. And most of the time he was correct.

I lost touch with Fruth shortly after he became a branch manager with Paine Webber and moved to Austin, except for indirect contact through Otto Glaser, a close friend and self-appointed organizer of periodic Merrill Lynch/Galleria alumni gatherings and a "pseudo-newsletter" about alumni doings. We resumed contact after he returned to Houston and formed a small RIA firm, Richard J. Fruth and Associates, Inc. Glaser, who became part of my writing group, wrote a chapter for *How to Invest Today* on bonds and Chapter 4 for this book, became associated with Fruth as vice president for the firm in 1996. Shortly thereafter, Fruth's position in the Nelson ratings rose to number eight; a strong climb indeed to be among the top ten. Thereafter, in late 1996, despite the relatively small size of his firm, he attained the ranking of number one, tops among all balanced funds in the English-speaking world.

Richard J. Fruth and Associates, Inc. was also selected by Charles Schwab & Co., Inc. as a reliable and responsible RIA to which they could refer some of their valued clients who wanted discount brokerage rates but also had recognized the need for seasoned senior investment thinking. They wanted and needed guidance and advice as well as discounts. Needless to relate, this accolade from Schwab added to my rationale for recommending him and his firm as a source of responsible and talented help for portfolio sizes adaptable to his approaches.

Interview with the Top Money Manager

I interviewed Richard J. Fruth during 1997. After asking about his background, I asked about his modus operandi—how consistently he used it, how he picked items to include in a client's portfolio, and when he should buy them and when distribute them from the portfolio. He answered me in general and also gave me a few specific examples, including Kmart and Duracell Company. I think it is most informative to read his own words:

LYNN: How long have you been in the business?

FRUTH: I started as a stockbroker with Merrill Lynch in 1970. Prior to that I had been a chemical engineer. In 1977 I joined Drexel Burnham, where I continued to handle the account relationships that I had built before and then went into branch management. In 1986 I moved to Paine Webber as manager in Austin, Texas, and in 1992 left to form my own firm, Richard J. Fruth and Associates, Inc.

LYNN: Why did you set up your own shop?

FRUTH: Over time it had become increasingly obvious that I had to choose for whom I was going to work—my clients or the brokerage firm. The full-service wire houses frequently wanted me to push the "product of the day." We were told the firm would do the evaluation of the merits of the investment that the home office was pushing, and we were told not to do our own research. Since the research provided by the brokerage firms tended to favor their investment banking clients, I found it highly advantageous to do my own research.

LYNN: What is your modus operandi?

FRUTH: We handle individual and retirement accounts. Our minimum account size is $200,000, and we charge 1 percent a year to manage the assets. We are basically balanced-account managers, that is, our accounts are primarily in common stocks with some bonds and any available funds held in a money-market fund. We do not use margin, options, commodities, or limited partnerships. The majority of our accounts are domiciled at Charles Schwab & Co., Inc.

LYNN: Why do you use Charles Schwab & Co., Inc.?

FRUTH: Charles Schwab is a real visionary. He has put together a wonderful firm that is attuned to the marketplace. They foresaw not only the need for discounted commissions for the individual who did not want advice as well as the need for independent advisers, RIAS, who could manage a client's assets on a fee basis rather than a commission basis. Over the past eight years, this part of Schwab has grown to over 4,000 advisers managing over $80 billion in assets! This phenomenal growth has taken place not only because the marketplace wanted it, but also because Schwab ponied up the talent and the funds to build a division, Schwab Institutional, to service the RIAS. The back-office support, trading desks, the annual Institutional Conference, and the AdvisorSource program have been immensely helpful.

LYNN: What is the AdvisorSource Program?

FRUTH: Schwab has selected a small number of RIAS around the country to whom they refer clients.

LYNN: Tell me more, Dick.

FRUTH: Each Schwab office has a representative who explains the concept of professional account management to appropriate Schwab clients. If clients are interested, they are then referred to participants in the AdvisorSource Program. Some advisers manage a portfolio of mutual funds; others such as ourselves manage a portfolio of individual stocks and bonds.

LYNN: How do you make your stock and bond selections?

FRUTH: We have a proprietary computer program that I spent over ten years developing. Each week we run the program, and it analyzes all NYSE, ASE, and OTC issues for certain technical criteria we feel are important. The program then "nominates" about ten to twenty issues a week for more detailed study. We then look at the fundamental aspects of each stock nominated. At this point, about two-thirds are culled from the list. The remaining third are then looked at from a technical aspect, and this gets the list down to one or two candidates, or sometimes none. If an issue makes it this far, we begin to watch it on a daily basis for an opportune entry point, a time for our move.

LYNN: Could you give us an example of a stock that your program selected?

FRUTH: Yes. Duracell showed up in our program in the fall of 1995 (see Figure 9.2). We liked what we saw, but the timing wasn't right. The stock was overbought, that is, extended on the upside. We waited for the stock to pull back and bought it several points lower in January of 1996. Apparently we were not the only ones who liked Duracell, because Gillette took the company over in the fall of 1996. This was a very substantial gain for us in a short period of time. It may seem strange to say that I was somewhat disappointed, but I felt we had a great growth stock and, frankly, I was sorry to see it merged into Gillette. But in fact we received Gillette stock in exchange,

Figure 9.2 Duracell Stock: Bar Chart

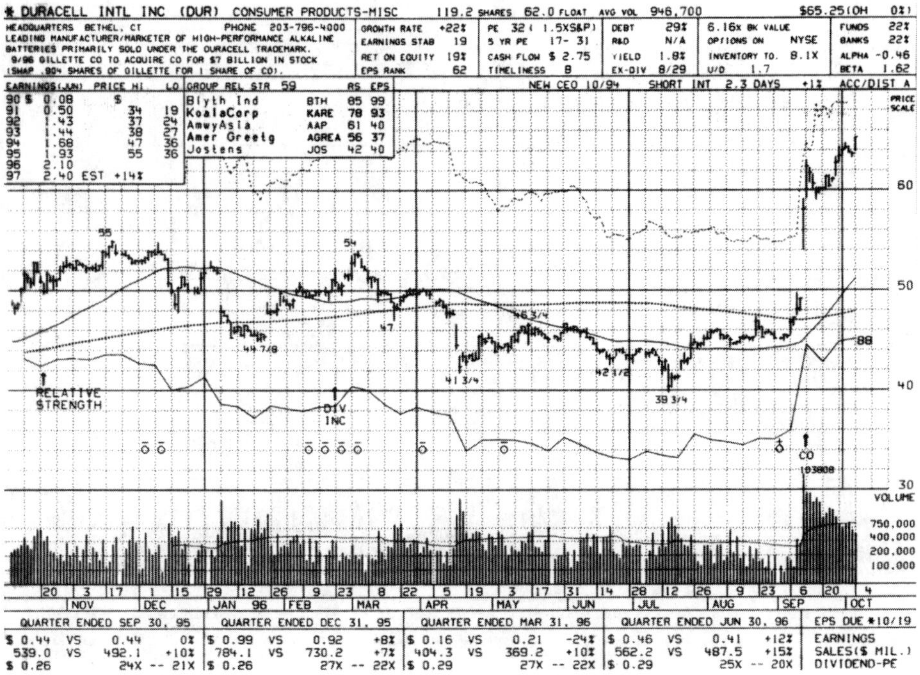

Source: Telescan

and it has performed very well since then, so we have held on to it.

LYNN: What portion of an account was in Gillette?

FRUTH: We like to buy stocks in what we call "unemotional quantities." By this we mean approximately 5 percent of the account. For an aggressive account, we might buy slightly more, or for a more conservative account, slightly less. We don't like to expose more funds to an idea, so that, in the event we are wrong or early, we are not significantly hurt by the position.

LYNN: Do your accounts have a lot of turnover?

FRUTH: No. We hope to find those quality growth stocks that you can hold for a long time. The big money has been made in stocks like Wal-Mart that advanced for ten years before its big growth phase ended.

LYNN: So you like blue chips, long-term holdings. Do you use other strategies?

FRUTH: Yes. We try to listen to what the market is telling us. The market oftentimes will signal clearly what you should be doing.

LYNN: Go on, tell me more. Any really dramatic cases you can cite?

Figure 9.3 Kmart Stock: Bar Chart

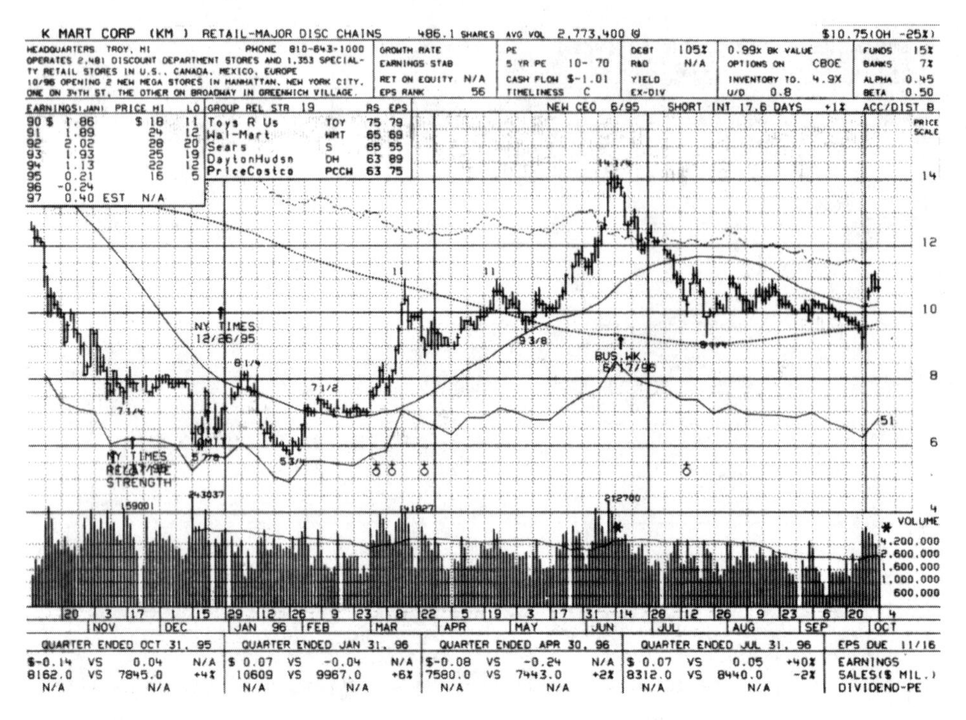

Source: Telescan

FRUTH: Well, in 1995 Kmart stock was in a serious decline (see Figure 9.3). The issue had traded in the mid-20s and was declining because they were not turning the company around fast enough. Meanwhile, 1995 was a good year in the market, and many investors had taken gains and were looking at their portfolios for tax-loss candidates to sell. Kmart was one of a few that showed up and came under severe tax-loss selling. This was compounded by poor earnings and Wall Street's frustration with the slow turnaround. In fact, Kmart had completed modernization of two-thirds of their stores, closed the money-losing Pace Clubs, sold Borders Bookstores and Sports Authority. The senior management was obviously considered uninspiring and was under attack. To add to their worries, they had a covenant in their loan agreement with a group of twenty-some banks that if rating agencies downgraded their debt, the bank loan would be due immediately.

Well, it was obvious that debt would be downgraded. So some amateur analyst shot his mouth off and said Kmart would declare bankruptcy in order to continue to operate under Chapter 11. That was like yelling fire in a theater, and the run on the stock was on, trading under $7 a share.

I knew the stock was a steal. Kmart was current on its payments to the banks and vendors. New management was coming on board. The turnaround was well under way. No bank is going to foreclose on a loan that is current and has every aspect of continuing to make timely payments. In addition, Kmart is the nation's second-largest retailer, an employer of hundreds of thousands of people, and a major customer of hundreds of suppliers, who, in turn, were bank customers and borrowers.

Needless to say, the covenants were renegotiated. The stock that we had bought on uninformed emotional selling at $7 we happily sold six months later for $14 during an emotionally optimistic peak. I should point out that we bought this stock in "unemotional quantities," approximating 2 percent to 3 percent of an account's value. If my analysis had been wrong and Kmart dropped in half, our loss would not have seriously affected an account.

By the way, we considered this a speculation and bought it only in our most aggressive accounts. That was a pretty dramatic case, Larry.

LYNN: Then you don't use model or cookie-cutter accounts. They are tailored to each individual's profile?

FRUTH: That's right.

LYNN: How about foreign stocks? Do you invest abroad?

FRUTH: Yes, we currently own Royal Dutch, Shell Oil Co., Schlumberger, Inc., Roche Holdings, Novartis, Inc., and Imperial Chemical Industries, Ltd. We own Dutch, French, Swiss, and British securities. We invest only in countries where you can drink the water. No third-world or developing countries. We do not want to take on political and currency risks. As a matter of fact, we own Exxon, Colgate-Palmolive, Emerson Electric, Inc., Coca-Cola—all international companies who can manage foreign investment far better than we. There are plenty of quality companies listed here without our needing to go abroad.

LYNN: Thanks, Dick! It sounds like you and your team are sticking to a carefully predetermined discipline.

10 Tangible Assets and Real Estate

Robert Frater
and Charles Smith

UP UNTIL TWO centuries ago, land, or real estate, was the essential source of wealth. One century ago, physical capital—production assets—took its place. Today, in the information age, human capital—knowledge and cognitive skill—is the essential source of wealth, and it is widely distributed by means of universal education. Nevertheless, real estate is a major asset class that needs to be monitored.

Real Estate as an Investment

Whether you are purchasing your first home or investing in an office building or rental house, real estate ownership has its own special, magical fascination. Home ownership is a basic goal of most Americans; with the owning of real estate comes a pride and sense of security that is unequaled in other investments. We have all heard, "They are not making any more of it" and "It's solid as a rock." These adages refer to the underlying belief that real estate is the most fundamental of all investments. That has been proven periodically over the years, since real estate ownership has always been synonymous with wealth.

It is estimated that 50 percent of the land in the United States is owned by the government—federal, state, or local. Approximately 38 percent of the private U.S. land is considered "nonusable," leaving only 12 percent available for ownership and development. In this chapter we provide some checklists to help you participate in the ownership of a part of that 12 percent.

One of the problems making it difficult to monitor and control your real estate activities is the wide variation in forms of ownership. One can deal in real estate equity by owning rental houses, raw land, apartment complexes, hotels, or even ranch land. Your ownership position may be total, as in a 100 percent proprietorship (such as owning your own home), or via a limited partnership in which your financial interest is limited and a managing partner assumes the greater risk. You can own real estate in a corporate entity or the more recently popular REITs (real estate investment trusts).

The real estate investment trust, or REIT (pronounced "reet"), combines the capital of many investors to acquire real estate. A REIT is much like a mutual fund for real estate in that individual investors obtain the benefit of a diversified portfolio under professional management. Its shares are freely traded, often on a major stock exchange. Over 300 REITs are operating in the United States today. Their assets total over $100 billion, and about 70 percent of them trade on the national stock exchanges.

Whether you buy real estate personally or through a REIT depends on your own personal situation and preference. Because REIT shares are typically priced from $2 to $40 each, they allow you to have a professionally managed real estate investment for a minimal cost. Because REITs are publically traded, they offer daily valuation and immediate liquidity that is not available if you own real estate directly. However, that means that REIT shares fluctuate in value daily, depending on the emotions of the investing public at the moment. Ultimately, the value of a REIT, like a stock, reflects the value of the income the REIT earns and the underlying assets it owns.

REIT analysis and monitoring are performed essentially the same as those of a stock. However, the ultimate return you receive on a REIT has very little similarity to the stock market as a whole. Real estate has a negative correlation to the stock market, which means it is one of the best investments available to offset or stabilize a traditional stock portfolio.

Tangible Investments

It has been said that "diamonds are a girl's best friend." This may or may not be true, but they are certainly not her best investment. Nor is gold or silver!

Tangible investments usually refer to gold or precious metals, jewelry, and/or collectibles. This book does not discuss these three investment categories at length for several reasons:

- Stocks, real estate, and traditional investments increase or decrease in value over time because they are producing something of value for someone else that can be quantified as a car or electricity, etc. Though jewelry does bring pleasure, it does not provide food, shelter, or clothing, so it possibly could have no value to anyone other than the owner.
- The market for such assets as gold and silver is to a large extent political and as such is at the whims of government and personal impulses.
- Unlike the markets for bonds, stock, and real estate, the market and values for most tangibles are totally unpredictable.

Another problem that complicates monitoring of real estate is the valuation process. Unlike a stock portfolio, real estate is not valued each day by the New York Stock Exchange or NASDAQ, except in the case of REITS.

Real Estate Buying Checklist

Determine if there are problems before buying real estate rather than afterward. Using the Real Estate Buying Checklist (Figure 10.1) before you invest can help you avoid costly mistakes. You must evaluate or monitor many considerations when adding real estate to your portfolio. The most important are described in the following explanation of the checklist items.

Personal

Why are you buying it? Real estate is often purchased primarily for emotional reasons. Before investing, make sure your reasons are based on solid logic and not emotional whims.

How long do you plan to own it? Because the costs of buying and selling real estate are usually 7 percent of the total transaction, short-term holds in real estate are seldom profitable. If what you need is short term, renting is often better than buying.

What are your specific needs? If this property is to be your residence, for example, how many bedrooms do you need? How many bathrooms? Identify the features most important to you, and try to satisfy them based on the priorities you have established.

Figure 10.1 Real Estate Buying Checklist

Personal

Why are you buying it? ______________________

How long do you plan to own it? ______________________

What are your specific needs? ______________________

How much can you afford? ______________________

How much cash should you put down, or how much money should you borrow? ______________________

____

Location

Is the neighborhood going up in value? ______________________

Are the schools good? ______________________

What is the average price per square foot? ______________________

How large is the tract or dwelling compared to the average tract or dwelling in the area?

____

What repairs will be needed? ______________________

What are the taxes and condo or association dues? ______________________

Is it in the 100-year floodplain? ______________________

Government and Environmental Issues

How is it zoned? ______________________

Is it deed-restricted? ______________________

Are there environmental problems? ______________________

- Asbestos ______________________
- Lead paint ______________________
- Contaminated soil ______________________
- Radon or formaldehyde ______________________
- High-power lines ______________________
- Easements ______________________

Terms

Financing ______________________

Title ______________________

Contingencies ______________________

How much can you afford? If you are purchasing your first primary residence, most banks will loan an amount such that the payments do not exceed 33 percent of your gross income. It's important to note that these payments must also include taxes and insurance. Based on the current interest rate, you can calculate the amount of mortgage you would qualify for. If you are buying rental property, you should consider that if the property does not currently have a tenant, you will have to make the mortgage payments anyway. Make sure you have enough money to cover this contingency.

How much cash should you put down, or how much money should you borrow? For a primary residence, you should take a loan for 80 percent of the appraised value. This will allow you to avoid expensive mortgage insurance that otherwise would automatically be placed on the loan. It also allows you to avoid escrow of taxes and insurance. On rental property, most lenders will loan only 80 percent of appraised value. Under certain circumstances, however, lenders may go much higher.

Location

Is the neighborhood going up in value? Areas move from popular to unpopular for a number of reasons. Ideally, you want a neighborhood that is already strong or starting to improve. If the real estate has decreased in value recently as compared to nearby real estate, make sure the situation will not continue.

Are the schools good? Whether or not you have children and whether it is your primary residence or commercial property, the quality of the area schools affects the stability and future appreciation of the property. If the neighborhood schools are considered undesirable, the property may not appreciate as you hope.

What is the average price per square foot? Properties are ultimately valued based on the number of square feet in the land or dwelling. You should buy a house at or below the average price per square foot in its area.

How large is the tract or dwelling compared to the average tract or dwelling in the area? Generally you should buy a house equal to or smaller than the average house in the area. This gives more chance for appreciation, greater price stability, and the availability of enlarging if your situation changes.

What repairs will be needed? You should have inspections made that will determine the condition of the roof, appliances, equipment, etc. Murphy's law states, "If anything bad can happen, it will." That is not necessarily true with real estate, but there will always be surprises for the buyer who has not checked for problems in advance.

What are the taxes and condo or association dues? These payments are obligations. Make sure you know the amount, how stable they have been in the past, and that there are no delinquencies from the previous owner.

Is it in the 100-year floodplain? This is diagrammed in a map created by the Army Corps of Engineers. If your property is located within the 100-year floodplain, your property may be prone to flooding, and flood insurance may be expensive.

Government and Environmental Issues

How is it zoned? A zoning board determines how a property is zoned. If you plan to have an office in your home but the zoning restrictions do not allow this usage, you may be unable to use the property for the purpose you intend. Zoning can be complex, expensive, and nearly impossible to change. Make sure that the zoning fits your intentions for the property. Modifying zoning can take decades. Don't assume it can be done easily.

Is it deed-restricted? Like zoning, deed restrictions can limit the use of property, regardless of how it was used by the previous owner or whether your intentions are in good taste. Make sure you understand the deed restrictions before buying and that you can live within their constraints.

Are there environmental problems? One of the greatest real estate risks is the *unlimited* liability associated with real estate that has been contaminated by underground storage tanks, asbestos, or others of a growing list of contaminants. Under current law, the only way to protect yourself is to commission a "Phase 1 Environmental Study" before you buy property. Especially if the property has been used for commercial purposes in the past, you should have this study made *before you buy.*

Here are some potential environmental problems you should be careful of:

- *Asbestos*—Asbestos was often used for siding, flooring, and insulation. Asbestos removal can often exceed the value of the real estate.

- *Lead paint*—Lead-based paint was used in most buildings built before 1960. Even if the lead-based paint is removed from the outside of the building, the soil around the building is often contaminated in the removal process.

- *Contaminated soil*—Soils may be contaminated by automobile oil changes, chemical dumping, or bleeding of underground tanks (even if the tank is not located on the property you are buying). Seepage from your neighbor's property over time can contaminate your property. Even though you or the previous owners were not responsible for this, you could still be held liable for the cleanup.

- *Radon and formaldehyde*—These are chemicals used in building products such as blown-in insulation, foam, some wallboard, and other products. These products give off small quantities of gases that accumulate in today's energy-efficient, tightly sealed buildings . Even small amounts of these gases can severely affect health. Make sure the house is closed and sealed before any of these tests are made on the property.

- *High-power lines*—This will probably be the big environmental issue of the 1990s. Magnetic fields surround all high-power lines. The complete medical effect of these magnetic fields is not yet known. If they are determined to be a health problem, it could dramatically affect the value of the real estate adjacent to these power lines.

- *Easements*—Many properties have utility easements, building easements, etc. These are rights of others to use your property and may limit your ability to use or develop it as you might prefer. Make sure you are aware of all the easements that might affect your property.

Terms of Purchase

The terms under which a property may be purchased often are more important than the price. Along with the price, you should therefore consider financing, form of title, and any contingencies.

Financing

Sometimes the owner is willing to lend a portion of the purchase price. If the terms are more favorable than those available at a lending institution, it may be worthwhile to pay a higher price for the real estate than you could otherwise justify.

Title

Normally you want a **fee simple** title. This means you own the property absolutely, and a lending institution or other creditor only has a right to pursue you through the courts to take the property if you do not meet some obligations. Many other forms of titling, such as contract for deed, do not truly pass the title to the buyer until the last payment is made to the lender. Make sure the title you receive is the best possible available in your state for the type of real estate you are purchasing.

Contingencies

When purchasing real estate, you can put a contingency on your offer, stating you are not obligated to complete the transaction unless repairs are below a certain cost or until your current home is sold, etc. Make sure you understand the contingencies, and use the ones available to you to protect yourself from a transaction not in your best interest.

Establishing a Purchase Price

One of the most important aspects of the real estate decision-making process is the establishment of a purchase price. For an existing property which needs remodeling or has a motivated seller, you can establish the optimum price to pay by using this simple formula:

$$\left(\text{Value of Property After Remodeling} \times \text{Loan-to-Value Ratio}\right) - \text{Fix-Up Expenses} = \text{Amount to Pay}$$

Calculated in this way, the amount to pay leaves you with zero dollars invested after refinancing. This formula may seem impossible to actually implement in the marketplace, but sufficient market research will turn up motivated sellers. Additionally, this formula will work for an investor who does not wish to purchase a property needing extensive repairs, in which situation the fix-up expenses will be close to zero.

An example with numbers will be useful. Let's assume you are looking at a two-unit apartment building with an asking price of $120,000. This building is located in an area where most properties are in good condition, but the building you are looking at needs some repairs such as painting, roofing, and general fix-up. After consulting with painters, roofers, and other contractors, you estimate it will cost $30,000 to complete the repairs necessary to get the property ready to rent. You also consult with real estate brokers in the area and an appraiser; they estimate that after you fix up the property and spend the $30,000 on repairs, the building will be worth $175,000. A visit to your lender indicates an available loan-to-value (LTV) ratio of 80 percent for refinancing purposes. Given these amounts, you can estimate how much to pay as follows:

$$\left(\text{Value of Property After Remodeling} \times \text{Loan-to-Value Ratio}\right) - \text{Fix-Up Expenses} = \text{Amount to Pay}$$

$$(\$175{,}000 \times .80) - \$30{,}000 = \$140{,}000 - \$30{,}000 = \$110{,}000$$

Thus, if you pay $110,000 for the property and spend $30,000 in repairs, you will have $140,000 invested and a property worth $175,000. If you refinance the property after it is fixed up, obtaining a loan with an 80 percent LTV ratio, you can borrow $140,000 and have none of your own money tied up in the property.

Establishing a Target Cash Flow

While establishing an optimum purchase price is critical to long-term profitability, and while the purchase price does affect cash flow if debt financing is used, you should establish a cash-flow target for all rental properties separately from the purchase price. A separate cash-flow estimate serves two main purposes. The first is to make sure that you don't expect a negative cash-flow situation. The second is to determine an expected net operating income (NOI) so that a checks-and-balances system can support the estimated purchase price. This checks-and-balances system results because, if the price is too high, or if loan terms are not optimum, then the

Figure 10.2 Worksheet for Estimating Cash-Flow Targets

Monthly potential gross income		
(after remodeling): ________ units × $________ / unit		$__________
Less: Vacancy and collection loss		__________
Effective gross income		$__________
Less: Operating expenses		
Real estate taxes	$__________	
Insurance	__________	
Maintenance and management	__________	__________
Net operating income		$__________
Less: Loan payment		__________
Monthly cash flow before taxes		$__________

monthly payment on the loan will be more than the NOI resulting in a negative cash flow. A negative cash-flow situation is to be avoided, unless you confidently expect the property to appreciate substantially in value.

To estimate cash-flow targets, you can use the worksheet in Figure 10.2. It provides a monthly estimate for the first year of operation. To estimate the potential gross income (PGI), research what similar properties are renting for in the marketplace. For example, if you are purchasing a duplex and similar duplexes that have been remodeled are renting for $950 per month, then your two-unit building should generate $1,900 per month in PGI, assuming the units are always rented and all residents pay their rent.

However, it is rare for 100 percent of PGI to be collected. Even in markets where the vacancy rate is less than 5 percent, sometimes residents do not pay their rent. Operating expenses include real estate taxes, insurance, and maintenance expenses.

Using the same duplex as an example, we can enter numbers in the worksheet (see Figure 10.3). Use PGI of $1,900, and assume a 5 percent vacancy and collection loss. Assume also that you expect to pay real estate taxes of $2,400, or $200 per month. You estimate that your monthly insurance cost will be $50 and your maintenance and management expenses will be $300 per month. The monthly payment on your twenty-year $140,000 loan (at 8½ percent) will be $1,215. Inserting these numbers in the worksheet, you determine that your monthly cash flow will be only $40 per month on a pretax basis. The good news is that, after refinancing, you have zero dollars invested.

Figure 10.3 Worksheet for Estimating Cash-Flow Targets: Completed Example

Monthly potential gross income		
(after remodeling): 2 units × $ 950 / unit		$ 1,900
Less: Vacancy and collection loss		95
Effective gross income		$ 1,805
Less: Operating expenses		
Real estate taxes	$ 200	
Insurance	50	
Maintenance and management	300	550
Net operating income		$ 1,255
Less: Loan payment		1,215
Monthly cash flow before taxes		$ 40

Monitoring Monthly Cash and Tax Flows: Rental Property Monitor

Once you own the property and are collecting rents and paying expenses, it is critical to keep a close accounting of the cash inflows and outflows. Additionally, because real estate can produce tax benefits, it is advantageous to keep track of taxable income or loss. We refer to these taxable incomes or losses as "tax flows."

To keep track of this information, use copies of the Rental Property Monitor (Figure 10.4). It has twelve columns, starting with a column for the month and year on the far left. You should also keep copies of all expense receipts for tax purposes. We recommend a separate file for each property.

Figure 10.4 is straightforward, with column 2 showing rent received, column 3 the date paid, column 4 the monthly mortgage payment, column 5 the interest portion of the payment, column 6 the total of all other expenses such as management, painting, etc., and column 7 the monthly depreciation expense. The next four columns calculate monthly and year-to-date totals. The final column is used for tracking mortgage balance.

One benefit of keeping this type of monthly accounting is that you can monitor each month where you stand in terms of cash flow and tax flow. This monthly knowledge of tax flows allows for better tax planning. For example, if your taxes are due in December and you do not want to take the deduction in the current year, you can delay payment until January—assuming you are a cash-basis taxpayer. As another example, you may have a positive tax flow, which means you owe taxes from the operation of the property; in response, you decide to perform maintenance a little ahead of schedule to get the tax deductions this year instead of next year. The only way to maximize the benefits of this type of tax planning is by knowing each month where you stand in terms of year-to-date (YTD) taxable income.

The monthly cash flows and tax flows are computed as follows:

$$\text{Monthly Cash Flow} = \text{Rent Received} - \text{Mortage Payment} - \text{Other Expenses}$$

$$\text{Monthly Tax Flow} = \text{Rent Received} - \text{Interest Paid} - \text{Other Expenses} - \text{Depreciation}$$

The computations differ because of two main items:

1. Only the interest portion of your loan payment is tax deductible as an expense.
2. Depreciation is a noncash expense requiring no monthly cash outlay, but it is deductible for income tax purposes.

Using the numbers on the sample worksheet (Figure 10.5), we can determine the monthly cash and tax flows for January 1997 as follows:

Figure 10.4 Rental Property Monitor

Month and Year	Rent Received	Date Paid	Monthly Payment	Interest Paid	Other Expenses	Depreciation	Monthly Cash Flow	YTD Cash Flow	Monthly Tax Flow	YTD Tax Flow	Mortgage Balance

Figure 10.5 Rental Property Monitor: Completed Example

Month and Year	Rent Received	Date Paid	Monthly Payment	Interest Paid	Other Expenses	Depreciation	Monthly Cash Flow	YTD Cash Flow	Monthly Tax Flow	YTD Tax Flow	Mortgage Balance
Jan–97	$1,775.00	1/25	$500.00	$260.92	$1,699.29	$250.00	($424.29)		($435.21)		$4,270.00
Feb–97	$1,775.00	2/10	$500.00	$14.98	$75.00	$250.00	$1,200.00	$775.71	$1,435.02	$999.81	$3,785.21
Mar–97	$1,681.00	2/24	$3,000.00	$12.44	$2,723.69	$250.00	($1,555.13)	($779.42)	($1,305.13)	($305.32)	$797.65
Apr–97	$2,185.00	4/1	$500.00	$5.94	$803.23	$250.00	$881.77	$102.35	$1,125.83	$820.51	$303.59
May–97	$2,065.00	5/20	$306.92	$3.33	$665.15	$250.00	$1,095.28	$1,195.28	$1,146.52	$1,967.03	$0.00
Jun–97						$250.00					

Note: Negative numbers are shown in parentheses.

Monthly Cash Flow	=	$1,775.00	–	$500.00	–	$1,699.29	= –$424.29		
Monthly Tax Flow	=	$1,775.00	–	$260.92	–	$1,699.29	= $250.00	=	–$435.21

The worksheet reports that $1,775 in rent was collected. The monthly cash flow was a negative $424.29, indicating that cash outflows were larger than cash inflows. Subtracting interest, operating expenses, and depreciation from the rent leaves a negative taxable income of $435.21 for January.

The YTD columns from cash flow and tax flow, columns 9 and 11, are used to report the cumulative or year-to-date numbers. Note that the YTD cash flow for February is the result of adding January's and February's cash flow ($1,200.00 for February less January's outflow of $424.29 leaves $775.71). We use the same procedure to compute YTD or cumulative taxable income (+$1,435.02 for February and –$435.21 for January add to $999.81). You can use copies of Figure 10.4 for your own records.

Although real-estate-management software packages are available for computers, the small to medium investor who takes a hands-on approach will need paper files as well. In case of an audit, the IRS will require many cash receipts for small purchases, and you may also have to produce receipts to support checks written. Therefore, purchase a heavy cardboard file folder in which to keep all receipts by month along with the corresponding Rental Propery Monitors. For the typical small investor with fewer than a dozen properties, the system of combining file folders and worksheets is an easy way to keep up with cash and tax flows on a monthly and YTD basis.

Cash Return on a Real Estate Sale

For most assets, the profit is the difference between the purchase price and the sales price. For real estate, the calculation is not quite that easy.

To determine the amount of gain, you must know the **basis** of a property. The taxable gain for tax purposes is the difference between the amount you sell it for and its basis. Basis is determined by the method of acquisition. If you purchase the property, the basis will be equal to the price you paid less any depreciation plus any capitalized improvements. If you inherited the property, the basis is usually the value of the property as of the date of the decedent's death. If an estate-tax return is due, it is possible that you can elect to use the basis as of six months after the date of death. If you received the property as a gift, then the basis is the same as it is for the person giving you the property.

If you acquired the property by a trade for services or other property, or through foreclosure, the computation becomes even more confusing. In that case you should consult an accountant to make sure you understand the basis before selling the property. It is important to understand these things because it is some-

Figure 10.6 Worksheet for Computing Capital Gain (Net Profit)

Sale price of asset	$__________
Less: Sales commission and other costs (legal fees, closing costs paid by seller)	__________
Less: Initial basis of value	__________
Plus: Capitalized improvements	__________
Less: Depreciation deductions	__________
Capital gain (net profit)	$__________

times possible to sell property in which all the cash proceeds coming from the property are not sufficient to pay the tax bill you owe. In that case, obviously, you must consider whether you should sell the property, give it to a charity, or exercise some other alternative.

The profit associated with the sale of real estate is generally considered a **capital gain**. Capital gains have a more favored tax status. Under current law (June 1997), the maximum tax on a capital gain is 28 percent, but this changes periodically and may shortly do so again. The amount of capital-gains tax that is due on a transaction depends on the current law and is a popular issue for political debate. Figure 10.6 shows how to calculate a basic capital gain.

Some of the terms in Figure 10.6 may be unfamiliar. The *initial basis of value* is the basis at the time you acquired the property, as previously discussed. *Capitalized improvements* are additional construction or major improvements made to the property, such as a new roof, that were capitalized and have been depreciated over time. *Depreciation deductions* are the sum of all depreciation taken since you have owned the property. The *adjusted basis of value of capital gain* is the taxable gain (or loss) associated with the sale of the property. If it is a taxable gain, it is taxable in the year of disposition. If it is a taxable loss, there are limitations as to what income it can offset.

Notice that although indebtedness on the property reduces the amount of cash available to you, the amount of debt has no bearing on the taxable gain.

Whenever you sell real estate, you can compute your capital gain on a copy of the worksheet in Figure 10.6. Enter the data for each sale on a copy of the Real Estate Sale Monitor, shown in Figure 10.7. This provides a single summary of all your gains from your real estate investments.

The previous calculations and descriptions of the real estate transaction may seem intimidating at first. However, if you move slowly and cautiously to make sure you don't overpay, you will find the world of real estate offers ripe opportunities for you to take charge of your financial future.

Figure 10.7 Real Estate Sale Monitor

Property Description	Month and Year	Sale Price	Sales Commission	Other Costs*	Initial Basis*	Capitalized Improvements	Depreciation Deductions	Realized Net Profit

*Legal fees, closing costs paid by seller.

11 Conclusions and Summary

Lawrence Lynn

THIS CHAPTER TIES together the "loose ends" discussed thus far—stocks, bonds, real estate, options, and so on—into a meaningful whole.

Monitoring Your Total Account

Essentially, you can objectively monitor and control your estate or overall account in several ways. One commonly in use is to view the total or summary estate activity and its rate of gain or loss. Each year, you simply add together the results of your subcomponents—stock, options, mutual funds, bonds, real estate, etc.—and determine the degree (or lack) of progress for a single year, several years, or possibly for portions of a year (e.g., quarters). Using this modus operandi, you need not examine the activities in any depth but merely note the absolute rate of gain or loss. If you plot your overall account as shown in Figure 11.1, you observe the results of all the individual activities when focused together—that is, the sum product of your activities which contribute to your overall estate. The result might appear as shown in Figure 11.1, which shows overall total estate over time, or as in Figure 11.2, which shows income over time.

As you can see from Figure 11.1, the objective for total estate growth, was a true 10 percent annual, net of about 3 percent inflation, hence, an absolute 12 percent. In fact, the investor surpassed this objective by 1 percent, since the growth reached a net of nearly 14 percent a year before inflation. Monitoring against the desired objective shows no need for overall corrective control. Inspection of the estate's contents, which included stock, no bonds, active option writing, real estate only using real estate investment trusts (REITS), and one registered investment adviser account of about $150,000, also growing nicely, shows no need for any corrective controls. The component activities, in the aggregate, were essentially positive and contributory.

Using this method of monitoring, all you need to do is note how your overall results turn out. If they prove satisfactory, you can stop right there if you wish. If you fail to meet your target, you certainly must look further to better monitor or control the activities.

For example, if you set your overall objective at 12.5 percent per year and came out with 9 percent, clearly you have a failing somewhere. You must examine the components of the estate to discover where the inadequacies lurked. If you determine that last year your real estate component earned 15 percent, your common stock 15 percent, your benefit plans and bonds similarly, but options activities resulted in a major negative, surely you know what component was responsible. If this were to keep up, it could lead to drastic overall negatives, so it calls out loudly for correction.

The estate increase charted in Figure 11.1 is 12 percent. This result is about 1 percent higher than typical mid-capitalization corporate equities since 1926. This compares favorably with the essentially riskless 6.5 percent offered by U.S. Treasury bills during most recent years. These comparisons are not adjusted for the approximate 3-percent-per-year inflation that occurred in the United States from 1926 to 1996.

Of course, you could have measured your performance against the S&P 500 stock index. This is more meaningful than the Dow Jones Industrial Average (DJIA).

Figure 11.1 Total Estate Monitor: Total Assets over Time

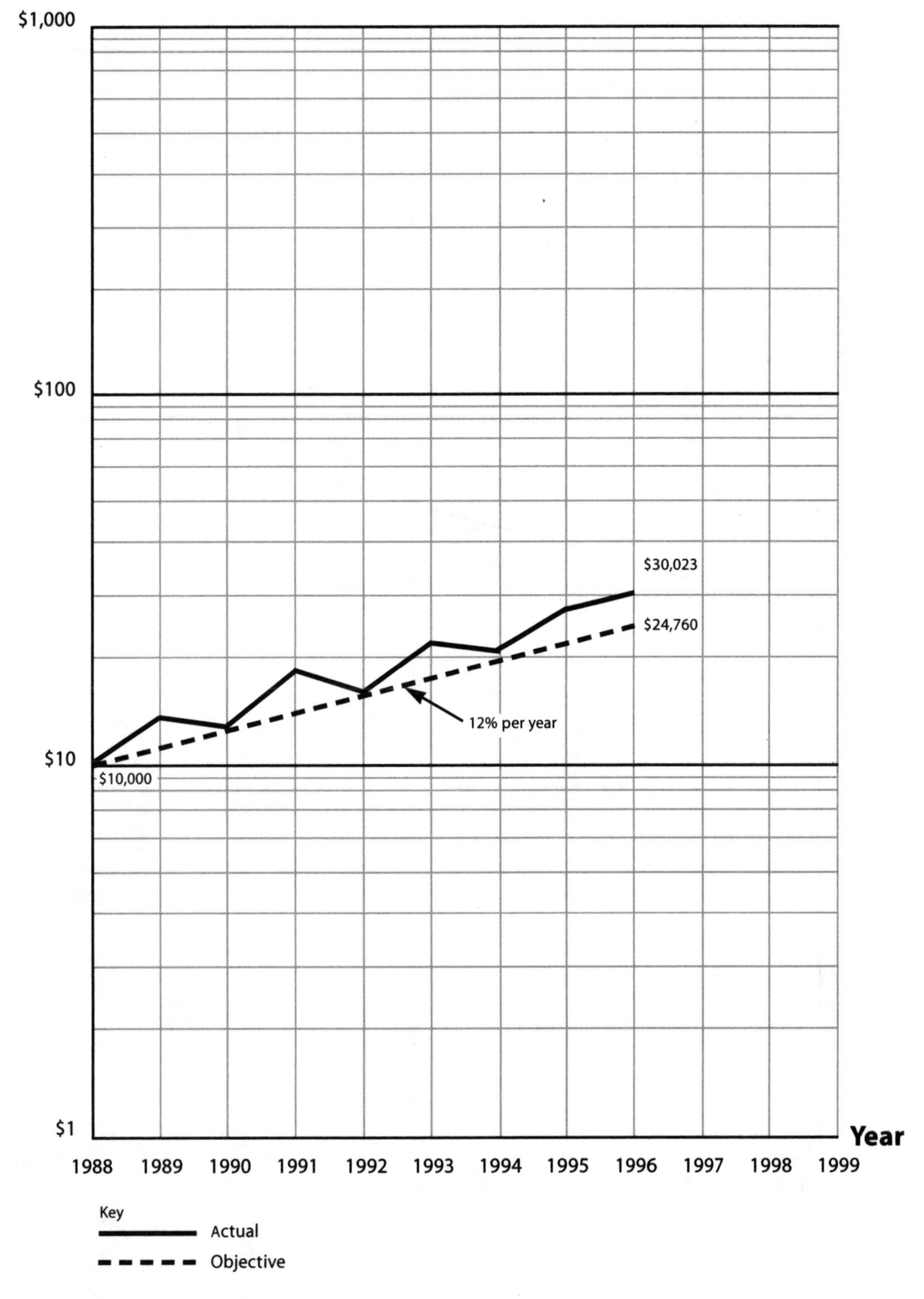

Figure 11.2 Total Estate Monitor: Income over Time

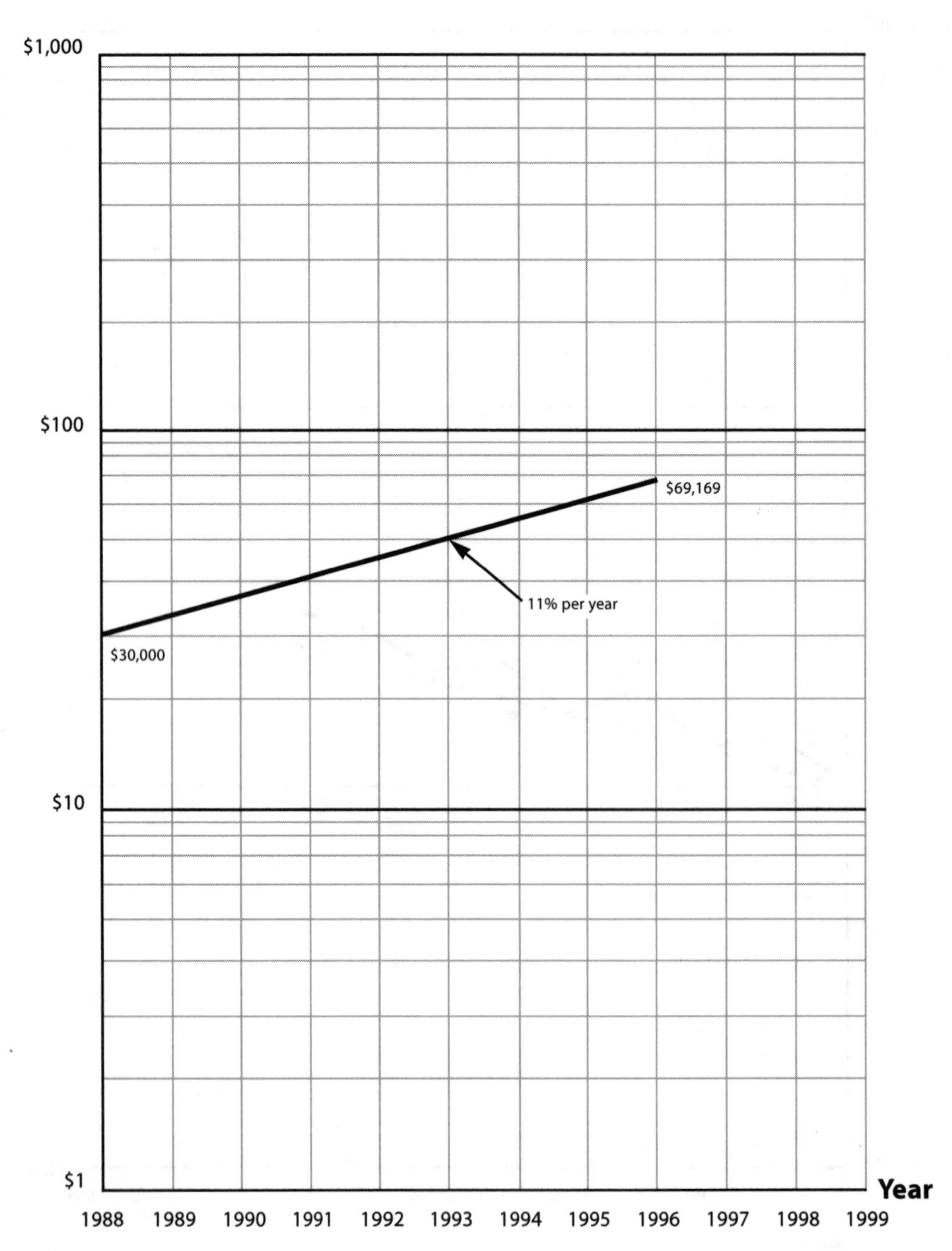

The reason is that the DJIA is based on the average of thirty of the most high-capitalization enterprises in the nation. Although they do represent a major segment of American industry, frequently they do not correctly reflect the many medium-cap or micro-cap industrial organizations that dot the American industrial landscape. The S&P 500 stock index, while admittedly also leaning to large companies, is far more indicative of typical overall business performance. Small-cap averages, such as the Russell 2000 or the Wilshire 5000, are weighted averages of many more corporations, but are not as commonly referred to as the DJIA or the S&P 500 as indicators of "how goes the market?"

Table 11.1 shows the recent history of the S&P 500 stock index and of an indexed fund or portfolio exactly mirroring its performance for 1989 through 1996. Superficially this sounds like an easy accomplishment for a fund. Yet it is a recorded fact that most mutual funds, supposedly with their "experts" guiding them, can't match or beat the S&P 500 (or the DJIA for that matter). For an estate to equal the average S&P 500 during 1989–1996, it would have had to achieve a performance of approximately 17 percent per year for the past eight years. Most funds and most incomes have not been that successful.

Another method of monitoring, shown in Figure 11.3, uses a chart showing the S&P stock index for 1989 versus the performance of a hypothetical couple

Table 11.1 Recent Performance of S&P 500 and an Indexed Portfolio

Calendar Year	S&P % Change	Indexed Fund*	
		Start of Year	End of Year
1989	31.6	10,000	13,160
1990	-3.1	13,160	12,752
1991	30.4	12,752	16,629
1992	7.6	16,629	17,892
1993	10.1	17,892	19,700
1994	1.3	19,700	19,956
1995	37.5	19,956	27,439
1996	23.1	27,439	33,777

*Reinvested dividends.

Figure 11.3 Total Estate Monitor:
Total Assets Versus the S&P 500

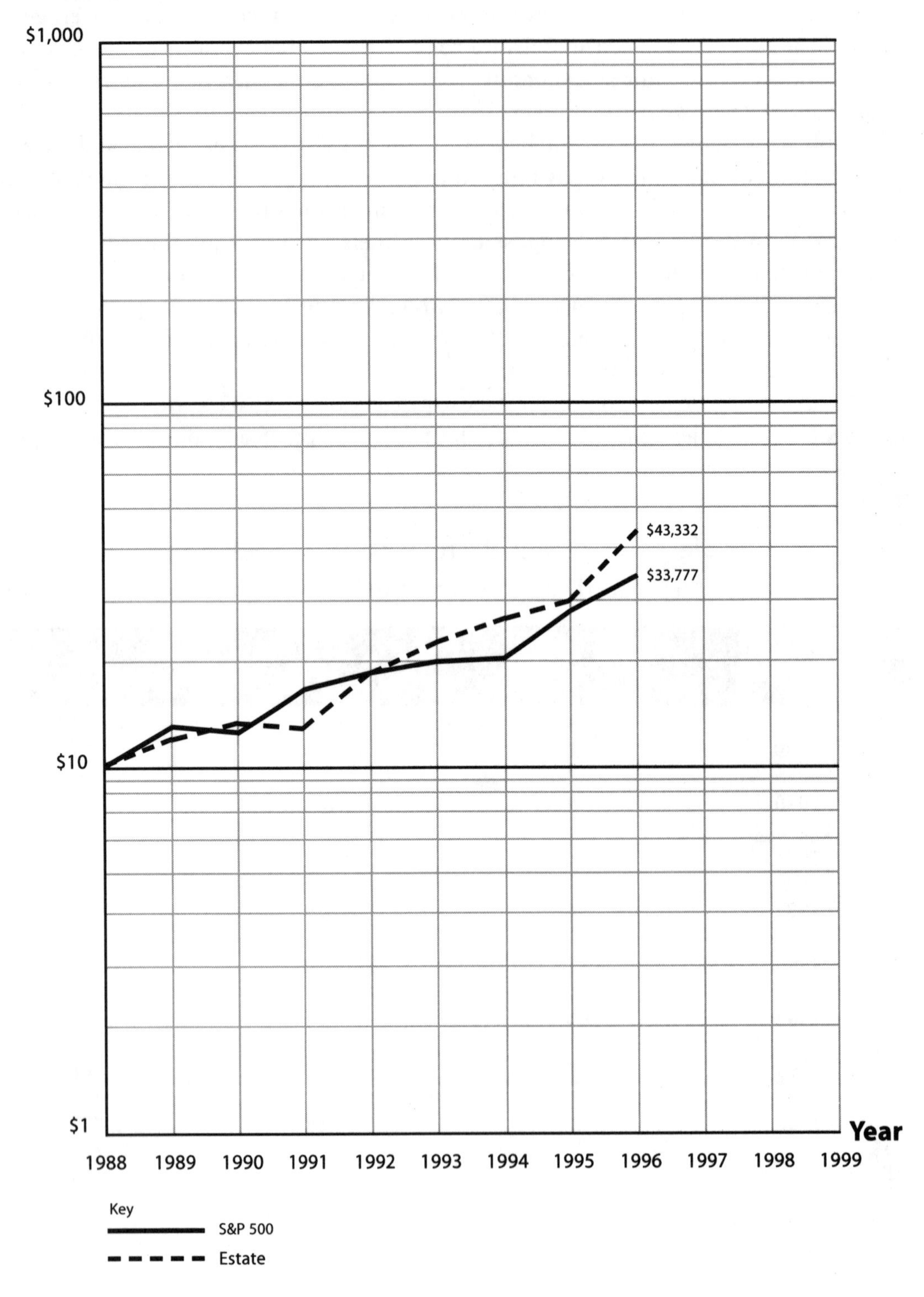

competing with it. During part of this time, 1990–1992, the couple's investment performance for the most part lagged the S&P 500, then it spurted ahead, caught up, and moved ahead of the popular index. If the estate target were to successfully match or beat the S&P 500, this couple would have achieved that difficult task.

To achieve better control, it would be instrumental to examine the internals of the estate of the couple in Figure 11.3. When we look into the various components of this couple's estate, using the charts from Chapters 1–10, not surprisingly, we find that the reason it underperformed the S&P 500 for a couple of years was that it was less heavily weighted with common stock than it should have been. In an overly conservative attempt to play safe, it was overweighted in bonds, CDs, and gold. It made inadequate use of aggressive option writing, even though the couple's few attempts at using this technique were favorable. They corrected these deficiencies in 1993–1995, applied improved techniques, and the estate outperformed the S&P 500 from 1993 onward.

How Are You Doing So Far?

Copy the blank Total Estate Monitor (Figure 11.4), and use it to log and follow your personal data. In order to correct the shortfalls from your objectives or targets, or to explain and understand possible overperformance, you will then have to explore individual asset-group results. In other words, you must look at the ingredients that make up your estate—stock, real estate, options, bonds, etc.—using the worksheets, charts, and monitors from earlier chapters. As you find these fugitive malingerers and underperformers, you must take steps to reduce them, correct them, or avoid them in the future.

If, as sometimes happens, you find that you consistently outperform your objectives, what should you do about it? First of all, you can congratulate yourself and do something to celebrate. Secondly, carefully examine the component investment segments to discover which of the components have done so well. Was it your handling of the selection of common stock? Was it your excellent techniques in naked-option writing that generated unusually high profits, which you judiciously reinvested to compound them further? Whatever it was, increased usage of this element might help you advance even further past your targets. Use it again, judiciously, and to a greater extent.

But the other answer to your present dilemma is that your objectives may have been set far too conservatively for your skills. Perhaps you have a uniquely talented registered investment adviser (RIA) who keeps generating gains of 20 percent to 30 percent per year, whereas your objectives were only an overall 12 percent absolute (9 percent after inflation, remember). If so, maybe you should sell out of some real estate and bonds and enlarge that RIA's operational segment.

In any case, you might want to expand your objectives to a more ambitious level and try to repeat these results. Your monitoring and control resulted in an enjoyable conclusion. Good luck to its continuation or betterment!

Figure 11.4 Total Estate Monitor

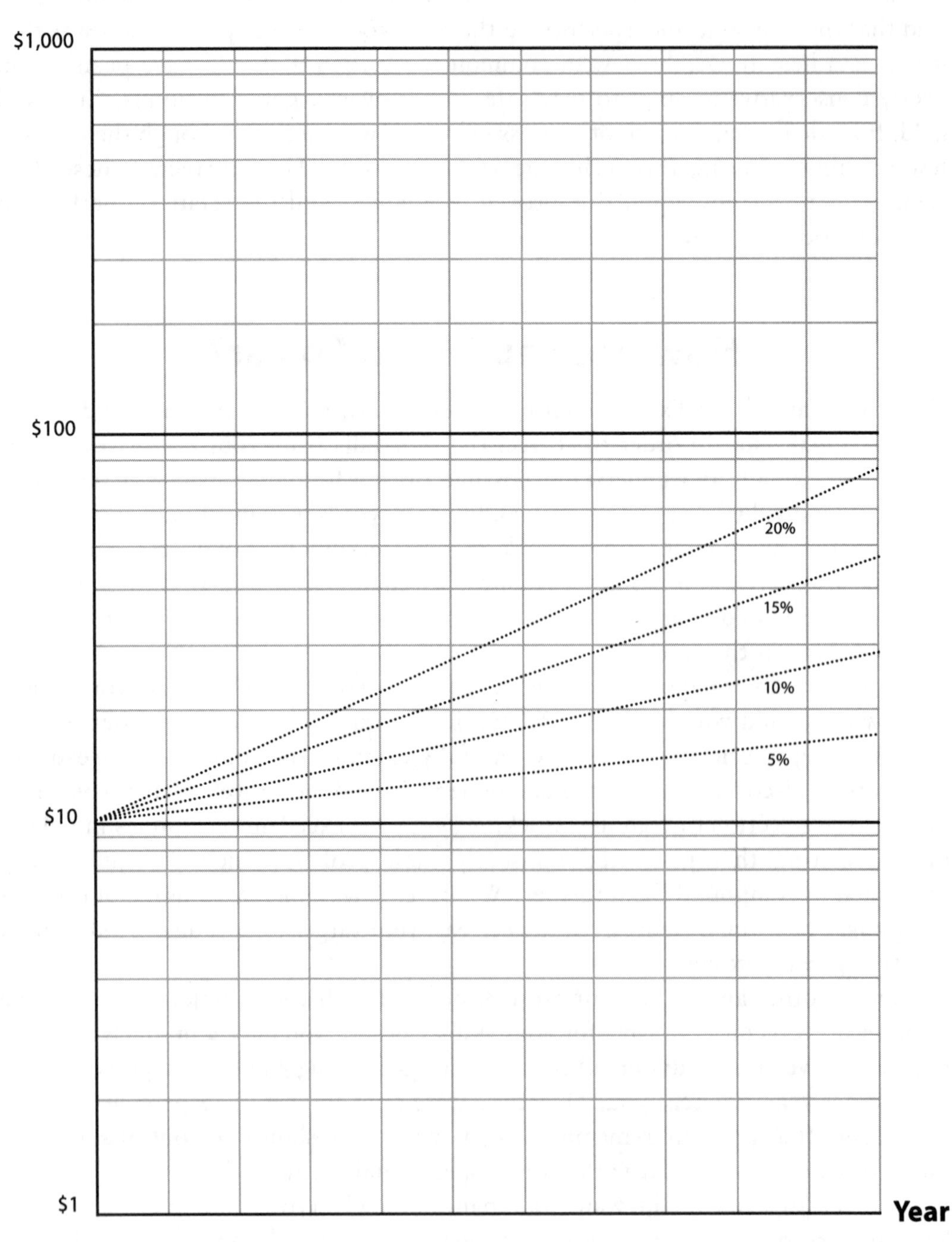

Appendix: Important Information Locators

Important Information Locator *for Investment Assets*

Bank Accounts:

Account #	Owner	Type	Bank Name	Phone #

Certificates of Deposit:

Account #	Owner	Maturity	Financial Institution	Phone #

Investment Accounts:

Account #	Owner	Type	Financial Institution	Phone #

Real Estate:

Description	Location of Title

Important Information Locator *for Retirement Accounts*

Annuities:

Contract #	Owner	Location of Policy	Insurance Company	Phone #

IRAs:

Account #	Owner	Plan Type	Firm Name	Phone #

Retirement Accounts:

Account #	Owner	Plan Type	Firm Name	Phone #

Important Information Locator *for Personal Records*

Important Papers:	Location	Notes
Auto Titles		
Birth Certificates		
Death Certificates		
Marriage License		
Home Deed		
Loan Agreements		
Tax Records		
Military Records		
Safe-Deposit Boxes		
Powers of Attorney		
Trusts		
Wills		
Other		

Important Information Locator *for Insurance Policies*

Life:

Insured	Policy #	Location of Policy	Insurance Company	Phone #

Disability:

Insured	Policy #	Location of Policy	Insurance Company	Phone #

Health:

Insured	Policy #	Location of Policy	Insurance Company	Phone #

Long-Term Care:

Insured	Policy #	Location of Policy	Insurance Company	Phone #

Important Information Locator *for Insurance Policies (Cont'd)*

Auto:

Make/Model	Policy #	Location of Policy	Insurance Company	Phone #

Homeowners:

Address	Policy #	Location of Policy	Insurance Company	Phone #

Liability:

Insured	Policy #	Location of Policy	Insurance Company	Phone #

Other:

Type/Insured	Policy #	Location of Policy	Insurance Company	Phone #

Important Information Locator: *People and Phone Numbers*

Accountant:

Name

Company

Address

Phone (office) Phone (home)

Attorney:

Name

Company

Address

Phone (office) Phone (home)

Bank:

Name

Company

Address

Phone (office) Fax (office)

Broker:

Name

Company

Address

Phone (office) Phone (home)

Clergy:

Name

Church

Address

Phone (office) Phone (home)

Doctor:

Name

Company

Address

Phone (office) Phone (home)

Executor:

Name

Company

Address

Phone (office) Phone (home)

Financial Planner:

Name

Company

Address

Phone (office) Phone (home)

Important Information Locator: *People and Phone Numbers (Cont'd)*

Other:

Name

Company

Address

Phone (office) Phone (home)

Other:

Name

Company

Address

Phone (office) Phone (home)

Other:

Name

Company

Address

Phone (office) Phone (home)

Other:

Name

Company

Address

Phone (office) Phone (home)

Other:

Name

Company

Address

Phone (office) Phone (home)

Other:

Name

Company

Address

Phone (office) Phone (home)

Other:

Name

Company

Address

Phone (office) Phone (home)

Other:

Name

Company

Address

Phone (office) Phone (home)

Bibliography

Burke, Michael. *The All New Guide to the Three Point Reversal Method.* New Rochelle, NY: Chartcraft, 1990.

Friedman, Albert J. *Financial Planner*, April 1982, 84–87.

Lynn, Lawrence, ed. *How to Invest Today.* New York: Henry Holt & Co., 1995.

Merrill, John F. *Beyond Stocks.* Houston: Tanglewood Publishing, 1997.

Nelson Publications, Quarterly Report, Port Chester, NY.

O'Neill, William. *How to Make Money in Stocks.* New York: McGraw-Hill, 1991.

Silvate, John D. *Financial Planner*, April 1982, 96–97.

Wolford, Larry E., and T. M. Clauretie. *Real Estate.* New York: John Wiley & Sons, 1992.

Sources of Other Resources

A. M. Best Company
Ambest Rd.
Oldwick, NJ 08858
908-439-3363

The Consumer Federation of America
1424 16th St., N.W., Suite 604
Washington, DC 20036
202-387-0087

Moody's Investors Service
99 Church St.
New York, NY 10007
212-553-0377

Morningstar, Inc.
225 W. Wacker Dr.
Chicago, IL 60606
800-735-0700

Standard and Poor's Ratings Group
25 Broadway
New York, NY 10004
212-208-1527

Index

A. M. Best Company, 120–21, 125–26
Accumulation, 85
Adjusted basis of value of capital gain, 173
Advance/decline ratio, 99
Alpha, 79
Annual capital gains and losses from option trades form, 75–76f
Annuities, 122
  bail-out options, 126
  deferred, 124–25
    equity-index, 124–25
    fixed, 124
    variable, 125
  immediate, 123–24
    joint, 123
    life-or-period-certain, 123
    period-certain, 123
    single-life, 123
  investment issues, 125–26
  tracking performance, 126–30
Annuity contract monitor, 129–30f
Annuity contract review worksheet, 127–28f
Assets, 24
  sources of, 25f
  summarizing for already retired persons, 141–44
  summarizing retirement and personal, 137–41
  types of, 25f

Bar charting, 84–91
  advantages, 91
  cup-and-handle formation, 85–86, 86f
  head-and-shoulders formation, 86–87, 88–89f
  software programs, 101
  trading channels, 87
  W formation, 86, 87f
Basis, property, 172
Bearish resistance line, 95
Bearish support line, 95
Beta, 79
Blended whole-life policies, 109–10
Bond monitor form, 37f, 40–43f
Bond ratio, 19f, 27
Bonds
  interest rates, 38–39
  monitoring, 39–44
  rating of, 36–38
  selection criteria, 36–39
Book value, 19f, 27
Bullish resistance line, 95
Bullish support line, 95
Burke, Michael, 91

Call feature, 39
Call option, 64–65
Capital gains, 173
Capitalization indicators, 27
Capitalized improvements, 173
Charles Schwab & Co., Inc., 153–54
Chartbooks, 89
Chiron Corp., 79–80
Closed-end investment companies, 50, 53–55
  fund monitor, 51f

Combinations, 67–68
Commodities, 10
Common stock ratio, 19f, 27
Computers, technical analysis and, 101
Consumer Federation of America (CFA), 122
Covered seller, 67
Cup-and-handle formation, 85
Current ratio, 19f, 24
Current yield, 38

Debt, 24, 25f
Deferred annuities, 124–25
  equity-index, 124
  fixed, 124
  variable, 125
Defined-contribution plans, 137, 138–39f
Depreciation deductions, 173
Dividend yield, 19f, 29–30
Dividends, 30

Earnings per share (EPS), 19f, 28
Earnings per share (EPS) relative strength indicator, 79
Epitope Corp., 70, 77–79
Equity, 24, 25f
Equity-index annuities, 124–25
Estate monitor, 10–14, 11–12f
Exercise dates, 66
Exercising, an option, 65–66

Fee simple titles, 165
Firm maintenance requirement (FMR) moneys, 68–69
Fixed annuities, 124
Fixed-income securities, 45–46f. *See also* Bonds
FMR. *See* Firm maintenance requirement (FMR) moneys
Foreign buy/sell ratio, 99
401(k) plans, 134
Fruth, Richard J., 151–57
Fundamental analysis, 99–100

Glaser, Otto, 152
Glaxo Wellcome, Ltd., 67
Graham, Benjamin, 152
Growth companies, 30
Growth investments, 5
Growth rate, 30
Guaranteed-cost whole-life policies, 109

Immediate annuities, 123–24
  joint, 123
  life-or-period-certain, 123
  period-certain, 123
  single-life, 123
Income investments, 5
Indicators
  capitalization, 27
  key stock, 18–30, 19f
Industry-group percent bullish, 98–99
Initial basis of value, 173
Insurance. *See* Life insurance
Insurance companies, rating of, 120–21
Interest, recording received, 47–48f
Interest coverage, 19f, 28
Interest rate, bond, 38–39
Intrinsic value (IV), 66
Investment accounts, management methods, 146–48
Investment categories, 5

Investment companies, 147–48
  fund monitor, 50, 51–52f
  types, 50
Investment objectives, 2, 5
Investment services bearish, 98
Investment-objective worksheet, 2–3f
Investments
  important information locators, 188–94
  value judgments for, 5–10

Joint annuities, 123
Junk bonds, 36

Leverage, 19f, 27
Life insurance, 103–4
  bail-out options, 121–22
  determining need and amount, 104
  permanent, 108–18
    universal-life, 110
    variable-life, 110–18
    whole-life, 108–10
  pitfalls, 118–20
  private rating firms, 120–21
  term, 107
Life insurance policy monitor, 105f
Life-or-period-certain annuities, 123
Lynn, Lawrence, 91

Maturity date, 38
McDonnell Douglas, 70
Metastock, 101
Moody's Investors Service Inc., 36, 121
Mutual funds (open-end investment companies), 50
  fund rating, 55–56
  net asset value, 56–61
  open-end, 55
  payout, 56
  performance measures, 61–62

Naked options, 67
NAV. *See* Net asset value (NAV)
Neckline, 86
Nelson Publications, 149
Net asset value (NAV), 55, 56–61
Net profit margin, 19f, 29
NYSE percent bullish, 99

Objectives. *See* Investment objectives
O'Neill, William, 85
Open-end investment companies (mutual funds), 50
  fund monitor, 52f
  fund rating, 55–56
  net asset value, 56–61
  payout, 56
  performance measures, 61–62
Operating profit margin, 19f, 29
Options. *See* Stock options
Options monitor, 74f

Participating whole-life policies, 109
P/E (price/earnings) ratio, 19f, 28–29
Penny stocks, 10
Pensions. *See* Defined-contribution plans; Retirement
Period-certain annuities, 123
Permanent life insurance, 108–18
  components, 108f
  universal-life, 110
  variable-life, 110–18
  whole-life, 108–10
Personal assets

for already retired persons, 141–44
summarizing, 137–41
Planning
investment objectives and, 2
origins, 2
Point & figure (P & F) charting, 91–97
advantages, 97
chart patterns, 93–95
software programs for, 101
trading patterns, 95–97
Points, 64
Preferred stock ratio, 19f, 27
Premium, 66
Price/earnings (P/E) ratio, 19f, 28–29
Profit margins, 29
Property. *See* Real estate
Put options, 65
Put/call ratio, 98

Ratio writer, 67
Real estate, 159
buying checklist, 161–65
determining profit on sale of, 172–74
establishing purchase price, 165–66
establishing target cash flow, 166–68
monitoring cash and tax flows, 169–72
purchase terms, 165
Real estate investment trusts (REITS), 160
Registered investment advisers (RIAS), 146
determining performance level, 151
selecting, 148–50
Regulation T, 68
Resistance lines, 95
Retained earnings, 24
Retirement
accounting for, 134–37
planning, 131–34
Retirement assets, summarizing, 137–41
for already retired persons, 141–44
Return on equity (ROE), 19f, 29
Return on investment (ROI), 19f, 29
Return vs. risk, 8, 9f
Risk vs. return, 8, 9f

Savant Technical Investor, 101
Schwab, Charles, 153–54
Second-to-die/survivorship insurance, 118
Sentiment indicators, 98–99
Seven-day advance/decline ratio, 99
Single-life annuities, 123
SMA. *See* Special miscellaneous account (SMA)
Software programs, technical analysis and, 101
Special miscellaneous account (SMA), 68–69
Speculative investments, 5, 8–10
Standard and Poor's, 36, 121
Stock options, 63–64
calls, 64–65
exercising, 65–66
intrinsic value (IV), 66
limitations on positions, 68–69
monitoring, 73–77
naked, 67
puts, 65

reasons for using, 69–73
selecting, 77–80
writing, 66–67
Stock performance monitor, 22–23f
Stock portfolio monitor, 30–33, 32f, 34f
Stocks
determining time to sell, 100
key indicators for, 18–30
prepurchase analysis, 18, 20–21f
selecting, 18
Straddles, 67
Supercharts, 101
Support lines, 95
SYSCO Inc., 18, 21f, 23f, 24

Tangible investments, 161
Technical analysis, 83–84
bar charting, 84–91
advantages, 91
cup-and-handle formation, 85, 86f
head-and-shoulders formation, 86–87, 88–89f
trading channels, 87
W formation, 86, 87f
fundamental analysis and, 99–100
point & figure (P & F) charting, 91–97
advantages, 97
chart patterns, 93–95
trading channels, 95–97
sentiment indicators, 98–99
using computers for, 101
Templeton, John, 152
Term life insurance, 107
Three-point reversal method, 91
Time-value (TV), 66
Trading channels
bar charting, 87
point & figure (P & F) charting, 95–97
Turnover ratio, 19f, 24

Underwriting, 115
Unit investment trusts, 50–53
Universal-life insurance, 110, 118
Universal-life policy, 113–14

Value judgments, 5–10
Value selection chart, 5, 6–7f
Vanish, 119
Variable annuities, 125
Variable-life insurance, 110–18

Whole-life insurance, 108–10, 111–12f
for two people, 118
Writer, 66–67
Writing, 66–67

Yield-to-maturity, 38–39

Zenix Investment Fund, Inc., 53–54

About the Contributors

Dr. Lawrence Lynn, the senior author and editor, received undergraduate and graduate degrees in chemical engineering from Texas A&M and Columbia Universities, respectively. He began his career in product and process development at Celanese Corp. of America, went on to General Foods, Inc., and thereafter was vice president of Riviana Foods, Inc. He entered general management and was president and CEO of Pine-O-Pine Co. in Houston before changing to investment banking–brokerage, first at Merrill Lynch and then at Drexel Burnham Lambert. He retired from Drexel as senior vice president—investments in 1984.

Dr. Lynn has taught the fundamentals of investing for the last twenty years at the Westchester campus of Houston Community College and in the adult-education division of Spring Branch School District, Houston, TX. His articles have appeared in professional journals such as *Chemical Engineering*, *Industrial Engineering Chemistry*, *Modern Plastics*, and *Food Engineering*.

Dr. Lynn is coauthor of *Your Vision* (New York: Master Media, 1994) and the principal author and editor of *How to Invest Today* (New York: Henry Holt & Company, 1995). *Your Vision* was chosen as a principal selection for the Doubleday Book Club.

Kenneth Altvater graduated from the University of Texas at Austin with a B.S. in economics, after which he began his career with American General Corp. in sales, administration, and training. After twenty more years as senior vice president and trust officer at Southern National Bank and River Oaks Trust Company, a prestigious Texas trust company, he became president of the Allocation Co., Inc. Here, he provides contract-plan administration for ERISA-qualified contribution plans. At River Oaks Trust Company, he administered plans with assets in excess of $200 million and annual fees in excess of $1 million. These credentials make Mr. Altvater an excellent source for the chapter on retirement planning and management.

George Eckhardt, Jr., vice president at Merrill Lynch, started out as a career Army officer with a B.S. degree in business administration from The Citadel. He entered the brokerage field in 1972 and thereafter became a Certified Financial Planner, specializing in retirement and estate planning. He is a member of the Circle of Excellence, a group of the most highly rated financial consultants at Merrill Lynch. Mr. Eckhardt is the contributing author of the chapter on the planning and monitoring of insurance, estate planning, and annuities.

Robert Frater, also a Certified Financial Planner, earned his B.S. at the University of Wisconsin–Stout. He is a nationally recognized financial planner and vice president of Houston Asset Management, Inc. Mr. Frater has purchased and developed over $10 million in real estate. Currently he is redeveloping the Texas First Telephone/Telegraph building into condominiums. He coauthored the chapter on real estate investments.

Dr. James Galbraith, author of the chapter on stock selection key indicators, received his college education at the University of Toronto and the University of

Idaho, specializing in geology and chemistry. He has had twenty-nine years of diversified technical experience in research projects requiring statistical analysis in Canada, the United States, and South America. He is currently an independent consultant geostatistician in Houston and an independent representative for 1st Global Partners, an investment advisory firm of Dallas. Dr. Galbraith has authored or coauthored fifteen articles appearing in such journals as the *Journal of Geochemical Exploration*, *Ground Water Journal*, and *The Analyst*. Some of his publications have been for the U.S. Department of Energy and The Brazilian Geological Congress.

Otto Glaser graduated from the University of Houston in 1954 with a degree in accounting. After two years of military service and four years with Radoff Bros., Inc., he entered investment brokerage in 1961. He was a senior broker for Merrill Lynch, Houston/Galleria office, for twenty-two years and vice president of A. G. Edwards & Sons, Inc., in Houston for twelve years. He is a vice president and Registered Investment Advisor with Richard J. Fruth and Associates, Inc. His thirty-five years as an investment broker have been spent working primarily with individual clients, directing a significant part of his efforts to the purchase and sale of bonds for both individuals and institutions. His contribution to this book is in the area of fixed-income investments.

John Markle, B.S., Michigan State University, began his financial career with E. F. Hutton and Co. after a period in the hotel-management industry. He served as a broker at Prudential-Bache before joining Merrill Lynch, where he has practiced a dozen years, most recent as vice president, Houston/Westlake office. He is an expert on point-and-figure charts, which he has used successfully for fifteen years. He contributed the chapter on technical analysis.

Lynn E. Marx received her B.S. degree from the University of Pittsburgh. She began her career in sales, administration, and training with CIGNA Corp. and moved on to her current position as assistant manager of the Houston branch of Sun Financial Group. She is a nationally known speaker in the areas of retirement and estate planning who has conducted over 100 seminars attended by more than 3,000 people. She has created educational presentation materials and financial analysis programs for financial planning professionals and is president of the Wealth Preservation Group of Houston, Texas.

Dr. Charles Smith is a professor at the University of Houston, where he teaches real estate classes and serves as coordinator for real estate studies. He did his undergraduate work at McNeese State University and his graduate studies at Louisiana State University, Baton Rouge, and Texas A&M University. Dr. Smith has taught real estate management, market analysis, appraisal, and other related courses. His many articles have been published by, among others, *Journal of Real Estate Appraisal, Journal of Real Estate Business, Akron Business and Economic Review, Journal of Real Estate Research, Journal of Property Management, Louisiana REALTOR, and Texas REALTOR*. His consulting and expert-witness assignments have extended from California to Louisiana. Dr. Smith has contributed to the real estate chapter.